Fodor's

BERMUDA

31st Edition

Where to Stay and Eat
for All Budgets

Must-See Sights
and Local Secrets

Ratings You Can Trust

Fodor's Travel Publications   New York, Toronto, London, Sydney, Auckland
www.fodors.com

FODOR'S BERMUDA

Editor: Molly Moker

Writers: Linda Coffman, Sirkka Huish, Simon Jones, Dale Leatherman, Susan MacCallum-Whitcomb

Production Editor: Carrie Parker

Maps & Illustrations: David Lindroth and Mark Stroud, *cartographers;* Bob Blake, Rebecca Baer, *map editors;* William Wu, *information graphics*

Design: Fabrizio La Rocca, *creative director;* Guido Caroti, *art director;* Tina Malaney, Chie Ushio, Nora Rosansky, Jessica Walsh *designers;* Melanie Marin, *associate director of photography*

Cover Photo: (Warwick Long Bay, South Shore Park, Warwick Parish, Bermuda): SIME/eStock Photo

Production Manager: Angela L. McLean

COPYRIGHT

Copyright © 2012 by Fodor's Travel, a division of Random House, Inc.

Fodor's is a registered trademark of Random House, Inc.

All rights reserved. Published in the United States by Fodor's Travel, a division of Random House, Inc., and in Canada by Random House of Canada, Limited, Toronto. Distributed by Random House, Inc., New York.

No maps, illustrations, or other portions of this book may be reproduced in any form without written permission from the publisher.

31st Edition

ISBN 978-0-679-00957-3

ISSN 0192-3765

SPECIAL SALES

This book is available at special discounts for bulk purchases for sales promotions or premiums. Special editions, including personalized covers, excerpts of existing books, and corporate imprints, can be created in large quantities for special needs. For more information, write to Special Markets/Premium Sales, 1745 Broadway, MD 3-2, New York, NY 10019, or e-mail specialmarkets@randomhouse.com.

AN IMPORTANT TIP & AN INVITATION

Although all prices, opening times, and other details in this book are based on information supplied to us at press time, changes occur all the time in the travel world, and Fodor's cannot accept responsibility for facts that become outdated or for inadvertent errors or omissions. So **always confirm information when it matters,** especially if you're making a detour to visit a specific place. Your experiences—positive and negative—matter to us. If we have missed or misstated something, **please write to us.** Share your opinion instantly through our online feedback center at fodors.com/contact-us.

PRINTED IN THE UNITED STATES OF AMERICA

10 9 8 7 6 5 4 3 2 1

CONTENTS

MAPS

ABOUT
THIS BOOK

Our Ratings

At Fodor's, we spend considerable time choosing the best places in a destination so you don't have to. By default, anything we recommend in this book is worth visiting. But some sights, properties, and experiences are so great that we've recognized them with additional accolades. Orange **Fodor's Choice** stars indicate our top recommendations; black stars highlight places we deem **Highly Recommended**; and **Best Bets** call attention to top properties in various categories. Disagree with any of our choices? Care to nominate a new place? Visit our feedback center at www.fodors.com/feedback.

Hotels

Hotels have private bath, phone, TV, and air-conditioning, and do not offer meals unless we specify that in the review. We always list facilities but not whether you'll be charged an extra fee to use them.

> For expanded hotel reviews,
> visit **Fodors.com**

Restaurants

Unless we state otherwise, restaurants are open for lunch and dinner daily. We mention dress only when there's a specific requirement and reservations only when they're essential or not accepted—it's always best to book ahead.

Credit Cards

We assume that restaurants and hotels accept credit cards. If not, we'll note it in the review.

Budget Well

Hotel and restaurant price categories from ¢ to $$$$ are defined in the opening pages of the respective chapters. For attractions, we always give standard adult admission fees; reductions are usually available for children, students, and senior citizens.

Listings			Hotels & Restaurants	Outdoors	
★ Fodor's Choice	✍	E-mail	▦ Hotel	⅄	Golf
★ Highly recommended	✉	Admission fee	⇥ Number of rooms	⚑	Camping
⊠ Physical address	⊙	Open/closed times	☌ Facilities	**Other**	
⊹ Directions or Map coordinates	Ⓜ	Metro stations	⑩ Meal plans	☺	Family-friendly
⌂ Mailing address	⊟	No credit cards	✗ Restaurant	⇨	See also
☎ Telephone			⌲ Reservations	⊠	Branch address
🖷 Fax			⚏ Dress code	☞	Take note
⊕ On the Web			↘ Smoking		

Experience Bermuda

WORD OF MOUTH

"Bermuda has such a rich culture and that's why we did our "second honeymoon" there. We were captivated by everything there. Beautiful beaches and sunsets, horse and buggy rides - so many spectacular things to see. It is an experience unlike any other place!"

—Knowing

"Bermuda is much more lush, floral, has pretty pink and aqua homes, and a more islandy feel. The island has a more proper British etiquette feel, but can be as casual as you want it to be. We have been several times and love Bermuda for its beauty."

—girlonthego

WELCOME TO BERMUDA

TOP REASONS TO GO

★ **Gorgeous beaches.**
Bermuda's pink-sand beaches, lapped by turquoise water, are some of the world's most beautiful.

★ **Island sophistication.** The island combines British old-world charm with modern luxuries.

★ **St. George's.** Lose yourself (and the crowds) on the winding side streets and mazelike back alleys of this 400-year-old town.

★ **Spectacular spas.** The island boasts several state-of-the-art spas and myriad treatments.

★ **World-class golf.**
Bermuda is unmatched when it come to top-notch golf courses, complete with breathtaking ocean views.

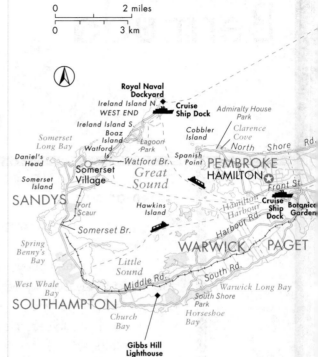

1 Hamilton and Central Parishes. The city of Hamilton, in the heart of Pembroke, is a bustling little capital referred to as "town" by locals. Along with major historical sites, Hamilton has the broadest array of restaurants, shops, bars, and museums. Paget Parish, adjoining Pembroke to the south, is best known for its enviable selection of south-shore beaches and Paget Marsh and the Botanical Gardens. Sleepy Devonshire Parish, adjoining Pembroke to the east, is the geographical center of the island, but most travelers merely pass through it. Serious sports enthusiasts are the exception, because the National Sports Centre, National Equestrian Centre, Bermuda Squash Racquets Association, and Ocean View Golf Course are all there. Warwick has Bermuda's longest beach; Warwick Long Bay Beach is rarely crowded, even in peak season.

GETTING ORIENTED

When Bermuda was developed back in the early 1600s, surveyors carved out the area around St. George's (then the capital) and divided the rest of the archipelago into eight districts. These parcels of land were deeded to—and named after—the Bermuda Company's original investors: Hamilton, Smith's, Devonshire, Pembroke, Paget, Warwick, Southampton, and Sandys. Although parish boundaries no longer delineate property ownership, they continue to function as the island version of state or province lines, and Bermudians remain parochially proud of them. Whether from the **West End** (anything west of the city of Hamilton), the **East End** (anything east of the city of Hamilton), or the **Town** (the city of Hamilton and its surrounding parishes), allegiances are quite publicly paraded when Cup Match—the annual cricket festival where east faces west—rolls around in July or August.

2 St. George's and Eastern Parishes. Air travelers first touch down in St. George's, just as the crew of the *Sea Venture* did in 1609. Their shipwreck kick-started Bermuda's settlement, and the town is today a UNESCO World Heritage Site. In the East you'll also find Hamilton Parish (not the city of Hamilton), which is home to the Bermuda Aquarium, Museum and Zoo, the Crystal Caves, Shelly Bay Park, and the infamous Swizzle Inn. In Smith's Parish, which borders Harrington Sound, you'll find Spittal Pond Nature Reserve, the Verdmont Museum, and John Smith's Bay.

3 Dockyard and Western Parishes. At the farthest West End tip in the parish of Sandys (pronounced *Sands*) you will find Bermuda's single largest tourist attraction: the Royal Naval Dockyard. A former British bastion, the complex has been converted to house the Bermuda National Museum, Dolphin Quest, and Snorkel Park Beach, plus shops and restaurants. Southampton is home to Horseshoe Bay, the most popular pink-sand beach.

BERMUDA PLANNER

When To Go

The important thing to remember when planning your trip is that subtropical Bermuda is in the Atlantic—not the Caribbean. High season is April through October, when the sun shines brightest and the warm waters beckon. This is when the island teems with activity, sightseeing options are plentiful, and the events calendar is full. Off-season—November through March—the weather is often perfect for golf or tennis, but the pace is considerably slower.

CLIMATE

Bermuda has a mild climate. In winter (December through March) temperatures range from around 55°F at night to 70°F in early afternoon. High winds can make the air feel cooler, however. The hottest times are between May and September, when temperatures range from 75°F to 85°F. It's not uncommon for the mercury to reach 90°F in July or August, and it often feels hotter due to humidity. Although summer is somewhat drier, rainfall is spread fairly evenly throughout the year. In August and September, hurricanes occasionally hit the island.

Getting Here

Bermuda is accessible by air and cruise ship. Most major airlines offer non-stop services to L.F. Wade International Airport in St. George's. Daily direct flights take two to three hours from East Coast cities, three hours from Toronto, and seven hours from London's Gatwick Airport.

Throughout the summer months there are regular cruise-ship arrivals. The government controls the number of sailings to prevent overcrowding on the small island, but most of the major cruise lines are represented. If you're arriving by sea, you're more than likely to step off the ship at King's Wharf or Heritage Wharf in Dockyard. Only a handful of cruise ships each year dock at Hamilton and St. George's.

Getting Around

Bermuda has a great public transport system, with buses covering the entire island. Buying a daily or weekly travel pass is perhaps the safest and cheapest way to do your sightseeing. They are valid for unlimited public transportation across all zones. Travel passes can be bought at Hamilton's bus station or ferry terminal, and cost $12 for one day, $28 for three days, and $45 for seven-days. The cost is $3 to $4.50 for single rides. Only exact change is accepted.

You can't rent a car in Bermuda; only full-time residents are issued driving licenses. The island's small size and the number of inhabitants does not leave a lot of space for extra vehicles on the road. You can, however, rent a scooter, the island's most popular mode of transportation. Expect to pay about $75 a day or about $200 a week to rent a good-quality scooter. Having two wheels will give you the freedom to go wherever you please, but the roads are narrow and winding, and accidents are frequent.

You can phone for a taxi pickup anywhere on the island or flag one down on the street, but taxis can be pricey if you're not with a large group. You'll pay $6.40 for the first mile and $2 for each subsequent mile. Drivers will also expect a tip. A surcharge of $1 is added for every piece of luggage you put in the trunk, and a 25% surcharge is added after midnight and on Sundays and holidays.

About the Restaurants

You will have no problem finding top-notch dining options in Bermuda, as restaurants are plentiful. Whether you are looking for traditional Bermudian or American fare, or Caribbean, Chinese, or Indian, the island has most cuisines covered. But good food does not come cheaply in Bermuda, and the portions will probably be a lot smaller than you are used to. You'll pay about $100 a head for a decent meal, and don't be surprised to see a 17 percent service charge added to the final tab. Most restaurants are in the Front Street area of Hamilton, with others concentrated in and around Dockyard and St. George's. Feel free to ask to look at menus and prices before taking your seat at a table. To try to save a few dollars it's worth asking about set menus and early-evening specials. Eat-as-much-as-you-can Sunday brunches are very popular with tourists and locals alike.

About the Hotels

You won't see many big-name hotels in Bermuda, as the island's charm is in its great selection of tucked-away resorts, cottage colonies, and intimate guest houses. The island's two largest—and probably best known—hotels are the Fairmont properties. But the best thing about Bermuda's accommodations is that most of them enjoy the tranquillity of being well hidden down small parish roads. For city living opt for Hamilton, for beach properties try the south shore, and for a taste of Bermuda's history, St. George's is your best bet. Your budget is more than likely going to determine where you stay; properties outside of Hamilton tend to be less expensive. Beware of the 7.25% government occupancy tax and a 10% service charge added to hotel bills. For the best deals, plan to visit during the winter. Some hotels also offer discounted rooms for repeat visitors.

WHAT IT COSTS IN US DOLLARS

	¢	$	$$	$$$	$$$$
Restaurants	under $10	$10–$20	$21–$30	$31–40	over $40
Hotels		under $110	$110–$200	$201–$300	$301–$400	over $400

Restaurant prices are per person for a main course at dinner. The bill usually includes a 17% service charge. Hotel prices are for two people in a standard double room in high season, excluding 7.25% tax and 10% service charge.

Essentials

Banks Bank of Butterfield, HSBC Bermuda, and Capital G banks are located in Hamilton. Branches are generally open Monday through Friday from 9 am to 4 pm. Smaller branches are in St. George's, with additional ATMs scattered across the island at gas stations and supermarkets.

Emergencies Call 911 for any type of emergency. The **King Edward VII Hospital** (✉ *7 Point Finger Rd., Paget* ☎ *441/236–2345*) has a 24-hour hour emergency room; the daytime-only **Lamb Foggo Urgent Care Centre** (✉ *1 Hall St., Southside* ☎ *441/298–7700*) is in St. David's. The **American Consulate** (✉ *Crown Hill, 16 Middle Rd., Devonshire* ☎ *441/295–1342*) can be visited from Monday through Friday, 8 am to 4:30 pm.

Visitor Information Centres are open Monday through Friday from 9 am to 5 pm at the ferry terminal on Front Street in Hamilton, near the ferry stop at Dockyard, and at the Museum at The Globe Hotel on Duke of York Street in St. George's. **Bermuda Department of Tourism** (☎ *441/292–0023*).

Taxis Bermuda Radio Cabs (☎ *441/295–4141*). **BTA** (☎ *441/296–2121*). **Co-Op Taxi Services** (☎ *441/292–4476*).

Bike Rentals Oleander Cycles (☎ *441/236–5235*). **Smatt's Cycle Livery** (☎ *441/295–1180*). **Wheels Cycles** (☎ *441/292–2245*).

BERMUDA TODAY

Bermuda has always been a land of adventure. Since it was first discovered in 1503, explorers and castaways have sought their fortune on the island. Today's adventurers head to Bermuda for water sports, golf, and scooter riding. Great shopping, pink sand, and spas provide retreat for those in search of relaxation. As in much of the world, tourism is struggling in Bermuda, and many large-scale developments are on hold. Thankfully the international business sector remains stable, and in true Bermudian spirit, locals continue to smile as they enjoy the island's rich natural bounty.

Today's Bermuda

...is tiny. Bermuda in all its glory is indeed little more than an easy-to-miss small dot on most world maps. Off the east coast of North Carolina in the northwest Atlantic, it's the fifth smallest country in the world—just 53 square kilometers, compared to the U.S's nearly 10 million square kilometers. That means you can travel the island's length in a little over an hour, and from north to south in 15 minutes. Don't let its size fool you, though; Bermuda is a main player in the business world, housing many big-name multinational companies.

...is not just one island. Most visitors wrongly assume Bermuda is just one island, when in fact there are islands everywhere you look. It has six principal islands, which are linked by bridges to create the main land, and a staggering 120 other islands scattered around the shore. Island hopping isn't really an option in Bermuda though, as there is no scheduled boat service, and many of the islets are surrounded by hazardous reefs. Some of the islands are also private residences, while others are mere rocks.

...is still very British. Bermuda's British traditions are obvious, from driving on the left side of the road to afternoon tea, to wig-wearing lawyers strolling to court. The national sports are cricket and football, there are "bobbies on the beat" (policemen on foot), and red letterboxes on street corners. Bermuda is one of the oldest British Overseas Territories, but that said, it's completely self-governing, with its own laws. Everyone, including Britons, is treated as a foreigner, as only Bermudians can own property, land, or vote.

...is not cheap. The World Bank rates Bermuda as one of the most affluent countries in the world, and it won't take long to

WHAT WE'RE TALKING ABOUT

Bermudians love to talk, so much so that you'd think neighbors hadn't seen one another for years when they stop in the street for a natter each morning.

Whether **gambling** should be made legal to boost tourism is a talking point that just won't

go away. Gambling has always been illegal here, and in May 2010 lawmakers voted against opening a casino in Bermuda. Locals are split over whether it would help boost the economy or ruin the island's unique appeal.

The **cost of living** is on the rise in Bermuda, and many Bermudians are struggling to keep up with the widespread wealth of international business. Bermuda is experiencing new levels of poverty as the unemployment rate increases. Even with the recession there

understand why. Start saving your dollars for Bermuda's high cost of living. Hotel accommodations are expensive, a bag of groceries costs more than $50, and gasoline is three times more than in the U.S. That being said, budget travelers should note that free walking tours are offered in Hamilton and St. George's, the Botanical Gardens have free entry, and the Gibb's Hill Lighthouse is a bargain at just $2.50.

...is crammed full of people. Bermuda is the third most densely populated place on earth. There's an average of more than 3,000 people per mile, which means there are more than enough happy faces to welcome you. For a bit of breathing space, head to Tucker's Town in St. George's Parish, the least populated spot on the island.

...is strict about cars. Bermuda has several laws governing the size and quantity of vehicles on the road. Only Bermudians or full-time residents are allowed driving licenses, and even they can only have one car per household. Licensing fees are determined by the length of vehicle.

...relies on the weather. Bermudians rely on rain to fill up their water tanks, as there is no public water system. As soon as it starts to rain, Bermudians talk at length about whether it's a passing shower or "tank rain." And when they aren't talking about the weather, they are hooked to the island's very own weather TV channel.

...is crazy about golf. Bermuda has golf courses everywhere you look, so it's no surprise that it's a popular pastime for many locals. There's a wide selection of government and privately-owned golf courses across the island, making it a golfer's paradise. The PGA Grand Slam of Golf is held here in October, but there are also several annual tournaments, such as team knock-outs, couples' classics, and par 3 championships.

...is proud of its traditions. Bermuda's history is rich and varied because of its Portuguese immigrants, English settlers, and African slaves. The traditions Bermudians are most proud of include Gombey dancers in colorful costumes, tucking into a codfish and potatoes breakfast, and greeting everyone with a "Good Morning" or "Good Afternoon." But it's the Cup Match holiday which really brings islanders together, with the east taking on the west for a traditional two-day cricket match.

has been no letup in the cost of food and housing. Government is tackling this by building low-cost housing and encouraging companies to employ Bermudians rather than expatriates.

The worsening **crime rate** is one of Bermuda's biggest concerns, as guns start to make their way onto the island. There have been unprecedented levels of gun crime since 2009, but there is little danger to tourists, as these serious crimes remain gang-related.

Bermudians remain at loggerheads about what is best for the country, as do the country's rival **political parties**, the Progressive Labour Party and the One Bermuda Alliance. The PLP have been in power since 1998, but there is likely to be an election in December 2011.

QUINTESSENTIAL BERMUDA

Pretty in Pink

According to local lore, Bermuda's sand has a faint rosy hue because it's so romantic here that even the beaches blush. Scientists, conversely, contend the coloring is derived from calcium carbonate and crushed bits of coral combined with the pulverized skeletons of microscopic scarlet protozoa (*Foraminifera* to be exact) that thrive on the surrounding reefs. Whatever the reason, this fine sand remains a Bermuda trademark. The pink-o-meter hits highest along the south shore, where "blushing beaches" include Horseshoe Bay (a classic curving strand) and Warwick Long Bay (Bermuda's longest expanse of sand). Other pocket-size beaches and secluded coves, though, are easy enough to find. Bermuda may only cover 21 square mi, yet the islands comprising it have a combined 75 mi of coast, so wherever you stay the beach is never more than a mile away.

The Long and Short of It

When it comes to the island's most recognizable symbol, Bermuda shorts might trump the infamous Bermuda Triangle. Originally part of a military uniform, the garment is a source of amusement to visitors—and a matter of national pride to natives. Elsewhere the term "Bermuda shorts" is loosely applied to any casual knee-length shorts. The real ones here are characterized by their fabric and tailoring (linen or wool blends, hitting 2 inches above the knee). Worn by businessmen with kneesocks and a blazer, they're considered the smartest of attire. If you want to join the local fashion and flash a little leg, just be sure to play by the rules. Rather than going for the seersucker-and-sandals look, get outfitted at a traditional retailer—like the English Sports Shop on Front Street in Hamilton, where genuine Bermuda shorts start at $50.

Although it's only 650 mi east of the United States, Bermuda seems like a world apart. Feeling at home on this oh-so-friendly archipelago, however, isn't hard. Just sample a few local pleasures and you'll be kicking back like a native "Onion" in no time.

A Perfect Match

On the Thursday and Friday before the first Monday in August, Bermuda takes a two-day holiday ostensibly to let residents watch the Cup Match: an annual cricket game pitting the West End against the East End. Locals clearly take the event seriously. Cup Match fever, for instance, takes hold weeks in advance, when team colors start flying from houses and vehicles island-wide. But Cup Match is also an excuse for some serious partying. While the players concentrate on whacking a leather ball through a wicket, the spectators generally focus on fun. Pulsating music, outrageous fashions, and delectable foods (anyone for mussel pie?) add to the carnival-like atmosphere. The Bermuda government even relaxes its anti-gambling laws so that locals can indulge in Crown & Anchor, a betting game first brought here by British sailors in the 19th century.

The Beat of a Different Drum

Bermuda has its own musical mélange that embraces both British and African traditions. Sample the former when the Bermuda Regiment's brass-and-drum corps "beats retreat." The pomp-filled sunset ceremony—a military staple since the 1700s—usually runs at least once a month in rotating venues around the island. Red coats and pith helmets are replaced by peacock-color capes and mile-high headdresses when local Gombey troupes take center stage. The hypnotic dancers and drummers, whose distinctive style dates back to the days of slavery, pop up unexpectedly around the island November through March. Other months you can catch them in action on Wednesday during the Hamilton's Harbour Nights festivities.

IF YOU LIKE

Life in the Past Lane

You don't have to be here long to realize there's much more to Bermuda than sea, sand, and rum swizzles. As one of Britain's oldest colonies, the island has more than 400 years of history and, thanks to thoughtful preservation policies, the architecture to prove it.

The jewel in the crown, in terms of period charm, is the UNESCO-designated town of **St. George's.** As Bermuda's original capital, it has a distinctly colonial feel, and wandering its crooked, cottage-lined lanes is akin to time travel. See the statue of Sir George Somers (who was shipwrecked here in 1609), and view a replica of his vessel before ambling over to King's Square to catch a "ducking stool" reenactment.

The British, keenly aware of Bermuda's strategic significance, kept it well protected from 1612 to 1956—which is why this tiny country has the world's highest concentration of **historic forts.** Start working through the list at the National Museum of Bermuda: a converted fortress that's now the centerpiece of the Royal Naval Dockyard. Fort St. Catherine, a 17th-century edifice, complete with moat and sprawling ramparts, is another must-see.

The **African Diaspora Heritage Trail,** part of the international Slave Route Project, shows that Brits weren't the only ones who helped shape Bermuda. This self-guided tour crisscrosses the island, identifying 11 sites related to Black Bermudians. Highlights include the poignant slave graveyard at St. Peter's Church and Cobb's Hill Methodist Church, which was built by and for blacks before Emancipation.

Tee Time

Bermuda is a renowned golfing destination and close enough to the United States and Canada to be pitched as "putting distance" from the eastern seaboard. The courses are as scenic as the island itself. But don't let their pretty appearance fool you. Many have holes by the sea or atop ocean-side bluffs, so wind and that big water hazard (the Atlantic!) can play havoc with your game.

Laid out by Charles Blair Macdonald in 1921, the classic course at **Mid Ocean Golf Club** in Tucker's Town is one of the most spectacular on the island—and one of the most highly regarded in the world. If you can wrangle an introduction from a member (or have your concierge do it on your behalf), you might find yourself on the links with celebs like Michael Douglas and Catherine Zeta-Jones, who own a home in Bermuda

Port Royal Golf Course in Southampton Parish is understandably popular. The affordable public property, fresh from a $14-million makeover, has an impressive pedigree: it's a Robert Trent Jones design and a favorite of Jack Nicklaus. Plus, it boasts Bermuda's most recognizable hole (the sublime 16th), which has been photographed for countless glossy golfing magazines.

You can see why they say "good things come in small packages" at the **Fairmont Southampton Resort's Golf Course.** The property's 18-hole par-3 executive course, designed by Ted Robinson, is on a hillside, and its challenging terrain offers a good warm-up for Bermuda's full-length courses. Better still, playing here for an afternoon won't break your piggy bank.

Just Add Water

Boat-loving Bermudians like to drop anchor, crack open a case of beer, and float the day away—an activity that should not be knocked until it is tried. Yet seeing what lies beneath the turquoise waves can be equally enjoyable. Warm, clear water with visibility up to 150 feet, rich marine life, unique topography, and perhaps most important, reliable outfitters, combine to make Bermuda an ideal place for underwater exploration.

Wreck divers know that not all of Bermuda's history lessons can be learned on dry land. Due to the island's treacherous coral reefs, hundreds of shipwrecks from various eras lie in its waters—and companies like **Triangle Diving** and **Blue Water Divers** will take you out to see them. Both operate wreck tours for experienced scuba enthusiasts as well as lesson-and-dive packages for first-timers.

Not ready to dive in? Consider taking an underwater walk. **Hartley's Under Sea Adventures** lets you don a specially designed helmet, then descend about 10 feet for some face time with fish. Although the equipment may look strange, the science is sound (helmets operate on the same principal as a tumbler overturned in water) and the experience is unforgettable.

From April to November all you need are fins and a mask to enjoy the Dockyard's **Snorkel Park Beach.** This sheltered, easy-to-access inlet features exotic sea creatures, submerged artifacts (such as centuries-old cannons), and even floating rest stations. You can rent snorkel gear—along with an assortment of other equipment, including kayaks, pedalos, and Jet Skis—at the site.

Suite Dreams

Many holiday hot spots invite visitors to bed down in ho-hum "all inclusives." But Bermuda is different. The island is dotted with one-of-a-kind accommodations, where big names in luxury lodging are interspersed with posh family-run resorts, old-school cottage colonies, and quaint, sometimes quirky, bed-and-breakfasts.

Bermuda is fresh off a hotel-building boom. The first to debut is the **Newstead Belmont Hills Golf Resort & Spa,** which opened in spring 2008 in Paget Parish. Boutique-style decor and divine water views make it a hit with overnighters; and if you wish you were lucky enough to actually live here, fractional ownership opportunities are available.

As its unusual name suggests, **Salt Kettle House** in Paget Parish isn't your ordinary bed-and-breakfast. Set on a peninsula overlooking Hamilton Harbour, it has cabbage-rose upholstery inside and colorful lounge chairs outside that combine to give it a "Laura Ashley Goes to the Beach" vibe. However, it is British-born owner Hazel Lowe—famed for dishing out advice as well as breakfast—who really keeps visitors coming back.

Tucked away in a quiet alleyway, **Aunt Nea's Inn at Hillcrest** offers the ultimate in St. George's charm. It's a family-run guest house that you won't want to leave because of all its history and quirky features. The unique feel of its rooms, which are filled with antiques, make it one of the quaintest places to stay on the island.

LIKE A LOCAL

Enjoy Salt Cod Fish and Potatoes
Bermudians love to eat, and on Sundays they never miss this traditional brunch dish. The custom dates back to the 18th century, when Bermuda sloops traded with Newfoundland and brought cheap and plentiful salt cod back to Bermuda to feed the slaves. The fish is served with a hardboiled eggs, bananas, avocado, and boiled potatoes with a tomato-and-onion-based sauce on the side.

Save Summer for After May 24
Bermuda Day—May 24—marks the official start of summer, and the date is forever etched on a Bermudian's mind. Regardless of the rising temperatures, true Bermudians would rather swelter in long pants than switch to their summer wardrobe before the all-important date. Bermudians won't even dip their toes in the water or take their boats out a day earlier than May 24. It's a public holiday, and is celebrated with a running and cycling race, followed by a parade.

Speak Bermudian
To the untrained ear you might think Bermudians sound awfully posh with their English-sounding accents. But listen carefully and you'll pick up a new lingo of "Bermewjan Vurds." The native tongue strings words together and has a tendency to swap the letter "w" for the letter "v." "Up the Country" means anything west of Hamilton and "down the country" means anywhere east of Hamilton. If you're "going shrew de trees" you're getting married. If you like the taste of something it's "well." An empty cocktail is at "low tide" and depending on how drunk you are you will be labeled anything from "hot" to "full hot."

Give color-coded instructions
Every cottage here is proudly painted in a pastel color, and no one dares to paint his or her home a color like that of their neighbor. Names and numbers of buildings are often irrelevant, as directions are dished out in a color-by-numbers kind of way. You'll be told to take a right at the pink building and then a left when you get to the yellow house. It's much the same story when ordering a taxi; the operator will take an address, but "what color is your place?" will automatically be asked.

Mind your Manners
You won't get very far in Bermuda until you learn the unwritten rule of greeting complete strangers with a "Good Morning" or a "Good Afternoon," followed quickly with "How are you?" It doesn't matter where you are, every conversation has to be started with those all important words—a simple hi or hello just won't cut it. Try to get on a bus or buy something in a store without starting with the friendly greeting and see what happens. You have been warned.

Respect Religion
With more churches per square mile than any other country, there's a house of worship on just about every street. Most Bermudians get dressed up in their Sunday best for weekly worship, whether Catholic, Methodist, Seventh Day Adventist, Jehovah's Witnesses, or Muslim. Locals love reading the marriage and death notices in the paper, as weddings and funerals are huge affairs with plenty of gate-crashers. It doesn't matter whether you know the person or not, it is simply assumed that any church service has an open door policy.

WEDDINGS AND HONEYMOONS

1

It's no wonder so many couples exchange wedding vows in Bermuda. For starters, this subtropical paradise has loads of secluded pink beaches. Factor in easy access from the United States; a well-established infrastructure that includes English-speaking wedding personnel; and a remarkably high romance quotient (the island even has an honest-to-goodness Lovers Lane), and you can understand why Bermuda is an ideal spot to tie the knot.

The Big Day

Find a Wedding Planner. There's a whole host of wedding planners ready and willing to do the hard work for you. Try **Bridal Suite** (☎ 441/292–2025 ⊕ *www. bridalsuitebermudaweddings.com*) or **Bermuda Bride** (☎ 441/295–8697 ⊕ *www. bermudabride.com*). Most larger resorts have their own wedding planners.

Get Your License. To get married in Bermuda, the couple must complete and send a Notice of Intended Marriage form to the **Bermuda Registrar General** (☎ 441/297–7709 ⊕ *www.registrygeneral.gov.bm*) within three months of their intended wedding date. A fee of $300 (plus $30 for the certificate) must accompany the form. The Notice of Intended Marriage is then published in the local newspaper. There is a waiting period of 15 days, and if no formal objection is raised, the license will be issued. The license to marry is valid for three months from the date of issue.

Scout the Perfect Backdrop. The obvious choice for a Bermuda destination wedding is right on the beach with the waves lapping at your feet and the sand between your toes. Another popular choice is the sunset clifftop ceremony looking down over the turquoise water. Many hotels will set up gazebos on their beaches or in their gardens. You can also go for the more unusual grounds of historic properties like the World Heritage Centre in St. George's or Fort Hamilton overlooking the capital city.

Dress Smart. It's your day and you can wear whatever you want. That said, most brides go for formal dresses rather than wedding gowns, and grooms like to go for linen pants and short-sleeved shirts. Similar smart-casual outfits are accepted for guests. Bare feet on the beach is a must.

Add Some Local Flavor. Bermudians serve two wedding cakes; the groom's cake is plain, often a pound cake, and the multitier bride's cake is a dark fruitcake. Another tradition is for the bride and groom to walk hand-in-hand beneath a Bermuda moongate—an archway made of limestone and coral usually found at the entrance to gardens. It's said that all who do so are assured everlasting luck.

The Honeymoon

Many resorts offer honeymoon suites and special packages for newlyweds, so be sure to inquire when booking your stay. The following hotels are our top honeymoon picks.

Cambridge Beaches. Sunsets, candlelit dinners, and beautiful scenery are all at this resort, which offers the ultimate pampering experience.

Elbow Beach. This cottage colony set in lush gardens welcomes its honeymooners with a bottle of bubbly. There are beautiful beachfront cottages, and the spa has couples treatment rooms.

The Reefs. This cliffside luxury resort has breathtaking views. You'll get champagne and chocolate-covered strawberries on your arrival and you can book a gourmet dinner right on the beach.

GREAT ITINERARIES

BUMMING AROUND BERMUDA: SEA, SAND, AND SIGHTS

Day 1: Horseshoe Bay

Chances are you came for that legendary pink sand, so don't waste any time finding it. If you think variety is the spice of life, spend the day bouncing from beach to beautiful beach along the south shore. (The No. 7 bus will get you there and back from the city of Hamilton.) Otherwise, just choose one and settle in. Our pick is the flagship beach at **Horseshoe Bay**: a gently curving crescent lapped by turquoise water and backed by South Shore Park. It does get crowded here—but for good reason. Unlike most Bermudian beaches, Horseshoe Bay has lifeguards (in season) plus a snack bar, changing rooms, and beach gear–rental facilities. Families should note that there's also a protected inlet, dubbed Horseshoe Baby Beach, which is perfect for young children. Looking for something more private? Picturesque trails through the park will lead you to secluded coves like Stonehole and Chaplin bays. Whichever you opt for, bring a hat, plenty of water, and a light cover-up if you plan to stay until evening. Don't forget to slather on the SPF either: bad sunburns and road rashes (caused by skimming the road on a scooter) are the two most common ailments visitors to Bermuda experience. When the sun goes down—and you have sand in every crevice—stroll over to the lively **Henry VIII pub and restaurant** for an evening bite or a late-night libation.

Day 2: The Town of St. George's

Founded in 1612, **St. George's** qualifies as one of the oldest towns in the Western Hemisphere and deserves a place on any traveler's itinerary. This UNESCO World Heritage Site has a smattering of worthwhile museums, the Bermuda National Trust Museum at the Globe Hotel and Tucker House being chief among them. Historic buildings such as St. Peter's Church also should not be missed. Organized walks and road train tours cover the highlights. Yet the real delight here is simply wandering the walled lanes and quaint alleys lined with traditional shops, pubs, and cottages. All of those roads eventually lead to **King's Square**, where you can try out the replica stocks. Nearby is another device formerly used to punish unruly folk—the seesaw-like ducking stool—which serves as the focal point for reenactments starring the Town Crier and a wet wench. (These are staged at noon May through October, Sunday through Thursday; other months on Monday, Wednesday, and Saturday only.) If you have time and shoe leather to spare, continue your history lesson outside St. George's at **Fort St. Catherine**, a hilltop defense built in the 17th century. Stop for a little swimming or snorkeling just below it in snug **Achilles Bay** or at **Fort St. Catherine Beach**; then cap the day back in town by enjoying a casual meal at the **White Horse Tavern** on the water's edge.

Day 3: The City of Hamilton

Bermuda's capital city is minuscule by mainland standards. Still, it dominates island life and has all the ingredients for a great day out. Since there's a little bit of everything here, you can plot a course according to your individual tastes. Shoppers should make a beeline for the **Front Street** area to spend a few hours—and a wallet-full of money—in the stores and galleries. Prefer sightseeing? Simply pick up a brochure for a self-guided tour at the Visitor Information Centre (VIC) and

Map labels:
Achilles Bay
Fort St. Catherine
King's Square
St. George's
National Museum of Bermuda & Dolphin Quest
Royal Naval Dockyard
Castle Harbour
Somerset Village
Harrington Sound
SANDYS PARISH
Great Sound
Spittal Pond
HAMILTON
Front St.
Fort Hamilton
Bermuda Underwater Exploration Institute
Botanical Gardens
Paget Marsh
ATLANTIC OCEAN
SOUTHAMPTON PARISH
Horseshoe Bay

hit the streets. Outside the city, visit **Fort Hamilton**: a must-see for history buffs and a great spot for photo ops. Alternatively, you can investigate sunken treasure and seashells without ever getting wet at the **Bermuda Underwater Exploration Institute** (about a 15-minute walk from the city center), or get out on the water itself. Excursion options from Hamilton range from archipelago tours and glass-bottom boat trips to low-cost ferry rides. Afterward, gear up to see Hamilton by night. Pubs and clubs start filling around 10 pm, leaving plenty of time for dinner at one of the area's surprisingly diverse restaurants. **Port O' Call** (conveniently positioned on Front Street) and **Ascots** (just outside the city in the Royal Palms Hotel) are both Fodor's Choices.

Day 4: The Dockyard
Once a military stronghold and now a magnet for tourists, the **Royal Naval Dockyard** offers a full day of history mixed with a heaping helping of adventure. Its centerpiece is the **National Museum of Bermuda**, where you can find exhibits on whaling, sailing, shipbuilding, and shipwrecks set within an imposing stone fortress. Once you've checked out the displays—and taken in the stunning views from the ramparts—head to the **Old Cooperage**.

This former barrel-making factory is the perfect place to stock up on unique souvenirs, because it houses both the Bermuda Craft Market (perhaps the island's best-stocked, best-priced craft outlet) and the Bermuda Arts Centre (a high-end co-op with gallery and studio space). After lunch in an area eatery, join one of the educational in-water programs offered by **Dolphin Quest** at the Keep Pond, or baby your budget by swimming with the fishies right next door at the inexpensive **Snorkel Park Beach**. Spring through fall, adrenaline junkies can try Jet Skiing (courtesy of H20 Sports); then toast their achievements at the nearby **Frog & Onion Pub**. If you're interested in a more placid on-the-water experience, take the slow, scenic ferry to Somerset Island and disembark at **Watford Bridge**. From there, explore quiet Somerset Village before sitting down for dinner at the **Somerset Country Squire**, a traditional tavern overlooking Mangrove Bay.

Day 5: Go Green
For many travelers Bermuda is synonymous with golf greens, so dedicated duffers will want to spend at least one day putting around. Even neophytes can get into the swing of things at the **Bermuda Golf Academy**. For other kinds of "green experiences," feel genteel at the **Botanical**

Gardens or go wild at **Paget Mash**, both near the city of Hamilton. The former is a Victorian venue with formal flower beds and subtropical fruit orchards; the latter a 25-acre tract that covers five distinct ecosystems (including primeval woodlands that contain the last surviving stands of native palmetto and cedar). **Spittal Pond**, on Bermuda's south shore, is another eco-destination. November to May it's a major draw for bird-watchers, thanks to the 30-odd species of waterfowl that stop here; in April it attracts whale-watchers hoping to spy migrating humpbacks from the preserve's oceanfront cliffs. You can access more "undiscovered" spots by traversing all or part of the **Bermuda Railway Trail**. With its lush greenery and dramatic lookouts, this 18-mi recreational route is best seen on foot. Of course, if your boots aren't made for walking, bicycling is permitted, too. (When renting equipment, just remember to request a pedal bike, otherwise you might end up with a motorized scooter.) If you like packaged excursions, **Fantasea Bermuda** has a surf-and-turf deal that combines a shoreline cruise with a guided cycle tour along the trail, and a cool-down swim at a Somerset beach.

Tips:
Before going swimming, check Horseshoe Bay Beach's notice board for **jellyfish updates**. Although the Portuguese man-of-war variety looks like an innocuous blue plastic bag, its sting is extremely painful and poisonous.

Bermuda has loads of beaches—but **few lifeguards**. The only places you can find them are at Horseshoe Bay, John Smith's Bay, Clearwater Beach, and Turtle Bay from May to October.

The **northern end of Court Street** in the City of Hamilton is off the typical tourist trail, so you can find some great local eateries and a taste of day-to-day Bermuda life. Be warned, this area is not advisable after dark.

In high season Hamilton hosts **Harbour Nights**, a street festival complete with craft vendors and live entertainment every Wednesday evening.

Since certain outdoor activities are only offered seasonally, you should **confirm operating times** to avoid disappointment. Also try to make any sporting reservations before you arrive in Bermuda—tee times and boat charters are in especially high demand.

Always be cautious if you're tooling around on a scooter. The island's notoriously narrow, twisting roads have a particularly high accident rate, and drinking-and-driving is a problem. Don't be scared, just be aware.

ON THE
CALENDAR

Bermuda is a year-round destination with an active events calendar, so we've highlighted the top annual offerings. For more options, consult **Bermuda Tourism** (☎ *800/237–6832* ⊕ *www.gotobermuda.com*). Local publications are another reliable resource. The free, widely distributed tourist magazine **The Bermuda.com Guide** provides a monthly overview, while the island's newspapers, the **Bermuda Sun** (⊕ *www.bermudasun.bm*) and **The Royal Gazette** (⊕ *www.royalgazette.com*) publish weekly calendars each Friday. Events are also listed on the papers' Web sites. Further info can be found online at ⊕ *www.thisweek.bm* and ⊕ *www.bermuda.com*. Entertainment Web sites **BlackandCoke.com** and **Bermynet.com** offer visitors a glimpse of Bermuda's night, sporting, and cultural life.

WINTER

December

Christmas Boat Parade. Every other year the Christmas Boat Parade sees decorated vessels of every size and description float through Hamilton Harbour. The event, which can draw 20,000 spectators, usually takes place on the second Saturday of the month and is topped off by festive fireworks. The event will take place in 2011 and following odd-numbered years. ⊕ *www.bermudaboatparade.bm*.

Hamilton Jaycees Santa Claus Parade. Father Christmas visits Front Street in the Hamilton Jaycees Santa Claus Parade, usually held the first Sunday in December. Santa is accompanied by marching bands, majorettes, and floats.

Annual Christmas Walkabout in St. George's. Properties specially decked out for the holiday season open their doors to the public during this early-evening event hosted by the Bermuda National Trust. Choir concerts, Christmas-theme readings, and eggnog sipping are also on the agenda. ☎ *441/236–6483* ⊕ *www.bnt.bm*.

Boxing Day. Following Commonwealth tradition, Bermuda makes December 26 a public holiday. Harness racing and cycling competitions are scheduled, and Gombey troupes mark the day by dancing in the streets.

January

Bermuda Festival of the Performing Arts. For more than 30 years the Bermuda Festival of the Performing Arts, the largest of its kind on the island, has featured international performers. Plays, ballets, chamber orchestras, and jazz jams are staged over two months at the City Hall Theatre and other venues. ☎ *441/295–1291* ⊕ *www.bermudafestival.org*.

	Bermuda International Race Weekend. On your mark! Bermuda International Race Weekend kicks off the third weekend of the month. The event begins Friday night with the Front Street Mile. It also includes a marathon, half-marathon, and a 10k (6.2-mi) charity walk. ☎ *441/296-0951* ⊕ *www. bermudaraceweekend.com.*
SPRING March–April	**Bermuda International Film Festival.** Starting in late March, the prestigious Bermuda International Film Festival shows dozens of independent feature, documentary, and short films from around the world, awarding prizes in four categories. In addition to seven days of screenings, you can expect panel discussions, parties, and popcorn. ☎ *441/293-3456* ⊕ *www. biff.bm.* **Palm Sunday Walk.** The Palm Sunday Walk is an annual 5- to 8-mi stroll sponsored by the Bermuda National Trust. Following a different route each year, the event allows thousands of walkers to access private properties that would otherwise be off-limits. ☎ *441/236-6483* ⊕ *www.bnt.bm.* **Bermuda Kite Festival.** Good Friday is a public holiday and traditionally *the* day for kite flying. Residents like to make their own from tissue paper, glue, and wooden sticks; then show them off during the annual Bermuda Kite Festival. Held at Horseshoe Bay in Southampton, it includes a kite contest plus classic fun and games. ☎ *441/295-0729.*
April	**Annual Exhibition.** Much like a state fair, Bermuda's Annual Exhibition showcases agriculture via livestock competitions, horticultural displays, and down-home entertainment. This three-day event at the Botanical Gardens typically runs the third weekend in April. The gardens (free other days) charge admission for the exhibition. ☎ *441/239-2351* ⊕ *www. bdaexhibition.bm.* **Peppercorn Ceremony.** Members of St. George's Masonic Lodge pay their rent on the Old State House with great pomp and circumstance during the Peppercorn Ceremony. A single peppercorn is solemnly passed over to the mayor in a stylish (if somewhat surreal) display that includes a march by the Bermuda Regiment. ☎ *441/297-1532.*
May	**Bermuda Heritage Month.** May is Bermuda Heritage Month, when a host of commemorative, cultural, and sporting activities are scheduled. The climax is Bermuda Day (May 24), a

public holiday that includes a parade around Hamilton, a cycling race, and dinghy races in St. George's Harbour. Traditionally, this is also the first day that locals swim, swearing the water is too cold earlier in the year. ☎ 441/292–1681.

Bermuda End-to-End. On the first Saturday in May Bermuda End-to-End lets you get exercise and meet residents while raising money for charity. The full 24-mi walking course mostly follows the Railway Trail, but alternate routes (including ones for swimmers, boaters, and equestrians) are also available. ☎ 441/292–6992 ⊕ www.bermudaendtoend.bm.

SUMMER

June

Newport–Bermuda Race. Seasoned yachtsmen chart a challenging 635-mi course from Rhode Island to St. David's Lighthouse during the biennial Newport–Bermuda Race. One of the sailing world's preeminent blue-water events, it's held late June in even-numbered years and is hosted by the Royal Bermuda Yacht Club. ☎ 441/295–2214 ⊕ www. bermudarace.com.

Bermuda Ocean Race. The smaller-scale Bermuda Ocean Race out of Annapolis sets sail in even-numbered years. ☎ 410/849–8523 ⊕ www.bermudaoceanrace.com.

Harbour Nights. Harbour Nights, a street festival featuring Bermudian artists, crafts, Gombey dancers, face painting, and the like, takes place every Wednesday night in summer on Front Street in the City of Hamilton.

July–August

Cup Match Cricket Festival. The Cup Match Cricket Festival is a spirited two-day celebration centered on the match between rival Somerset and St. George's cricket clubs. (Locals sport red-and-navy if they're Somerset fans, dark blue–light blue if they're St. George's fans.) The highlight of Bermuda's events calendar, it's scheduled either the last Thursday and Friday in July or the first Thursday and Friday in August in conjunction with two public holidays: Emancipation Day and Somers Day. ☎ 441/234–0327, 441/297–0374.

August

Non-Mariners Race. The quirky Non-Mariners Race is decidedly nonsensical. On the first Sunday in August landlubbers hastily cobble together "non-boats" on the beach; then attempt to race them in Mangrove Bay. No paddles, oars, engines, or sails are permitted, and contraptions that manage to float far are disqualified. ☎ 441/234–2248.

FALL	
September	**International Sand Sculpture Competition.** Bermuda's fine pink sand is put to good use during Horseshoe Bay's one-day International Sand Sculpture Competition, typically held on the Saturday before Labour Day. Teams of up to six people are encouraged to get creative and build the craziest scultures possible on a 15x15-foot patch of beach. Prizes are awarded in seven categories. ☎ *441/295–4597.*
October	**King Edward VII Gold Cup.** The weeklong King Edward VII Gold Cup sees match-race skippers (America's Cup competitors among them) vie for the titular trophy and a $100,000 purse. Races are in Hamilton Harbour, and the Royal Bermuda Yacht Club opens its doors for the event, making this one especially appealing to spectators. ☎ *441/295–6361* ⊕ *www.kingedwardviigoldcup.com.*
	PGA Grand Slam of Golf. Go fore it! Mid-month the Port Royal Golf Course proudly hosts the PGA Grand Slam of Golf. Only an ultra-elite foursome—winners of the year's Masters Tournament, U.S. Open, British Open, and PGA Championship—qualify to play. ☎ *561/624–8400* ⊕ *www.pga.com.*
November	**Reconvening of Parliament.** On the first Friday in November the Reconvening of Parliament kicks off when the governor, in full regalia, arrives at Hamilton's Cabinet Building in a horse-drawn landau. His Speech from the Throne (detailing new policies and initiatives) usually begins around 11 am, so arrive by 10:15 to secure a good spot. ☎ *441/292–7408.*
	World Rugby Classic. Former international players from around the globe represent their respective countries in matches at the National Sports Centre in Devonshire Parish. Afterward fans can mix with the players in a "tavern tent" behind the touchline. ☎ *441/295–6574* ⊕ *www.worldrugby.bm.*
	Remembrance Day. Remembrance Day is a public holiday held in memory of fallen soldiers from Bermuda and its allied nations. A parade with Bermudian, British, and U.S. military units, the Bermuda Police, and war-veterans' organizations takes place on Front Street in Hamilton, and commemorative wreaths are laid at the Cenotaph near the Cabinet Building.

Exploring Bermuda

WORD OF MOUTH

"Bermuda is one of my favorite places in the world—the beaches, the scenery, the people are lovely. There are quite a few sights to see for being a little island, such as the aquarium, numerous forts, the Royal Dockyard, Hamilton, etc. We usually rent motorbikes (which can be dangerous—I don't particularly recommend it) or they have a good system of public busses to get around."

—luvsun

Updated by
Sirkka Huish

Bermuda is justifiably famous for pink-sand beaches, impossibly blue water, and kelly-green golf courses. But that's only the beginning. Thanks to its colorful past, this small sliver of land also has a surprising number of historic sites. In addition to countless quaint old cottages, it's said to have the oldest continually inhabited town of English origin in the Western Hemisphere and—because of its strategic Atlantic location—more forts per square mile than any other place on earth.

Bermuda has a distinctive culture, too: one that combines a reverence for British traditions dating back to colonial days with a more relaxed attitude befitting a subtropical island. You'll most likely see the British influences within the government, legal, and educational systems. In court, for instance, local lawyers may still wear formal flowing robes— yet there's a good chance that they're sporting Bermuda shorts beneath them. You'll also see "bobbies" (policemen) directing traffic, red telephone boxes and post boxes, and hear lots of cricket talk, as it's the island's national sport.

African and Caribbean influences are more subtle, but they can be spotted through the music and dance of calypso and reggae. Look out for the island's Gombey dancers; they may only look like colorful characters wildly jumping up and down, but they actually have a history embedded in African tribal music.

There is certainly no shortage of things to see in Bermuda. The town of St. George's, at the island's East End, is the original 1600s settlement and a UNESCO World Heritage Site. It has streets full of well-preserved history, as well as a whole host of Bermuda National Trust properties. The city of Hamilton (not to be confused with the parish of the same name farther northeast) is home to Bermuda's principal harbor and most of its shops. It's also the main departure point for sightseeing boats, ferries, and the pink-and-blue buses that ramble all over the island. The Royal Naval Dockyard, at the West End, is a former British shipyard that has been transformed into a stunning tourist attraction. Spend a day there shopping or museum and art-gallery hopping.

All three of these destinations can be explored easily on foot. The rest of the island, however, is best discovered by taxi, motor scooter, or even bicycle—but only if you're fit, because Bermuda is hilly! The main roads connecting the parishes are North Shore Road, Middle Road, South Road (also known as South Shore Road), and Harbour Road. Their names make it easy for you to get your bearings, and almost all the traffic traversing the island's 21-mi length is concentrated on them, although some 1,200 smaller roads also crisscross it.

Bermuda has long been thought of as a pricey vacation destination, but since the Bermudian dollar is on par with the American one, visitors from the States don't have to fret over the declining value of the greenback. Since U.S. bills are so widely accepted, vacationers don't have to bother with currency exchanges, either.

EXPLORING BERMUDA

Bermuda's compact size and small-town feel make it incredibly easy to navigate. The one drawback is that visitors can't rent cars. But who needs four wheels when you can get where you want to go with just two? The majority of Bermuda's visitors head straight to a bike-rental shop to get a nifty little 50cc scooter, perfect for zipping from one end of the island to the other. If you prefer to play it safe (roads are narrow and winding), there's also an excellent bus and ferry transport system linking all the island's main points.

Pay Hamilton a visit for the hustle and bustle of city life, serene St. George's packs a history punch, and the Royal Naval Dockyard is sightseeing central. Our best advice for touring the island? Try not to cram too much in. Nothing happens in a hurry in Bermuda, so planning a packed agenda is going to leave you feeling frustrated. This is your vacation after all, and the island's uncrowded pink-sand shores serve up relaxation perhaps better than any. Take time to enjoy the beauty.

HAMILTON AND CENTRAL PARISHES

With a permanent resident population of 1,500 households, Hamilton doesn't qualify as a major metropolis. Yet it has enough stores, restaurants, and offices to amp up the island's energy level. Moreover, it has a thriving international business community (centered on financial and investment services, insurance, telecommunications, global management of intellectual property, shipping, and aircraft and ship registration), which lends it a degree of sophistication seldom found in so small a center.

The central parishes cover the large area of Paget, Warwick, and Devonshire. These parishes are much sleepier than Hamilton, and provide great nature and beach respites when you tire of city life. Convenient bus and ferry connections connect the parishes, so trips outside of Hamilton are easy and a fun way to get off the tourist track.

TIMING   Although it's possible to buzz through Hamilton in a few hours, you should plan to give it a day if you're going to take in some of the museums, Fort Hamilton, and the Bermuda Underwater Exploration Institute. Serious shoppers should set aside another half day to browse around the shops. Set aside one day for some of the nature sites in the central parishes, and another day if you want to relax at the beaches.

A GOOD WALK IN HAMILTON

Any tour of Hamilton should begin on **Front Street**, a tidy thoroughfare lined with ice cream–color buildings, many with cheery awnings and ornate balconies. The Visitor Information Centre next to the Ferry Terminal at No. 8 is a good starting point. Continue west and swing down Point Pleasant Road to **Albuoy's Point** for a splendid view of Hamilton Harbour. Afterward, retrace your steps, passing the Ferry Terminal Building where passengers board boats for sightseeing excursions. (You can also depart from here on more affordable round-trip rides to the Dockyard and St. George's via the Sea Express ferry.) Stroll toward the intersection of Front and Queen streets, where you can see the Birdcage, a much-photographed traffic box named for its designer, Michael "Dickey" Bird.

Turn up Queen Street to see the 19th-century **Perot Post Office**. Just beyond it is the **Museum of the Bermuda Historical Society/ Bermuda National Library**. Follow Queen Street away from the harbor to Church Street to reach the **City Hall & Arts Centre**, which houses the Bermuda National Gallery, the Bermuda Society of Arts Gallery, and a performing arts venue. Saturday mornings from November through

June you can continue on to the **Farmers Market**, which sets up about five minutes north on Canal Road.

Returning to the City Hall steps, turn east on Church Street and pass the Hamilton Bus Terminal. One block farther, the imposing **Cathedral of the Most Holy Trinity** looms up before you. Next, past the cathedral near the corner of Church and Parliament streets, you'll come to **Sessions House**. Keep going down Parliament to Front Street for a look at the **Cabinet Building** and, in front of it, the Cenotaph for fallen Bermudian soldiers. From here you might head back to Front Street for a leisurely stroll past (or into) the shops, then linger over lunch in one of the many cafés overlooking the harbor.

If you're up for a longer walk (about 15 minutes east from the Cenotaph) or are traveling by scooter or taxi, head to the **Bermuda Underwater Exploration Institute (BUEI)**. **Fort Hamilton** is another worthwhile destination, though the road to it— north on King Street, then a sharp right on Happy Valley Road—is a bit too steep for casual walkers. The moated fort has gorgeous grounds, underground passageways, and great views of Hamilton and its harbor.

WHAT TO SEE
TOP ATTRACTIONS

Bermuda Underwater Exploration Institute (BUEI). The 40,000-square-foot Ocean Discovery Centre showcases local contributions to oceanographic research and undersea discovery. Guests can ogle the world-class shell collection amassed by resident Jack Lightbourne (three of the 1,000 species were identified by and named for Lightbourne himself); or visit a gallery honoring native-born archaeologist Teddy Tucker to see booty retrieved from Bermudian shipwrecks. The types of gizmos that made such discoveries possible are also displayed, including a replica of the bathysphere William Beebe and Otis Barton used in their

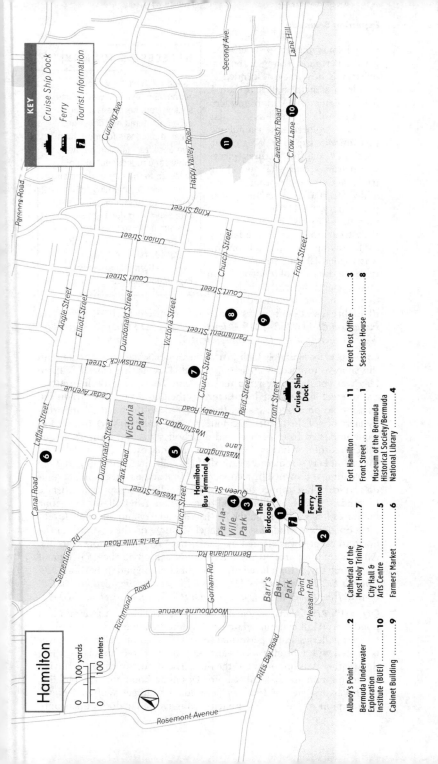

Hamilton

KEY

⛴ Cruise Ship Dock
🚢 Ferry
ℹ Tourist Information

0 —— 100 yards
0 —— 100 meters

Albuoy's Point **2**
Bermuda Underwater
Exploration
Institute (BUEI) **10**
Cabinet Building **9**

Cathedral of the
Most Holy Trinity **7**
City Hall &
Arts Centre **5**
Farmers Market **6**

Fort Hamilton **11**
Front Street **1**
Museum of the Bermuda
Historical Society/Bermuda
National Library **4**

Perot Post Office **3**
Sessions House **8**

record-smashing 1934 dive. (Forget the Bermuda Triangle: the real mystery is how they descended ½ a mile in a metal ball less than 5 feet in diameter!) A more modern "submersible," Nautilus-X2, lets wannabe explorers take a simulated seven-minute trip to the ocean floor. Special events, like lectures, glowworm cruises, and whale-watching trips, are available, too, for an added fee. If all that activity makes you hungry, the Harbourfront restaurant is a lovely choice for lunch. Pedestrians may access the facility by following the sidewalk on the water side of Front Street. Motorists must drive out of town on Front Street, round the traffic circle, and exit at the lane signposted for the

> **HEEEEERE'S JOHNNY!**
>
> "Good morning. I love you!" Johnny Barnes calls, waving and smiling. And he means it. The eccentric retired bus driver has greeted motorists for more than two decades, standing on the Crow Lane roundabout at the entrance to the City of Hamilton every weekday morning from about 6 to 10 rain or shine. Late risers who don't get to see him in person can look for the bronze Desmond Fountain–designed statue of Johnny near the Bermuda Underwater Exploration Institute.

BUEI, because it's only accessible to in-bound vehicles. ✉ *40 Crow La., Hamilton* ☎ *441/292–7219* ⊕ *www.buei.org* ➲ *$12.50* ⊙ *Weekdays 9–5, weekends 10–5; last admission at 4.*

Cathedral of the Most Holy Trinity. After the original Anglican sanctuary on this site was torched by an arsonist in 1884, Scottish architect William Hay was enlisted to design a replacement. True to his training, he set out to erect a Gothic-style structure in the grand European tradition. Mission accomplished. Inside, the clerestory in the nave is supported by piers of polished Scottish granite; soaring archways are trimmed in stone imported from France; and the choir stalls and bishop's throne are carved out of English oak. The pulpit, meanwhile, is modeled on the one in Hay's hometown cathedral (St. Giles in Edinburgh), and the whole thing is crowned by a copper roof that stands out among Bermuda's typical white-topped buildings. Yet for all the European flourishes, Bermuda Cathedral still has a subtropical flair. After all, the limestone building blocks came from the Par-la-Ville quarry and one of its loveliest stained-glass windows—the Angel Window on the east wall of the north transept—was created by local artist Vivienne Gilmore Gardner. After sauntering around the interior, you can climb the 155 steps of the church tower for a heavenly view of Hamilton and its harbor. ✉ *29 Church St., Hamilton* ☎ *441/292–4033* ⊕ *www.anglican.bm* ➲ *Cathedral free; tower $3* ⊙ *Cathedral daily 8–5; tower weekdays 10–4.*

★ **City Hall & Arts Centre.** Set back from the street behind a fountain and pond, City Hall contains Hamilton's administrative offices as well as two art galleries and a performance hall. Instead of a clock, its tower is topped with a bronze wind vane—a prudent choice in a land where the weather is as important as the time. The statues of children playing in the fountain are by local sculptor Desmond Fountain. The building itself was designed in 1960 by Bermudian architect Wilfred Onions, a champion of balanced simplicity. Massive cedar doors open onto an impressive lobby notable for its beautiful chandeliers and portraits of mayors past and present. To the left is City Hall Theatre, a major venue for concerts, plays, and dance performances. To the right are the civic offices, where you can find souvenirs such as pens, T-shirts, and paperweights showing the Corporation of Hamilton's logo. A handsome cedar staircase leads upstairs to two upper-floor art galleries. (An elevator gets you there, too.) ✉ *17 Church St., Hamilton* ☎ *441/292–1234* ☽ *City Hall weekdays 9–5; National Gallery and Society of the Arts weekdays 10-4, Sat. 10-2.*

Bermuda National Gallery. On the first landing, in the East Exhibition Room, the Bermuda National Gallery is home to Bermuda's national art collection. The permanent exhibits include paintings by island artists as well as European masters like Gainsborough and Reynolds; African masks and sculpture; and photographs by internationally known artists, such as Bermudian Richard Saunders (1922–87). The fine and decorative art pieces in the Bermuda Collection reflect the country's multicultural heritage. Temporary exhibits are also a major part of the museum's program, and on any given day you can see a selection of local work along with a traveling exhibit from another museum. For a comprehensive look at the collections, join one of the free docent-led tours offered Thursday at 10:30 (private ones can be arranged on request). Lectures and other special programs are listed in the gallery's online calendar. Parents should note that some of these are targeted specifically at children. Furthermore, drawing stations where they can create their own artwork are available within the gallery. ☎ *441/295–9428* ⊕ *www.bng. bm* ✉ *Donations accepted*

Bermuda Society of Arts Gallery. Farther up the stairs, in the West Wing, the Bermuda Society of Arts Gallery displays work by its members. Its frequently changing juried shows attract talented local painters, sculptors, and photographers. Art collectors will be pleased to learn that many pieces may also be purchased. ☎ *441/292–3824* ⊕ *www.bsoa.bm* ✉ *Donations accepted*

☽ ★ **Fort Hamilton.** This imposing moat-ringed fortress has underground passageways that were cut through solid rock by Royal Engineers in the 1860s. Built to defend the West End's Royal Naval Dockyard from land attacks, it was outdated even before its completion, but remains a fine example of a polygonal Victorian fort. Even if you're not a big fan of military history, the hilltop site's stellar views and stunning gardens make the trip worthwhile. On Monday at noon, from November to March, bagpipes echo through the grounds as the kilt-clad members of the Bermuda Islands Pipe Band perform a traditional skirling ceremony. Due to one-way streets, getting to the fort by scooter can be a bit challenging. From downtown Hamilton head north on Queen Street, turn right on Church Street, then turn left to go up the hill on King Street. Make a sharp (270-degree) right turn onto Happy Valley Road and follow the signs. Pedestrians may walk along Front Street to King Street. ✉ *Happy Valley Rd., Hamilton* ☎ *441/292–1234* ✉ *Free* ☽ *Daily 8-sunset.*

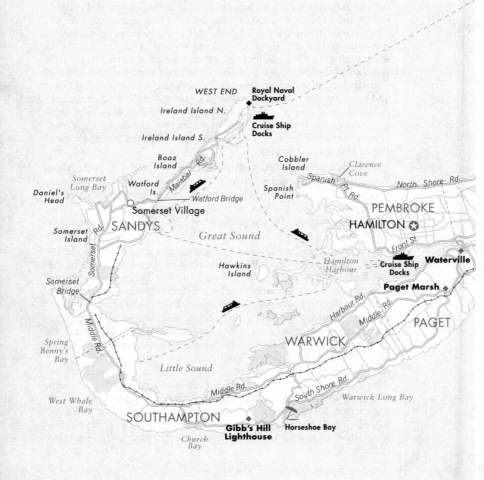

ATLANTIC OCEAN

WEST END — Royal Naval Dockyard
Ireland Island N.
Cruise Ship Docks
Ireland Island S.
Boaz Island
Cobbler Island
Clarence Cove
Somerset Long Bay
Watford Is.
Malabar Rd.
Spanish Pt. Rd.
North Shore Rd.
Daniel's Head
Watford Bridge
Spanish Point
PEMBROKE
Somerset Village
SANDYS
HAMILTON
Great Sound
Somerset Island
Front St.
Somerset Rd.
Hamilton Harbour
Cruise Ship Docks — Waterville
Hawkins Island
Paget Marsh
Somerset Bridge
Harbour Rd.
Middle Rd.
PAGET
Spring Benny's Bay
Middle Rd.
Little Sound
WARWICK
West Whale Bay
Middle Rd.
South Shore Rd.
Warwick Long Bay
SOUTHAMPTON
Gibb's Hill Lighthouse
Horseshoe Bay
Church Bay

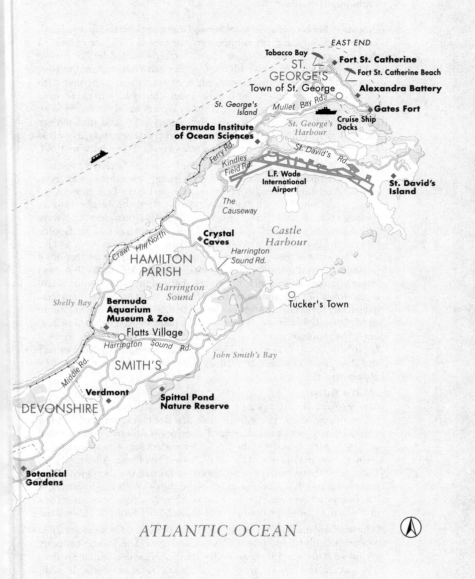

EAST END

Tobacco Bay
ST.
GEORGE'S
Town of St. George
Fort St. Catherine
Fort St. Catherine Beach
Alexandra Battery

St. George's
Island
Mullet Bay Rd.
Gates Fort

Bermuda Institute
of Ocean Sciences
St. George's
Harbour
Cruise Ship
Docks

Ferry Rd.
St. David's Rd.

Kindley
Field Rd.
L.F. Wade
International
Airport
St. David's
Island

The Causeway

Castle
Harbour

Crystal
Caves
Harrington
Sound Rd.

Crawl Hill North
HAMILTON
PARISH

Harrington
Sound
Tucker's Town

Shelly Bay
Bermuda Aquarium
Museum & Zoo
Flatts Village
Harrington Sound Rd.

John Smith's Bay

Middle Rd.
SMITH'S

Verdmont
Spittal Pond
Nature Reserve

DEVONSHIRE

Botanical
Gardens

ATLANTIC OCEAN

0   2 miles
0   3 km

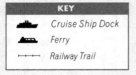

KEY	
⛴	Cruise Ship Dock
🚢	Ferry
⊢⊢⊢	Railway Trail

Museum of the Bermuda Historical Society/Bermuda National Library. Mark Twain admired the giant rubber tree that stands on Queen Street in the front yard of this Georgian house, formerly owned by Postmaster William Bennet Perot and his family. Though charmed by the tree, which had been imported from what is now Guyana in the mid-19th century, Twain lamented that it didn't bear rubbery fruit in the form of overshoes and hot-water bottles. The library, about which he made no tongue-in-cheek comment, was established in 1839, and its reference section has virtually every book ever written about Bermuda, as well as a microfilm collection of Bermudian newspapers dating back to 1784.

To the left of the library entrance is the Historical Society's museum. The collection is eclectic, chronicling the island's past through interesting—and in some cases downright quirky—artifacts. One display, for instance, is full of Bermudian silver dating from the 1600s; another focuses on tools and trinkets made by Boer War prisoners who were exiled here in 1901 and 1902. Check out the portraits of Sir George Somers and his wife, painted around 1605, and of William Perot and his wife that hang in the entrance hall. The newest exhibit is a selection of portraits of prominent Bermudians painted in the 1970s. ■TIP→ Don't forget that you can also pick up your free copy of the letter George Washington wrote in 1775; addressed to the inhabitants of Bermuda, it requests gunpowder for use in the American Revolution. ⊠ *13 Queen St., Hamilton* 🕾 *441/295–2905 library, 441/295–2487 museum ⊕ www.bnl.bm* 🖾 *Library free; museum donations accepted ⊗ Library Mon.–Thurs. 8:30–7, Fri. 10–5, Sat. 9–5, Sun. 1–5; closed Sun. and at 6 Mon.–Thur. in July and Aug.; museum weekdays 10–2, closes at 1 in winter. ☞ Tours by appointment.*

WORTH NOTING

Albuoy's Point. It's always a pleasure to watch sailboats and passenger ferries zigzag around the many islands that dot Hamilton Harbour. For a ringside seat, grab a bench beneath the trees at Albuoy's Point, a small waterside park. Nearby is the Royal Bermuda Yacht Club, founded in 1844 and granted the use of the word "Royal" by Prince Albert in 1845. Today luminaries from the international sailing scene hobnob with local yachtsmen and business executives at the club's 1930s headquarters. If you're around between April and November, you might even catch one of the many club-sponsored racing events. ⊠ *Off Front St., Hamilton*

Botanical Gardens. Established in 1898, the Botanical Gardens are filled with exotic subtropical plants, flowers, and trees. The 36-acre property features a miniature forest, an aviary, a hibiscus garden with more than 150 species, and collections of orchids, cacti, fruits, and ferns. In addition to these must-see sights is an intriguing must-smell one: the Garden for the Sightless. Designed primarily for the blind, it has fragrant plants (like geranium, lemon, lavender, and spices), plus Braille signage. Weather permitting, free 60- to 90-minute guided tours of the Botanical Gardens begin at 10:30 Tuesday, Wednesday, and Friday. ⊠ *18 Berry Hill Rd., Paget Parish* 🕾 *441/236–5902* 🖾 *Free ⊗ Daily sunrise–sunset.*

Camden. This gracious white house within the gardens is the official residence of Bermuda's premier. Tours of the interior are given Tuesday and Friday noon to 2, except when official functions are scheduled. ☎ 441/236–5732.

Masterworks Museum of Bermuda Art. Behind Camden sits the island's first purpose-built state-of-the-art museum: the Masterworks Museum of Bermuda Art. Like its former incarnation (the Masterworks Foundation), the new venue's theme is "Bermuda through the Eyes of Artists," and the soaring main gallery is devoted to island-inspired works by such internationally renowned figures as Georgia O'Keeffe, Andrew Wyeth,

> ### WHAT'S IN A NAME?
>
> Bermudians cultivated onions long before Americans did. In fact, throughout the 19th century they were one of the island's major exports, and its people were so closely identified with the tear-inducing plant that anyone born and bred here came to be known as an "Onion." Though competition eventually put an end to the lucrative trade, this nickname for locals stuck.

and Winslow Homer. Two other galleries display (and sell) paintings by native-born artists. ☎ 441/236–2950 ⊕ *www.bermudamasterworks. com* ☒ *$5* ☉ *Mon.–Sat. 10–4.*

Cabinet Building. Bermuda's Senate (the upper house of Parliament) sits in a dignified Cabinet Building built in 1841 and remodeled almost a century later. The most rewarding time to be here is during the formal opening of Parliament, traditionally held on the first Friday of November. His Excellency the Governor, dressed in a plumed hat and full regalia, arrives on the grounds in a landau drawn by magnificent black horses and accompanied by a police escort. A senior officer, carrying the Black Rod made by the crown jewelers, next asks the speaker of the House, elected representatives, and members of the Senate chamber to convene. The governor then presents the Throne Speech from a tiny cedar throne dating from 1642. A more somber ceremony is held in front of the building every Remembrance Day (November 11), when the governor and other dignitaries lay wreaths at the Cenotaph, a limestone memorial to Bermuda's war casualties erected in 1920. At other times of the year, assuming Parliament is in session, you may visit the Senate chambers on Wednesday from November to July to watch debates that are alternately lively and long-winded. Note that the gallery to the left of the main entrance is intended for public use. ☒ *105 Front St., Hamilton* ☎ *441/292–5501* ⊕ *www.gov.bm* ☒ *Free* ☉ *Mon.–Fri., 9–5.*

Farmers Market. One of the best places to mingle with Onions and, yes, buy a few edible ones is the Farmers Market held every Saturday from 8 to 12, November through June. It features up to 30 vendors who sell only Bermuda-grown, -caught, or -made products. Along with organic produce, fresh fish, and assorted home-baked items, goodies like hand-crafted soaps and honey derived from island wildflowers are for sale. The market, at the Bull's Head Car Park, is about a five-minute walk north of City Hall. ☒ *Canal Rd., Hamilton* ☎ *441/238–1862.*

Front Street. Running along the harbor, Hamilton's main thoroughfare bustles with small cars, motor scooters, bicycles, buses, and the occasional horse-drawn carriage. In past years some have lamented that it also bustles with hordes of tourists, particularly during cruise-ship season. But the fact that only occasional callers will now be docking in Hamilton should help alleviate any overcrowding. As for actual attractions, the prime ones here are the high-class low-rise shops that line the street. (Don't overlook small offshoots and alleyways like Chancery Lane, Bermuda House Lane, and the Walkway, where you'll stumble upon hidden-away boutiques.) The Visitor Information Centre, next to the Ferry Terminal at No. 8 Front Street, is a good place to strike out from when you're ready to explore the rest of Hamilton. Open Monday through Saturday 9–4, it's the place to go for pamphlets, maps, and to have your questions answered. It also has brochures for self-guided city walking tours. ⊠ *Hamilton* ☎ *441/295–1480.*

Paget Marsh. Take a walk on the wild side at Paget Marsh: a 25-acre tract of land that's remained virtually untouched since presettlement times. Along with some of the last remaining stands of native Bermuda palmetto and cedar, this reserve—jointly owned and preserved by the Bermuda National Trust and the Bermuda Audubon Society—contains a mangrove forest and grassy savanna. These unspoiled habitats can be explored via a boardwalk that features interpretive signs describing the endemic flora and fauna. When listening to the cries of the native and migratory birds that frequent this natural wetland, you can quickly forget that bustling Hamilton is just minutes away. ⊠ *Lovers La., Paget Parish* ☎ *441/236–6483* ⊕ *www.bnt.bm* ☒ *Free* ☉ *Daily sunrise–sunset.*

NEED A BREAK?

Lemon Tree Café. When you're in the mood for a picnic in the park, pick up supplies at the Lemon Tree Café right beside the Par-la-Ville Park entrance. Weekdays, from breakfast to late afternoon, chefs whip up hot meals, sandwiches, and wicked French pastries that you can take out or enjoy on the patio. For a taste of Bermuda's social scene, stop by instead for Friday-night happy hour. ⊠ 7 Queen St., Hamilton ☎ 441/292–0235.

Par-la-Ville Park. Next to the Perot Post Office is the Queen Street entrance to Par-la-Ville Park (there's another entrance on Par-la-Ville Road). Once Perot's private garden, it has winding paths, luxuriant blooms, plentiful benches, and a photogenic Bermuda moongate. Long popular with people-watchers, it now attracts art lovers, too. Return visitors will notice that the Bermuda National Gallery has created a Sculpture Garden in the park by installing several major outdoor works. ⊠ *Par-la-Ville Rd., Hamilton*

Perot Post Office. To some, this rather austere 1840s structure is simply a place to mail a letter. To stamp collectors, on the other hand, the lovingly restored, fully operational post office named for Hamilton's first postmaster is a veritable shrine. William Bennet Perot was certainly a genial fellow: he would meet arriving steamers, collect the incoming mail, stash it in his beaver hat, and then stroll around Hamilton to deliver it, greeting each recipient with a tip of his chapeau. But it was his resourcefulness that made him most famous among philatelists. Tired of individually hand-stamping outgoing letters, Perot began printing stamps in 1848. Of the thousands he produced, only 11 still exist—and several

CLOSE UP

The Bermuda Triangle Demystified

Long before the myth of the Bermuda Triangle became legend, Bermuda had already earned a reputation as an enchanted island. It was nicknamed "The Devil's Islands" by early sea travelers, frightened by the calls of cahow birds and the squeals of wild pigs that could be heard on shore. But perhaps the most damning tales were told by sailors terrified of being wrecked on Bermuda's dangerous reefs. The island's mystical reputation is believed to have inspired Shakespeare's *The Tempest*, a tale of shipwreck and sorcery in "the still-vexed Bermoothes."

The early origin of the Triangle myth stretches as far back as Columbus, who noted in his logbook a haywire compass, strange lights, and a burst of flame falling into the sea. Columbus, as well as other seamen after him, also encountered a harrowing stretch of ocean now known as the Sargasso Sea. Ancient tales tell of sailboats stranded forever in a windless expanse of water, surrounded by seaweed and the remnants of other unfortunate vessels. It's true that relics have been found in the Sargasso Sea—an area of ocean between Bermuda and the Caribbean—but the deadly calm waters are more likely the result of circular ocean currents sweeping through the North Atlantic rather than paranormal activity.

In the past 500 years at least 50 ships and 20 aircraft have vanished in the Triangle, most without a trace— no wreckage, no bodies, nothing. Many disappeared in reportedly calm waters, without having sent a distress signal. Among the legends is that of Flight 19. At 2:10 on the afternoon of December 5, 1945, five TBM Avenger Torpedo Bombers took off from Fort Lauderdale, Florida, on a routine two-hour training mission. Their last radio contact was at 4 pm. The planes and 27 men were never seen or heard from again. The official navy report said the planes disappeared "as if they had flown to Mars."

The bizarre disappearances attributed to the Triangle have been linked to everything from alien abduction to sorcery. Although the mystery has not been completely solved, there are scientific explanations for many of the maritime disasters that have occurred in the Triangle. The most obvious answers are linked to extreme weather conditions with which any Bermudian fisherman would be well acquainted. "White squalls"—intense, unexpected storms that arrive without warning on otherwise clear days— are probable culprits, along with waterspouts, the equivalent of sea tornadoes. The most recent scientific theory on the infamous Triangle suggests that the freakish disappearance of ships and aircraft could be the result of large deposits of methane gas spewing up from the ocean floor. Huge eruptions of methane bubbles may push water away from a ship, causing it to sink. If the highly flammable methane then rises into the air, it could ignite in an airplane's engine—causing it to explode and disappear.

Fact or fiction, the Triangle is a part of local lore that won't disappear anytime soon. But don't let it scare you away—this myth isn't the only thing that makes Bermuda seem so magical.

—Kim Dismont Robinson

2

of those are owned by Queen Elizabeth. If you'd like to get your hands on one, be prepared to dig deep. In June 2005 a Perot-era one-penny stamp sold at auction for a record-breaking $244,000. ⊠ *11 Queen St., Hamilton* ☎ *441/292–9052* ☞ *Free* ☉ *Weekdays 9–5.*

Sessions House & Jubilee Clock Tower. This eye-catching Italianate edifice, erected in 1819, is where the House of Assembly (the lower house of Parliament) and the Supreme Court convene. The Florentine towers and colonnade, decorated with red terra-cotta, were added to the building in 1887 to commemorate

> ### GO FOR GOLD
>
> To sightsee like a VIP, sign up for a National Trust guided tour. The outing begins at Waterville with a "special-access" stroll through the historic house and surrounding gardens. After being served refreshments, groups continue on by taxi to Paget Marsh for an exclusive tour of the reserve. Contact the Bermuda National Trust 24 hours in advance at ☎ *441/236–6483.* You must have at least four people in your group.

Queen Victoria's Golden Jubilee. The Victoria Jubilee Clock Tower made its striking debut—albeit a few years late—at midnight on December 31, 1893. Bermuda's Westminster-style Parliament meets on the second floor, where the speaker rules the roost in a powdered wig and robe. (The island has approximately 14 times as many politicians per capita as Europe or North America, so maintaining order is no small feat.) Sartorial splendor is equally evident downstairs in the Supreme Court, where wigs and robes (red for judges, black for barristers) are again the order of the day. You're welcome to watch the colorful proceedings: bear in mind, though, that visitors, too, are required to wear appropriate attire. Call first to find out when parliamentary sessions and court cases are scheduled. ⊠ *21 Parliament St., Hamilton* ☎ *441/292– 7408 House of Assembly, 441/292–1350 Supreme Court* ⊕ *www.gov. bm* ☞ *Free* ☉ *Weekdays 8:30–5.*

Waterville. Bermuda's National Trust (the nonprofit organization that oversees the restoration and preservation of many of the island's gardens, open spaces, and historic buildings) has its offices in Waterville: a rambling estate overlooking Hamilton Harbour. Waterville was home to the Trimingham family for seven generations. In fact, their much-loved (and still dearly missed) department store started out here in 1842. The drawing and dining rooms, both laden with art and antiques donated by the family, are open to the public during business hours. Also worth seeing is a superb showcase garden planted by the Bermuda Rose Society. ⊠ *2 Pomander Rd., Paget Parish* ☎ *441/236–6483* ⊕ *www.bnt.bm* ☞ *Free* ☉ *Weekdays 9–5.*

ST. GEORGE'S AND EASTERN PARISHES

St. George's and Hamilton are about 10 mi and 200 years apart. The latter wasn't even incorporated as a town until 1792; and by the time Hamilton became capital in 1815, St. George's had already celebrated its bicentennial.

The settlement of Bermuda began in what is now the town of St. George's when the *Sea Venture*—flagship of an English fleet carrying supplies to Jamestown, Virginia—was wrecked on Bermuda's treacherous reefs in 1609. Four hundred years later, no visit to the island would be complete without a stop in this picturesque and remarkably preserved example of an early New World outpost.

Although St. George's is a living community—not a living-history museum—it retains the patina of authenticity. In fact, in 2000 it was named a UNESCO World Heritage Site. That designation puts it on a par with spots like the Great Wall of China and the Taj Mahal in India. But don't expect awe-inspiring edifices here. On the contrary, St. George's chief charm lies in tiny walled cottages, simple colonial churches, and labyrinthine alleys that beg to be explored.

Also over in the east of the island, you will find the parishes of Smith's and Hamilton. This is probably the quietest corner of the island, so it's a great spot to enjoy tranquil nature trails. However, tucked away in Hamilton Parish you'll find two of the island's biggest attractions; the Bermuda Aquarium Museum and Zoo and Crystal Caves. The east is also home to some of Bermuda's finest gold courses.

TIMING   Given its small size, St. George's has a disproportionately large number of historic buildings, plus pleasant gardens and enticing shops. They say you can't get lost here—but you can certainly lose track of time. So give yourself a day to explore its nooks and crannies. Allow another day to take in the nearby Bermuda Aquarium Museum and Zoo and Crystal Caves.

WHAT TO SEE

TOP ATTRACTIONS

Bermuda Aquarium, Museum & Zoo. The BAMZ, established in 1926, has always been a pleasant diversion. But following an ambitious decade-long expansion program, it rates as one of Bermuda's premier attractions. In the aquarium the big draw is the North Rock Exhibit, a 140,000-gallon tank that gives you a diver's-eye view of the area's living coral reefs and the colorful marine life it sustains. The museum section has multimedia and interactive displays focusing on native habitats and the impact humans have had on them. The island-theme zoo, meanwhile, displays more than 300 birds, reptiles, and mammals. Don't miss the "Islands of Australasia" exhibit, with its lemurs, wallabies, and tree kangaroos, or "Islands of the Caribbean," a huge walk-through enclosure that gets you within arm's length of ibises and golden lion tamarins. Other popular areas include an outdoor seal pool, tidal touch tank, and cool kid-friendly Discovery Room. ✉ *40 N. Shore Rd., Flatts Village, Hamilton Parish* ☎ *441/293–2727* ⊕ *www.bamz.org* ✉ *$10* ⊙ *Daily 9–5, last admission at 4; North Rock dive talk at 1:10 daily and seal feeding at 1:30 and 4 daily.*

Bermuda National Trust Museum at the Globe Hotel. Erected as a governor's mansion around 1700, this building became a hotbed of activity during the American Civil War. From here, Confederate Major Norman Walker coordinated the surreptitious flow of guns, ammunition, and war supplies from England, through Union blockades, into American

Fodor's Choice
★

A GOOD WALK IN ST. GEORGE'S

Start your tour in **King's Square**, then stroll out onto **Ordnance Island** to see a replica of *Deliverance II*: the ship built as a replacement for the *Sea Venture*. Behind you, just up the street is the **Bermuda National Trust Museum at the Globe Hotel**, and across the square is the **Town Hall**. Venturing up King Street, notice the fine Bermudian architecture of **Bridge House**. At the top of King Street is the **Old State House**, the earliest stone building in Bermuda.

Walk up Princess Street to Duke of York Street and turn right, following the sidewalk to the **Bermudian Heritage Museum**. Across Duke of York Street, you can find **Somers Garden**, where Sir George Somers's heart is reportedly buried. After walking through the garden, climb the steps to Blockade Alley for a view of the **Unfinished Church** on a hill ahead. To your left are Duke of Kent Street, Featherbed Alley, and the **St. George's Historical Society Museum, Printery & Garden**. Next, cross Clarence Street to Church Lane and turn right on Broad Alley

to reach the **Old Rectory**. Straight ahead (or as straight as you can go among these twisted streets) is Printer's Alley, which in turn links to **Nea's Alley**, where a whiff of 19th-century scandal still lingers.

Return to Church Lane and enter the yard of **St. Peter's Church**, a centuries-old sanctuary that, until the building of the Old State House, did double duty as the colony's only public meeting place. (The main entrance is on Duke of York Street.) From the church, continue down Duke of York Street until you reach Queen Street on your right. A short walk up it brings you to the **Bermuda Perfumery & Gardens** at Stewart Hall, which will be on the left. Turn around and walk back to Duke of York Street and go right until you get to Barber's Alley, turning left to reach **Tucker House**, which has been transformed from a prominent merchant's home into a museum. From there continue along Water Street, veering left again on Penno's Drive to visit the new **World Heritage Centre** at Penno's Wharf.

ports. It saw service as the Globe Hotel during the mid-19th century and became a National Trust property in 1951. A short video, *Bermuda, Centre of the Atlantic*, recounts the history of Bermuda, and a memorabilia-filled exhibit entitled "Rogues & Runners: Bermuda and the American Civil War" describes St. George's when it was a port for Confederate blockade runners. ■ TIP→ This is where you will also find the St. George's Visitor Information Centre. ⊠ *32 Duke of York St., St. George's* ☎ *441/297–1423* ⊕ *www.bnt.bm* ☎ *$5; $10 combination ticket includes admission to Tucker House and Verdmont* ☉ *Apr.–Nov., Mon.-Sat. 10–4; Nov.-Apr,, Mon., Wed., Sat., 10-4.*

★ **Bermuda Perfumery & Gardens.** In 2005 this perfumery moved from Bailey's Bay in Smith's Parish, where it had been based since 1928, to historic Stewart Hall. Although the location changed, the techniques it uses did not: the perfumery still manufactures and bottles all its island-inspired scents on-site using more than 3,000 essential oils extracted from frangipani, jasmine, oleander, and passionflower. Guides are

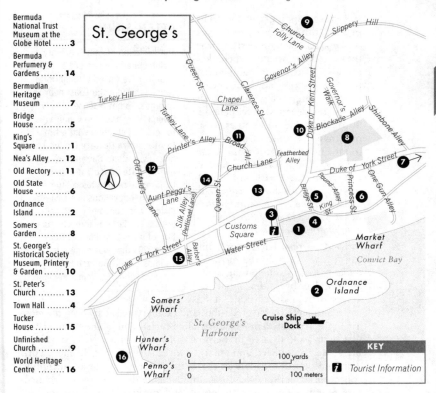

available to explain the entire process, and there's a small museum that outlines the company's history. You can also wander around the gardens and stock up on your favorite fragrances in the showroom. ✉ *Stewart Hall, 5 Queen St., St. George's* ☎ *441/293–0627* ⊕ *www. lilibermuda.com* ✇ *Free* ☉ *Mon.–Sat. 9–5.*

NEED A BREAK?

Bailey's Ice Cream. If you've got kids in tow—or are driving a scooter—you may want to skip the rum and stick to Bailey's— Bailey's Ice Cream, that is. The popular parlor, directly across from the inn, dishes up some two-dozen flavors of homemade all-natural ice creams, plus low-fat frozen yogurts and fat-free sorbets. ✉ *2 Blue Hole Hill, Bailey's Bay, Hamilton Parish* ☎ *441/293-8605.*

☾ **Fodor's Choice** ★

Crystal Caves. Bermuda's limestone caves have been attracting attention since the island was first settled. As far back as 1623, Captain John Smith (of Pocahontas fame) commented on these "vary strange, darke, and cumbersome" caverns. Nevertheless, it came as a surprise when two boys, attempting to retrieve a lost ball, discovered Crystal Cave in 1907. The hole through which the boys descended is still visible. But, thankfully, you can now view their find without having to make such a dramatic entrance. Inside, tour guides will lead you across a pontoon bridge that spans a 55-foot-deep subterranean lake. Look up to see stalactites dripping from the ceiling or down through the perfectly clear water to see stalagmites rising from the cave floor. Amateur spelunkers can also journey through geologic time at Crystal's smaller sister cave, Fantasy. After being closed to the public for decades, it reopened in 2001. Set aside 30 minutes to see one cave; 75 minutes if you plan to take in both. ✉ *8 Crystal Caves Rd., off Wilkinson Ave., Bailey's Bay, Hamilton Parish* ☎ *441/293–0640* ⊕ *www.bermudacaves.com* 🎫 *One cave $20; combination ticket $27* ⊙ *Daily 9:30–4:30; last combination tour at 4.*

⟳ ★ **Fort St. Catherine.** This restored hilltop fort is arguably the most formidable-looking one on the island. Surrounded by a dry moat and accessed by a drawbridge, it has

> **ATTEN-SHUN!**
>
> The evolution of British military architecture between 1612 and 1956 can be traced through fortifications that dot the coast near St. George's. To get a sense of how diverse they are, follow your visit to Fort St. Catherine with a trip to **Alexandra Battery** (about a mile away along Barry Road) and nearby **Gates Fort**. The former, built in the mid-1800s, features Victorian innovations like cast-iron facings and concrete emplacements. The latter is a reconstruction of a small militia fort from the 1620s that was named for Sir Thomas Gates, the first survivor of the *Sea Venture* to reach dry land.

enough tunnels, towers, redoubts, and ramparts to satisfy even the most avid military historian—or adrenaline-fueled child. The original fort was built around 1614 by Bermuda's first governor, Richard Moore, but it was remodeled and enlarged at least five times. In fact, work continued on it until late in the 19th century. On-site an intriguing collection of antique weapons complements the impressive architecture. Standing out among the pistols and muskets is an 18-ton muzzle-loading cannon, which was capable of firing 400-pound shells a full half mile. ✉ *15 Coot Pond Rd., St. George's Parish* ☎ *441/297–1920* 🎫 *$7* ⊙ *Weekdays 10–4.*

⟳ Fodor'sChoice ★ **Spittal Pond Nature Reserve.** This Bermuda National Trust park has 64 acres for roaming, though you're asked to keep to the well-marked walkways that loop through the woods and along the spectacular shoreline. More than 30 species of waterfowl—including herons, egrets, and white-eyed vireos—winter here between November and May, making the reserve a top spot for birders. Get your timing right and you may be able to spy migrating whales as well. History buffs may be more interested in climbing the high bluff to Portuguese Rock. Early settlers found this rock crudely carved with the date 1543 along with other markings that are believed to be the initials "RP" (for *Rex Portugaline*, King of Portugal) and a cross representing the Portuguese Order of Christ. The theory goes that a Portuguese ship was wrecked on the island and that her sailors marked the occasion before departing on a newly built ship. The rock was removed to prevent further damage by erosion, and a bronze cast of the original stands in its place. A plaster-of-paris version is also on display at the Museum of the Bermuda Historical Society in Hamilton. ✉ *South Rd., Smith's Parish* ☎ *441/236–6483* ⊕ *www.bnt. bm* 🎫 *Free* ⊙ *Daily sunrise–sunset.*

Fodor'sChoice **St. Peter's Church.** Because parts of
★ this whitewashed stone church date
back to 1620, it holds the distinc-
tion of being the oldest continuously operating Anglican church
in the Western Hemisphere. It was
not, however, the first house of worship to stand on this site. It replaced
a 1612 structure made of wooden
posts and palmetto leaves that was
destroyed in a storm. The present
church was extended in 1713 (the
oldest part is the area around the
triple-tier pulpit), the tower and
wings having been added in the
19th century. Befitting its age, St.
Peter's has many treasures. The red
cedar altar, carved in 1615 under
the supervision of Richard Moore
(a shipwright and the colony's first
governor) is the oldest piece of
woodwork in Bermuda. The late

> **ALL FIRED UP**
>
> In 1775 the Continental Congress
> imposed a ban on exports to colo-
> nies not supporting their trade
> embargo against England. Ber-
> muda depended on the American
> colonies for grain, so a delegation
> of Bermudians traveled to Phila-
> delphia offering salt in exchange
> for the resumption of grain ship-
> ments. Congress rejected the
> salt, but agreed to lift the ban if
> Bermuda sent gunpowder instead.
> A group of Bermudians, including
> two members of the esteemed
> Tucker family, then broke into the
> island's arsenal, stole the gunpow-
> der, and shipped it to Boston. The
> ban was soon lifted.

18th-century bishop's throne is believed to have been salvaged from
a shipwreck, and the baptismal font, brought to the island by early
settlers, is an estimated 900 years old. There's also a fine collection of
communion silver from the 1600s in the vestry. Nevertheless, it's the
building itself that leaves the most lasting impression. With rough-hewn
pillars, exposed cedar beams, and candlelit chandeliers, the church
is stunning in its simplicity. After viewing the interior, walk into the
churchyard to see where prominent Bermudians, including Governor Sir
Richard Sharples, who was assassinated in 1973, are buried. A separate
graveyard for slaves and free blacks (to the west of the church, behind
the wall) is a poignant reminder of Bermuda's segregated past. ⊠ *33
Duke of York St., St. George's* ☎ *441/297–2459* ⊕ *www.stpeters.bm*
⊠ *Donations appreciated* ☺ *Mon.–Sat. 10–4, Sun. service at 11:15.*

Tucker House. Tucker House is owned and lovingly maintained as a
museum by the Bermuda National Trust. It was built in the 1750s for
a merchant who stored his wares in the cellar (a space that now holds
an archaeological exhibit). But it's been associated with the Tucker
family ever since Henry Tucker, president of the Governor's Council
and a key participant in the Bermuda Gunpowder Plot, purchased it in
1775. His descendents lived here until 1809, and much of the fine silver
and heirloom furniture—which dates primarily from the mid-18th and
early-19th centuries—was donated by them. As a result, the house is
essentially a tribute to this well-connected clan whose members included
a Bermudian governor, a U.S. treasurer, a Confederate navy captain,
and an Episcopal bishop.

The kitchen, however, is dedicated to another notable—Joseph Haine
Rainey—who is thought to have operated a barber's shop in it during
the Civil War. (Barber's Alley, around the corner, is also named in his

honor.) As a freed slave from South Carolina, Rainey fled to Bermuda at the outbreak of the war. Afterward he returned to the United States and, in 1870, became the first black man to be elected to the House of Representatives. A short flight of stairs leads down to the kitchen, originally a separate building, and to an enclosed kitchen garden. ⊠ *5 Water St., St. George's* ☎ *441/297–0545* ⊕ *www.bnt.bm* ✉ *$5; $10 combination ticket includes admission to National Trust Museum in Globe Hotel and Verdmont* ⊙ *May–Oct., Mon.–Fri. 10–2; Nov.–Apr, Wed.–Fri. 10–2.*

Ⓒ **Verdmont House Museum.** Even if you think you've had your fill of old houses, Verdmont deserves a look. The National Trust property, which opened as a museum in 1956, is notable for its Georgian architecture. Yet what really sets this place apart is its pristine condition. Though used as a residence until the mid-20th century, virtually no structural changes were made to Verdmont since it was erected around 1710. Former owners never even added electricity or plumbing (so the "powder room" was strictly used for powdering wigs). The house is also known for its enviable collection of antiques. Some pieces—such as the early 19th-century piano—were imported from England. However, most are 18th-century cedar, crafted by Bermudian cabinetmakers. Among the most interesting artifacts are the pint-size furnishings and period toys that fill Verdmont's upstairs nursery. A china coffee service, said to have been a gift from Napoléon to U.S. President James Madison, is also on display. The president never received it, though, since the ship bearing it across the Atlantic was seized by a privateer and brought to Bermuda. ⊠ *6 Verdmont La., off Collector's Hill, Smith's Parish* ☎ *441/236–7369* ⊕ *www.bnt.bm* ✉ *$5; $10 combination ticket with Bermuda National Trust Museum in Globe Hotel and Tucker House* ⊙ *May–Oct., Tues–Thur. and Sat. 10–4; Nov.–Apr., Wed. and Sat. 10–4.*

WORTH NOTING

Bermuda Institute of Ocean Sciences. In 1903—long before environmental issues earned top-of-mind awareness—scientists began studying marine life at this mid-Atlantic facility formerly known as the Bermuda Biological Station for Research. Now researchers from around the world come here to work on projects dealing with hot topics like global warming, marine ecology, and acid rain. You can learn all about them on a free 90-minute tour that starts Wednesday morning at 10 in the reception building. Tours cover the grounds and laboratory. You might also see the station's 168-foot research vessel, R/V *HSBC Atlantic Explorer,* if it happens to be docked that day. ⊠ *17 Biological Station, Ferry Reach, St. George's Parish* ☎ *441/297–1880* ⊕ *www.bios.edu* ✉ *Donations accepted.*

Bermudian Heritage Museum. The history, trials, and accomplishments of black Bermudians are highlighted in this converted 1840s warehouse. Photographs of early black residents including slaves, freedom fighters, and professionals line the walls, and the works of black artisans are proudly exhibited. Look, in particular, for the display about the *Enterprise,* a slave ship that was blown off course to Bermuda while sailing from Virginia to South Carolina in 1835. Since slavery had already been abolished on the island, the 78 slaves on board were technically

Slavery in Bermuda

Within a few years of the colony's founding, slavery had become a fact of life in Bermuda. As early as 1616, slaves—most of whom were "imported" as household servants and tradespeople rather than field workers—began arriving, first from Africa and then from the Caribbean. In the mid-1600s they were joined by Native American captives (among them, the wife of a Pequod chief). The practice flourished to such an extent that by the time British legislation finally abolished it in 1834, slaves made up more than half of the island's population.

The date the abolition decree was issued, August 1, continues to be marked island-wide. Known as Emancipation Day, it's a time for cricket matches, concerts, and, of course, Gombey dancing: a colorful form of self-expression, rooted in African tradition, which slave owners had banned. If you can't time your trip to coincide with the festivities, you can still bone up on the backstory by following the African Diaspora Heritage Trail. Affiliated with UNESCO's international Slave Route Project, it highlights sites related to the Bermudian slave trade.

Some of the trail's 11 stops are already tourist staples. For instance, in St. George's, the slave graveyard at St. Peter's Church is a designated site; as is Tucker House, where Joseph Rainey (the first black man to be elected to the U.S. House of Representatives) sat out the Civil War. Also on the list is the Commissioner's House at the Royal Naval Dockyard, which has an exhibit that vividly evokes the age of slavery through artifacts like iron shackles and glass trade beads.

Other sites are obscure, but nonetheless illuminating. Take Cobb's Hill Methodist Church in Warwick Parish. Dedicated in 1827, seven years before Emancipation, it was the first sanctuary in Bermuda built by and for blacks. Because they struggled to complete it in their rare off-hours (often working by candlelight!), the church is both a religious monument and a symbol of human resilience. For further details on the African Diaspora Heritage Trail, pick up a brochure at any Visitor Information Centre.

—Susan MacCallum-Whitcomb

free—and the Local Friendly Societies (grassroots organizations devoted to liberating and supporting slaves) worked to keep it that way. Society members obtained an injunction to bring the slaves' case into court and escorted the "human cargo" to their hearing in Hamilton, where many spoke in their own defense. All except one woman and her four children accepted the offer of freedom. Today countless Bermudians trace their ancestry back to those who arrived on the *Enterprise.* Appropriately enough, the museum building was once home to one of the Friendly Societies. ⊠ *Water and Duke of York Sts., St. George's* ☎ *441/297–4126* ⊠ *$4* ⊘ *Mon.–Fri. 10–2.*

Bridge House. This 17th-century building owned by the National Trust currently contains private residence apartments, an art studio, and a shop. Previously it was home to several of Bermuda's governors—and at least one ghost. Mistress Christian Stevenson, who was condemned

Law and Order: Colonial Style

Back in Bermuda's early days, colonists convicted of offenses such as drunkenness, blasphemy, and slander would be locked in the stocks or forced to stand in the pillory for a set length of time. Either way, the punishment was uncomfortable and humiliating (especially when rapidly thrown rotten fruit was added to the equation!). Today, replicas of both stocks and pillory can be found on King's Square in St. George's, and curious souls are welcome to try them out.

It is, however, recommended that you stay well away from the other apparatus townsfolk used to chasten the unruly—the ducking stool—unless you fancy getting wet. Originally reserved for women who nagged or gossiped, the device is essentially an oversize wooden seesaw. The accused would be strapped to a seat on one end, then wheeled out over the harbor, and repeatedly dropped in.

A worse fate was "trial by water," otherwise known as "swimming the witch." In the 1600s suspected witches—typically women charged with such heinous crimes as bewitching hogs or having warts—would have their thumbs tied to their toes and be thrown into the harbor.

Those who sank, for whatever good it did them, were declared innocent. Those who floated were condemned. The unfortunates who fell into the latter category were hauled out to be hanged—and when it comes to the executioners' preferred locations, place names like Gallows Island and Gibbet Island are a dead giveaway.

—Susan MacCallum-Whitcomb

as a witch in 1653, proclaimed her innocence at this spot, and now seems reluctant to leave it. Other National Trust properties also qualify as "favorite haunts." For instance, the Old Rectory on Broad Alley is said to have a spirit who plays the spinet in the wee hours of the morning. Verdmont, in Smith's Parish, also has its share of resident ghosts: among them, an adolescent girl who died of typhoid there in 1844. ⊠ 1 *Bridge St., St. George's* ⊕ *www.bnt.bm.*

King's Square. In a town where age is relative, King's Square is comparatively new. The square was only created in the 19th century after a marshy part of the harbor was filled in. Today it still looks rather inauspicious, more a patch of pavement than a leafy common, yet the square is St. George's undisputed center. Locals frequently congregate here for civic celebrations. Visitors, meanwhile, come to see the replica stocks and pillory. Formerly used to punish petty crimes, these grisly gizmos—together with a replica ducking stool—are now popular props for photo ops. Reenactments of historical incidents, overseen by a town crier in full colonial costume, are staged in the square November through April on Monday, Wednesday, and Saturday at noon, and May through October on Monday through Thursday and Sunday at noon. ⊠ *Duke of York St., St. George's.*

Nea's Alley. While roaming the back streets, look for Nea's Alley. Nineteenth-century Irish poet Thomas Moore, who lived in St. George's during his tenure as registrar of the admiralty court, waxed poetic about both this "lime-covered alley" and a lovely woman he first encountered here: his boss's teenaged bride, Nea Tucker. Though arguably the most amorous, Moore wasn't the only writer to be inspired by Bermuda. Mark Twain wrote about it in *The Innocents Abroad,* and his exclamation "you go to heaven if you want to; I'd druther stay in Bermuda" remains something of a motto in these parts. Two 20th-century playwrights, Eugene O'Neill and Noel Coward, also wintered—and worked—on the island. More recently, Bermuda resident Peter Benchley took the idea for his novel *The Deep* from the ships lost offshore. ⊠ *Between Printer's Alley and Old Maid's La., St. George's*

The Old Rectory. Built around 1699 by part-time privateer George Dew, this charming limestone cottage is mainly associated with a later resident, Alexander Richardson (the rector of St. Peter's Church), who lived here between 1763 and 1805. In addition to handsome gardens, the house with its cedar beams, multiple chimneys, and "welcoming arms" entrance is a lovely example of traditional Bermudian architecture. ⊠ *1 Broad Alley, behind St. Peter's Church, St. George's* ☎ *441/236–6483* ⊕ *www.bnt.bm* ✉ *Donations accepted* ✆ *Nov.–Mar., Wed. 1–5.*

Old State House. A curious ritual takes place every April in King's Square as one peppercorn, regally placed upon a velvet pillow, is presented to the mayor of St. George's amid much pomp and circumstance. The paltry peppercorn is the rent paid annually for the Old State House by the Masonic Lodge St. George No. 200 of the Grand Lodge of Scotland. This fraternal organization has occupied the building since Bermuda's Parliament—the third oldest in the world after Iceland's and England's—vacated it in 1815 when the capital moved to Hamilton. The Old State House was erected in 1620 in what Governor Nathaniel Butler believed was the Italian style, so it's one of the few structures in Bermuda not to feature a flat roof. Builders used a mixture of turtle oil and lime as mortar, setting the style for future Bermudian buildings. ⊠ *4 Princess St., St. George's* ☎ *441/297–1206* ✉ *Free* ✆ *Wed. 10–4.*

Ⓒ **Ordnance Island.** Ordnance Island, directly across from King's Square, is dominated by a splendid bronze statue of Sir George Somers, commander of the *Sea Venture.* Somers looks surprised that he made it safely to shore—and you may be surprised that he ever chose to set sail again when you spy the nearby *Deliverance II.* It's a full-scale replica of one of two ships—the other was the *Patience*—built under Somers's supervision to carry survivors from the 1609 wreck onward to Jamestown. But considering her size (just 57 feet from bow to stern), *Deliverance II* hardly seems ocean-worthy by modern standards. ⊠ *Across from King's Sq., St. George's*

Somers Garden. After sailing to Jamestown and back in 1610, Sir George Somers—the British admiral charged with developing the Bermudian colony—fell ill and died. According to local lore, he instructed his nephew Matthew Somers to bury his heart in Bermuda, where it belonged. Matthew sailed for England soon afterward, sneaking the body aboard in a cedar chest so as not to attract attention from superstitious sailors, and eventually buried it near Somers's birthplace in Dorset. Although it can't be proven that Matthew actually carried out his uncle's wishes, it's generally believed that Admiral Somers's heart was indeed left behind in a modest tomb at the southwest corner of the park. When the tomb was opened many years later, only a few bones, a pebble, and some bottle fragments were found. Nonetheless, ceremonies were held at the empty grave in 1920, when the Prince of Wales christened this pleasant, tree-shrouded park Somers Garden. ⊠ *Bordered by Shinbone and Blockade Alleys, Duke of Kent and Duke of York Sts., St. George's* 🖭 *Free* ☉ *Daily 8–4.*

St. David's Island. In a place famous for manicured lawns and well-tended gardens, St. David's Island feels comparatively wild. However, the real highlight is—quite literally—St. David's Lighthouse. Built in 1879 of Bermuda stone and occupying the tallest point on the East End, this red-and-white-striped lighthouse rises 208 feet above the sea, providing jaw-dropping views of St. George's, Castle Harbour, and the reef-rimmed south shore. This is also a great place to spot humpback whales passing through Bermuda's waters in April and May. There's a small snack bar if you get hungry or thirsty. ■TIP➜ **The Black Horse Tavern, one of the island's top attractions, specializes in seafood concoctions like shark hash and curried conch stew.** ⊠ *Lighthouse Hill, St. George's Parish* 🕾 *441/236–5902* 🖭 *Free* ☉ *Daily 7:30–4.*

St. George's Historical Society Museum, Printery, and Garden. Furnished to resemble its former incarnation as a private home, this typical Bermudian building reveals what life was like in the early 1700s. Along with period furnishings, such as a 1620 statehouse table, it has assorted documents and artifacts pertaining to the colonial days. But it's the re-created kitchen—complete with palmetto baskets and calabash dipping gourds—that really takes the cake. Downstairs, the printery features a working replica of a Gutenberg-style press, as well as early editions of island newspapers. The beautiful cottage gardens behind the museum are also worth a visit. ⊠ *3 Featherbed Alley, near Duke of Kent St., St. George's* 🕾 *441/297–0423* 🖭 *$5* ☉ *Apr.–Nov., Mon.–Thurs. and Sat. 10–4; Jan.–Mar., Wed. 10–4.*

Town Hall. St. George's administrative offices are housed in a putty-color two-story structure that dates back to 1808. Inside the cedar-paneled hall—where the civic government still meets—you can see portraits of past mayors. Better yet, you can get some "face time" with the current one. Midday on Wednesday, November through March, the mayor greets visitors and gives a brief talk. ⊠ *5 King's Sq., St. George's* 🕾 *441/297–1532* 🖭 *Free* ☉ *Mon.–Sat. 9–4.*

Unfinished Church. Work began on this intended replacement for St. Peter's Church in 1874. But, just as it neared completion, construction was halted by storm damage and disagreements within the church community. Hence the massive Gothic Revival pile sat—unfinished and crumbling—until the Bermuda National Trust stepped in to stabilize the structure in 1992. With soaring stone walls, a grassy floor, and only the sky for a roof, it's the sort of atmospheric ruin that poets and painters so admire. Tourists are currently not able to go inside the ruins, but can admire the structure from the outside. ⊠ *Duke of Kent St., St. George's* 🕾 *441/236–6483* ⊕ *www.bnt.bm.*

☾ **World Heritage Centre.** Housed in an 1860 customs warehouse next to the Penno's Wharf Cruise Ship Terminal, the center has recently completed its multimillion-dollar renovation. You can now view an introductory film (*A Stroll through St. George's*) and visit the ground-floor Orientation Exhibits Gallery, which showcases several hundred years of civic history. In an effort to make the past palatable—even to very young guests—this gallery has engaging models, ranging from a miniaturized version of St. George's (circa 1620) to a full-scale mock-up of the deck of the *Sea Venture*. It also contains a costume corner where kids can dress up in period outfits. Developed under the auspices of the St. George's Foundation, the World Heritage Centre also has an education center, retail galleries, and regular talks, tours, and historical reenactments. ✉ *19 Penno's Wharf, St. George's* ☎ *441/297–5791* ⊕ *www. stgeorgesfoundation.org* ☞ *$5* ✆ *Mon.–Sat. 10–4.*

DOCKYARD AND WESTERN PARISHES

Bermuda is denser than you might imagine. But in contrast to Hamilton and St. George's, the island's West End seems positively pastoral. Many of the top sites here are natural ones: namely the wildlife reserves, wooded areas, and beautiful waterways of Sandys Parish. The notable exception is Bermuda's single largest tourist attraction—the Royal Naval Dockyard.

Its story begins in the aftermath of the American Revolution, when Britain suddenly found itself with neither an anchorage nor a major ship-repair yard in the western Atlantic. Around 1809, just as Napoléon was surfacing as a serious threat and the empire's ships were becoming increasingly vulnerable to pirate attack, Britain decided to construct a stronghold in Bermuda. Dubbed the "Gibraltar of the West," the Dockyard operated as a shipyard for nearly 150 years. The facility was closed in 1951, although the Royal Navy maintained a small presence here until 1976 and held title to the land until 1995.

The Bermudian government and development groups began to plan for civilian use of the Dockyard in 1980. Since then, $21 million in public funds and $42 million in private money has been spent to make the area blossom. Now trees and shrubs grow where there used to be vast stretches of concrete. Private yachts calmly float where naval vessels once anchored, and cruise ships dock at the terminal. Historic structures—like the Clocktower and Cooperage buildings—house restaurants, galleries, shops, even a movie theater. A strip of beach has been turned into a snorkel park. And at the center of it all are the National Museum of Bermuda and Dolphin Quest: two popular facilities that share a fortified 6-acre site.

Outside of the Dockyard, Sandys and Southampton are just a short bus ride away. You'll notice that Sandys (pronounced Sands) is made up of several islands, all connected by bridges, including the smallest drawbridge in the world. It's in this parish that you'll also find Somerset Village, which is a popular spot for swimming and fishing. Southampton is the place to head if you want to soak up some rays; don't miss Horseshoe Bay.

TIMING Allow a full day for exploring this area. Before setting out, check public transit schedules carefully (you'll find them online at ⊕ *www. gov.bm*). By water, the trip can take anywhere from 30 minutes to more than an hour depending on which ferry you choose. On land, Buses 7 and 8 depart from Hamilton about every 15 minutes and take an hour to reach the Dockyard via South or Middle Road.

WHAT TO SEE
TOP ATTRACTIONS

Fort Scaur. The British chose the highest hill in Somerset for the site of this fort, built in the late 1860s and early 1870s to defend the flank of the Dockyard from possible American attacks. British troops were garrisoned here until World War I; and American forces were, ironically, stationed at the fort during World War II. Today its stone walls are surrounded by 22 acres of pretty gardens, and the view of the Great Sound and Ely's Harbour from the parapet is unsurpassed. Be sure to check out the early-Bermuda Weather Stone, which is billed as a "perfect weather indicator." A sign posted nearby solemnly explains all. ⊠ *107 Somerset Rd., Sandys Parish* ☎ *441/236–5902* ⊠ *Free* ☾ *Daily 8–4.*

> **NO EXPERIENCE NECESSARY**
>
> The Dockyard was largely built by convicts transported from Britain and the other colonies. Burglars and privateers from Nova Scotia were, for instance, sent here well into the 19th century. Murderers who had their death sentence commuted were also shipped over. But given the harsh conditions, some must have wished they had never been shown such "mercy." Almost one quarter of these forced laborers (some 2,000 in total) died and were buried, mostly in unmarked graves, in a cemetery at the approach to the Dockyard, just off Malabar Road.

TEA TIME **Dining Room.** After Gibb's Hill was automated in 1969, the keeper's cottage at its base was converted into an eatery. Whether you're looking for a filling meal or just a refreshing drink to quench your thirst, this quaint little restaurant serves lunch and dinner daily. Bermudian, British, and Indian dishes are on the menu. ⊠ *68 St. Anne's Rd., Southampton Parish* ☎ *441/238–8679* ☾ *Daily 11:30–2 and 6–10.*

☾ ★ **Gibb's Hill Lighthouse.** This cast-iron lighthouse soars above Southampton Parish. Designed in London and opened in 1846, the tower stands 117 feet high and 362 feet above the sea. The light was originally produced by a concentrated burner of four large, circular wicks. Today the beam from the 1,000-watt bulb can be seen by ships 40 mi out to sea and by planes 120 mi away at 10,000 feet. The haul up the 185 spiral stairs is an arduous one—particularly if you dislike heights or tight spaces. But en route to the top you can stop to catch your breath on eight landings, where photographs and drawings of the lighthouse help divert attention from your aching appendages. Once on the balcony, you'll be rewarded by panoramic island views. ⊠ *68 St. Anne's Rd., Southampton Parish*

A GOOD TOUR OF DOCKYARD AND THE WEST END

To make the most of your visit to the West End, plan to combine sea and land transportation. Transit tokens, tickets, and passes work on both ferries and buses, allowing you to hop on and off wherever you please. If you have a bicycle or scooter, you can bring it on the ferry; however, you'll be charged an extra adult fare to take the latter, and space is sometimes limited. Once you arrive, the Dockyard itself can be covered easily on foot. But other sights are rather far apart. So plan to take a taxi, bus, or ferry if you're continuing on to Somerset or elsewhere.

The logical place to begin a tour is the Royal Naval Dockyard. Start your day by visiting the **National Museum of Bermuda** and **Dolphin Quest**, which are housed together in a stone fortress built between 1837 and 1852. To the left of the entrance is the **Snorkel Park**, a small protected reef where you can get up close to marine life. Across from the museum entrance, the tempting art gallery and permanent art-and-crafts market in the **Old Cooperage** also warrant a visit. To the west are a pottery shop, glassblowing center, and other businesses that occupy attractive old military warehouses;

just south is the **Clocktower Mall,** where you can find still more shops. The new Visitor Information Centre is close to the ferry stop. Finish your tour here, or continue via ferry to Somerset Island.

For an interesting change of pace, opt for the slow boat (not the one heading directly to Hamilton) out of the Dockyard. You'll pass by Boaz and Watford islands on your way to Somerset Island, fringed on both sides with beautiful secluded coves, inlets, and bays. Getting off the ferry at Watford Bridge, you can make a quick jaunt into **Somerset Village**, which consistently ranks among Bermuda's prettiest communities.

The next sights, reached via Somerset Road, are best visited by bus or scooter. About 2 mi east of Somerset Village, opposite the Willowbank Hotel, is the entrance to the **Heydon Trust Property**, which boasts both wide-open spaces and a tiny 1616 chapel. Around the bend on your left is **Fort Scaur**, a serene spot with sweeping views of the Great Sound. Linking Somerset Island with the rest of Bermuda is **Somerset Bridge**. Across the bridge, Somerset Road becomes Middle Road, which leads into Southampton Parish.

441/238–8069 ⊕ *www.bermudalighthouse.com* ⌂ *$2.50* ☉ *Daily 9.30–4:30. Closed mid-Jan.–mid-Feb.*

C
Fodor's Choice
★
National Museum of Bermuda. The Maritime Museum, ensconced in Bermuda's largest fort, displays its collections in a series of old munitions warehouses that surround the parade grounds and Keep Pond. Insulated from the rest of the Dockyard by a moat and massive stone ramparts, it is entered by way of a drawbridge. At the Shifting House, right inside the entrance, you can wander through rooms filled with relics from some of the 350-odd ships wrecked on the island's reefs. Other buildings are devoted to seafaring pursuits such as whaling, shipbuilding, and yacht racing. More displays are in the 19th-century Commissioner's House, on the museum's upper grounds. Built as both home and

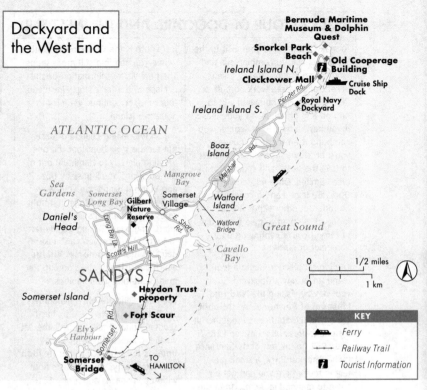

Bermuda Maritime Museum & Dolphin Quest

Snorkel Park Beach

Ireland Island N.

Old Cooperage Building

Clocktower Mall

Cruise Ship Dock

Pender Rd.

Royal Navy Dockyard

Ireland Island S.

ATLANTIC OCEAN

Boaz Island

Maldar Rd.

Mangrove Bay

Sea Gardens

Somerset Long Bay

Gilbert Nature Reserve

Somerset Village

Watford Island

Daniel's Head

Long Bay La.

E. Shore Rd.

Watford Bridge

Great Sound

Scott's Hill

Cavello Bay

SANDYS

Somerset Island

Heydon Trust property

Fort Scaur

Somerset Rd.

Ely's Harbour

Somerset Bridge

TO HAMILTON

0   1/2 miles

0   1 km

KEY	
⛴	*Ferry*
+—+—+	*Railway Trail*
🛈	*Tourist Information*

headquarters for the Dockyard commissioner, the house later served as a barracks during World War I and was used for military intelligence during World War II. Today, after an award-winning restoration, it contains exhibits on Bermuda's social and military history. A must-see is the Hall of History, a mural of Bermuda's history covering 1,000 square feet. It took local artist Graham Foster more than 3.5 years to paint. You'll also likely want to snap some photos of the goats that graze outside the building: their job is to keep the grass well mowed. ⊠ *Old Royal Naval Dockyard* ☎ *441/234–1418* ⊕ *www.bmm.bm* ☜ *$10* ☼ *Daily 9:30–4.*

Dolphin Quest. After immersing yourself in maritime history, you can immerse yourself—literally—in the wonderful world of dolphins. Dolphin Quest offers a range of in-water programs that allow adults and children ages five or older to pet, play with, and swim alongside its eight Atlantic bottlenose dolphins in the historic Keep Pond. There are even specially designed sessions, conducted from a submersible bench, for younger kids. Since entry to the Dolphin Quest area is free with museum admission, anyone can watch the action. Participation in the actual programs, however, costs $160 to $310, and advance booking is recommended. For $650 you can be a dolphin trainer for the day. ☎ *441/234–4464* ⊕ *www.dolphinquest.com.*

☾ ★ **Snorkel Park Beach.** Evidence of the Dockyard's naval legacy can be viewed at this protected inlet, accessed through a stone tunnel adjacent to the National Museum of Bermuda. Beneath the water's surface lie cast-iron cannons dating from 1550 to 1800, plus an antique anchor and gun-carriage wheel. The true attractions, however, are colorful fish (you might see more than 50 varieties) and other sea creatures including anemones, sea cucumbers, and assorted species of coral. Thanks to amenities like floating rest stations, snorkeling and scuba diving couldn't be easier. Everything is available to rent, including kayaks, pedalos, Jet Skis, and underwater scooters. This is a family beach by day, catering mainly to cruise-ship passengers, and a nightclub by night with beach parties and island barbecues. ⊠ *7 Maritime La., Sandys Parish* ☎ *441/234–6989* ⊕ *www.snorkelparkbeach. com* ⊠ *$5* ☉ *Apr.–Oct., Mon.–Sat. 9–4, Sun. 11–7; limited winter opening hours.*

SOME ASSEMBLY REQUIRED

Though it may appear to be yet another stalwart stone building, the Commissioner's House is actually an engineering landmark. Designed by a naval architect, it was the world's first prefabricated residence. The component parts—made of cast iron rather than standard wood—were constructed in England between 1823 and 1827, then shipped to Bermuda, where they were assembled and sheathed in local limestone.

WORTH NOTING

Clocktower Mall. A pair of 100-foot towers makes it impossible to miss the Clocktower Mall. (Observant folks will note that one of them features a standard clock, the other a tide indicator.) Inside this 19th-century building, the Royal Navy's administrative offices have been replaced by distinctly Bermudian boutiques—including specialty shops and branches of Front Street favorites. These are particularly popular on Sunday, because most stores outside the Dockyard area are closed. If you need pamphlets, bus and ferry tickets, or a phone card, the latter is open daily from 8 to 5. ☎ *Dockyard* ☎ *441/234–1709* ⊠ *Free* ☉ *Apr.–Dec., 9–6; Jan.–Mar., 10–5.*

Visitor Information Centre. Just in front of the mall is the former military parade ground, which now hosts special events (like the Beating of the Retreat Ceremony). The Visitor Information Centre is just across the water in a gazebo-shaped building, near the ferry stop. ☎ *441/799–4842.*

Heydon Trust Property. A reminder of what the island was like in its early days, this blissfully peaceful 43-acre preserve remains an unspoiled open space, except for a few citrus groves and flower gardens. Pathways with well-positioned park, benches wind through it, affording some wonderful water views. If you persevere along the main path, you'll reach rustic Heydon Chapel. Built in the early 1600s, it's Bermuda's smallest church. Nondenominational services featuring stirring Gregorian chants are still held in the single-room sanctuary weekdays at 7:30 am and 3 pm, Saturday 3 pm only. ⊠ *16 Heydon Dr., off Somerset Rd., Sandys Parish* ☎ *441/234–1831* ⊠ *Free* ☉ *Daily sunrise–sunset.*

The Bermuda Railway

The history of the Bermuda Railway—which operated on the island from 1931 to 1948—is as brief as the track is short. Bermuda's Public Works Department considered proposals for a railroad as early as 1899, and Parliament finally granted permission in 1922 for a line to run from Somerset to St. George's. But laying tracks was a daunting task, requiring the costly and time-consuming construction of long tunnels and swing bridges. By the time it was finished, the railway had cost investors $1 million, making it, per mile, the most expensive railway ever built.

"Old Rattle and Shake," as it was nicknamed, began to decline during World War II. Soldiers put the train to hard use, and it proved impossible to obtain the necessary maintenance equipment. At the end of the war the government acquired the distressed railway for $115,000. Automobiles arrived in Bermuda in 1946, and train service ended in 1948, when the railway was sold in its entirety to British Guiana (now Guyana). Then, in the 1980s, the government gave new life to the ground it had covered by converting the tracks into trails.

Today the secluded 18-mi recreational Bermuda Railway Trail runs the length of the island, offering fabulous coastal views along the way. Restricted to pedestrians, horseback riders, and cyclists, the trail is a delightful way to see the island away from the traffic and noise of main roads. You might want to rent a bike if you plan to cover the entire trail, as many enthusiastic travelers do. Do note, though, that many portions of the trail are isolated—so you should avoid setting out alone after dark. Regardless of when you go, it's wise to first pick up a free copy of the Bermuda Railway Trail Guide available at Visitor Information Centres.

—Revised by Susan MacCallum-Whitcomb

Old Cooperage Building. Ready to do some shopping? Inside this former barrel-making factory you can find the Bermuda Craft Market and the Bermuda Arts Centre. The former—arguably the island's largest and best-priced craft outlet—showcases the wares of more than 60 craftspeople, including quilters, candle makers, and wood carvers. The latter is a member-run art gallery that displays innovative high-end work. Exhibits change every month, and may include watercolors, oils, sculpture, and photography—much of which is for sale. Half-a-dozen artists also maintain studios on the premises, so leave some time to watch them at work. ⊠ *4 Maritime La., Dockyard* ☎ *441/234–3208 Craft Market, 441/234–2809 Arts Centre* ⊕ *www.artbermuda.bm* ⊠ *Free* ☉ *Craft Market: daily 10–5. Arts Centre: daily 10–5.*

Frog & Onion Pub. The supersize fireplace in which coopers used to forge their barrel bands is the focal point of the Frog & Onion Pub. Architectural interest aside, this naval-theme pub makes a great place for a lunch break, an afternoon libation, or even a quick game of pool. The menu has traditional fare (think Cornish pastie and fish-and-chips) as well as thirst-quenching ales made on-site by the Dockyard Brewing Company. ⊠ *The Old*

Cooperage, Dockyard ☎ *441/234–2900* ⊕ *www.frogandonion.bm.*

Somerset Bridge. The West End is connected to the rest of Bermuda by Somerset Bridge, and once you have crossed over it you're no longer, according to local lingo, "up the country." More than marking a boundary, Somerset Bridge is something of an attraction in its own right because it's reputed to be the world's smallest drawbridge. It opens a mere 18 inches, just wide enough to accommodate the mast of a passing sailboat. ⊠ *Between Somerset and Middle Rds., Sandys Parish*

Somerset Village. Its position on Mangrove Bay once made it a popular hideout for pirates. But judging by Somerset Village's bucolic appearance, you'd never guess that now. The shady past has been erased by shady trees, quiet streets, and charming cottages. As far as actual attractions go, this quaint one-road retreat has only a few eateries and shops—most of them offshoots of Hamilton stores. However, it provides easy access to the Gilbert Nature Reserve, a 5-acre woodland with paths that connect to some of the most scenic portions of Bermuda's Railway Trail. ⊠ *Sandys Parish.*

SEGWAY AWAY!

Segway Tours of Bermuda. In a land where cars are limited to one per household, alternate means of transportation matter—which explains why Bermuda's efficient public transit system is so revered and why horse-drawn carriages still do a roaring business. Now Segway Tours of Bermuda adds a higher-tech option: 90-minute Dockyard tours conducted year-round on übercool, two-wheeled Segway human transporters. The tours, which combine Bermuda's history and present day, depart daily from the yellow double-decker bus at 10, 12, 2 and 4. ☎ *441/504–2581* ⊕ *www.segway.bm.*

Where to Eat

WORD OF MOUTH

"While in town we had lunch at the Pickled Onion—excellent meal! A lunch for five was around $200 with a couple of drinks—not bad! The wahoo was fresh and the best we had on the Island all week."

—Tanya

"My favorites for 'local' would be Mad Hatters (tiny place, reservations essential, sit outside if the weather is good), North Rock Brewery (say hi to Doc and Tony for me) and, if you find yourself headed to Smiths parish or the east end of the island near breakfast time, Specialty Inn (diner-style, you're not going for the decor) for breakfast (or pizza)."

—txgirlinbda

Updated by
Sirkka Huish

What's incredible about the Bermuda restaurant scene isn't so much the number or quality of restaurants, but the sheer variety of cuisines represented on the menus, especially considering Bermuda is such a tiny island. It hosts a medley of global cuisines—British, French, Italian, Portuguese, American, Caribbean, Indian, Chinese, and Thai—palatable reminders of Bermuda's history as a colony.

Many superior independent and resort restaurants attract a constant and steady stream of internationally acclaimed chefs, assuring that the latest techniques and trends are menu regulars. At the same time, virtually all restaurant menus list traditional Bermudian dishes and drinks, so you have the opportunity to taste local specialties at almost any meal.

As you might expect, methods are not all that's imported. Roughly 80% of Bermuda's food is flown or shipped in, most of it from the United States. This explains why restaurant prices are often higher here than on the mainland.

Nevertheless, there are a number of delicious local ingredients that you should look for. At the top of the list is extraordinary seafood, like lobster (best during September through March), crab, oysters, mussels, clams, red snapper, rockfish, tuna, and wahoo. Additionally, many chefs work with local growers to serve fresh seasonal fruits and vegetables, such as potatoes, carrots, leeks, tomatoes, corn, broccoli, and Bermuda onions (one of the island's earliest exports); and in the fruit department, strawberries, cherries, bananas, and *loquats* (small yellow fruit used for preserves). Imports notwithstanding, Bermudian cuisine really begins and ends with local ingredients and traditional preparations, and therein lies the island's culinary identity.

While in Bermuda, try to eat like a local and put a couple of traditional dishes to the test. Bermuda is a seafood lover's paradise, with favorite dishes including mussel pie, shark hash, and codfish and bananas. As for soups, you can go for fish chowder, conch chowder, or traditional Portuguese black-eyed bean soup. Don't forget to kick back and relax after your meal with a Rum Swizzle, a Black and Coke, or a Dark 'n Stormy. Ginger beer—which is quite different from ginger ale—remains the Island's most popular soda for the kids.

WHAT IT COSTS IN U.S. DOLLARS				
¢	$	$$	$$$	$$$$
Restaurants under $10	$10–$20	$21–$30	$31–$40	over $40

Prices are per person for a main course at dinner. The bill usually includes a 17% service charge.

RESTAURANT REVIEWS

Listed alphabetically within region.

HAMILTON AND CENTRAL PARISHES

HAMILTON

The capital city has the largest concentration of eateries within a stone's throw from one another. It's best to explore the food options on foot, as most are based in and around Front Street, and it won't take long to find something to satisfy your craving. Don't forget to stroll down the side streets and alleyways, as some of the best restaurants are tucked away out of sight. Many restaurants have balconies overlooking the picturesque Hamilton Harbour, which makes this area a great spot for alfresco dining. Don't be surprised to see restaurant staff clearing away their tables and chairs around 10 pm, when the restaurants are transformed into clubs and the fun really begins.

$$$ ✕ **Barracuda Grill.** The tastefully decorated contemporary dining room—
SEAFOOD mahogany-framed chairs and banquettes, soft-gold lights over the tables—is reminiscent of sophisticated big-city restaurants, and the food that comes to the table is created by a culinary team dedicated to excellence. The island-style fish chowder or the lobster spring rolls are two good ways to start your meal. Moving on to entrées, you might try the grilled local yellowfin tuna, Bermuda rockfish, or seared fresh scallops. If you save room for dessert, opt for the chocolate-banana bread volcano or perhaps the gingerbread toffee pudding. There's also a great cocktail bar to sit at while you wait for your table. And if you're looking for a romantic dinner, reserve the "snug corner," which is a table for two, tucked away out of sight of other diners. ✉ *5 Burnaby St.* ☎ *441/292–1609* ⊕ *www.irg. bm* ⊘ *No lunch weekends.*

$ ✕ **Bermuda Bistro at the Beach.**
BERMUDIAN Despite what the name suggests, this restaurant is right in the heart of Hamilton. It's the ideal stop-off during a day of shopping, offering inexpensive and quick food—and plenty of it. Whether you want a hearty three-course lunch or just an afternoon snack, there's something for everyone on the menu, from burgers and sandwiches to fish and steaks. The restaurant's on-street patio is the perfect people-watching location. If you're feeling peckish on a night out, this is the place to come, as food is served until midnight every night. ✉ *103*

TOP 5 DINING

■ Enjoy eat-as-much-as-you-can Sunday brunch at the Fairmont Southampton Resort's Windows on the Sound restaurant (otherwise only open to guests).

■ Enjoy a lazy afternoon at the Swizzle Inn with a huge plate of nachos and a couple of jugs of Rum Swizzle.

■ Grab some jerk chicken and rice 'n' peas from the Jamaican Grill and picnic at Horseshoe Bay.

■ Have a fish sandwich with plenty of mayo from Bouchée. Cheap and delicious!

■ Savor surf 'n' turf at Waterlot Inn. Need we say more?

Front St. ☎ *441/292–0219* ⊕ *www.thebeachbermuda.com.*

$$ BRASSERIE ★ ✕ **Bolero Brasserie.** The waitstaff, dressed in waistcoats, long white aprons, and red ties, create an authentic European feel, while owner and chef Johnny Roberts takes great pride in preparing the finest food for his traditional bistro.

There's a classic brasserie menu featuring snails, ballotine of foie gras, roast rack of lamb, mushroom risotto, calf's liver, bacon and black pudding, and for something sweet: sticky toffee pudding, crème brûlée, and crêpes. Vegetarians and anyone with any special dietary requirements are also catered to. The impressive red decor includes a wall decorated with a multitude of various-size mirrors, and plenty of local artwork. There's also a balcony overlooking Front Street with great views of Hamilton Harbour. ⊠ *Bermuda House La., 95 Front St.* ☎ *441/292–4507* ⊕ *www.bolerobrasserie.com* ⊗ *Closed Sun. No lunch Sat.*

$$ FRENCH ✕ **Bouchée.** It's worth the walk west out of Hamilton to see why this charming spot is a firm favorite with locals and tourists alike. The atmosphere is sophisticated-casual, the menu is extensive, and the food is delicious. Recommended starters are the French pâté and pan-seared scallops. Then make the most of the local fish, usually sea bass, rockfish, or wahoo, cooked to your liking. To really fill up, treat yourself to the three-course set menu, available Friday and Saturday nights for $45. The portions are a healthy size, and the knowledgeable staff will keep you entertained. There is live entertainment at dinner on Saturday night. ⊠ *75 Pitts Bay Rd., near Woodburne Ave.* ☎ *441/295–5759.*

$$ AFRICAN ✕ **Café Cairo.** Experience the cuisine and ambience of North Africa at this relaxed restaurant. Boasting a menu of exotic flavors, this popular eatery shows Bermuda's culinary adventurous streak at its best, satisfying the well-traveled palates of both islanders and tourists. Specialties include Egyptian and Moroccan dishes; don't miss the hummus, kofta lamb, and couscous, or the shish kebab. After your meal, settle in on the low-seated sofas in the back room and enjoy a Turkish coffee. The balcony is great for people-watching, and you'll more than likely be offered a pipe of *sheesha* (fruit tobacco). It's one of the few Front Street restaurants to serve food until the early hours of the morning, and the place becomes a lively nightspot after 10. ⊠ *93 Front St.* ☎ *441/295–5155* ⊗ *Closed Sun.*

$$ ASIAN ♻ ✕ **Chopsticks.** The menu here is a mix of Szechuan, Hunan, Cantonese, and Thai favorites. Top Chinese choices include beef with vegetables in ginger sauce, sweet-and-spicy chicken, and sweet-and-sour fish. For Thai tastes, try beef with onion, scallions, and basil in hot chili sauce, Thai green curry, or shrimp *panang* (in coconut-curry sauce). The food is good, but you'll be paying more for smaller portions, compared to the U.S. The impressive decor includes a huge floor-to-ceiling waterfall, large bronze statues, and a hand-painted mural. As an alterna-

tive, takeout is also offered. ✉ *88 Reid St.* ☎ *441/292–0791* ⊕ *www. bermudarestaurants.com.*

$$ ✕ **Coconut Rock and Yashi Sushi**
ECLECTIC **Bar.** Whether you're in the mood for shrimp tempura and sashimi served in a quiet room with black-lacquer tables and paper lanterns, or you would rather have chicken chimichanga, fried tiger shrimp, or grilled sirloin steak surrounded by loud music videos on multiple screens at a popular nighttime venue—or if you want a little of both—these adjoining restaurants can satisfy. The underground restaurant is dark and dingy and remains well hidden beneath Hamilton's main shopping street. But it's an old favorite with locals, and the fusion of different flavors and good-size portions make it worth the wait for a table. ✉ *Williams House, downstairs, 20 Reid St.* ☎ *441/292–1043* ☺ *No lunch Sun.*

$ ✕ **Docksider.** Locals come to mingle at this sprawling Front Street sports
BRITISH bar. It's generally more popular as a drinking venue, as it can get quite overcrowded and rowdy. But if you want to catch the game on the big screen with everyone else, an all-day menu of standard pub fare is available, as well as local fish. Go for the English beef pie, fish-and-chips, or a fish sandwich, and sip your dessert—a Dark 'n Stormy—out on the porch as you watch Bermuda stroll by. Or if you can't make up your mind, you can always rely on the hearty full English breakfast to fill you up. Food is served until 10 pm. The pub has a good jukebox and there's often a DJ or a band on summer weekends. ✉ *121 Front St.* ☎ *441/296–3333* ⊕ *www.dockies.com.*

$$ ✕ **Flanagans Irish Pub & Restaurant.** Bermuda's only Irish pub has come
IRISH back bigger and better than before. Having undergone a complete renovation, this place is now looking like a traditional Irish pub with a real homey feel. The staff is welcoming and more than happy to talk you through the extensive menu. Consider homemade comfort food such as fish-and-chips, shepherd's pie, burgers, pasta, and seafood, including wahoo, rockfish, and snapper. Adjoining the restaurant is its sister sports bar, The Outback, which is full of TVs showing the latest games. ✉ *Emporium Bldg., 69 Front St., 2nd fl.* ☎ *441/295–8299* ⊕ *www.flanagans.bm.*

$$ ✕ **Flying Fish and Omakase Sushi Bar.** This restaurant, which was formerly
SEAFOOD called Primavera, sets the standard for seafood, as it specializes in the best local and imported fish. You can choose from oysters, Cape Cod clams, and Maine mussels, as well as a king crab leg, pan-roasted striped bass, and scallops and scampi. You can also handpick the lobster from the huge water tank in the middle of the restaurant. This ensures that live seafood is kept in the freshest of conditions until it reaches your plate. The sushi bar, Omakase, is upstairs, but you may order from the menu downstairs as well. Delicacies include the Bermuda maki roll stuffed with crabmeat, avocado, and cucumber. Several vegetarian rolls,

---

GOOD TO GO

Miles Market (96 Pitts Bay Road, Hamilton), a gourmet grocery store, is a quick-hit spot for ready-to-go hot or cold eats, especially handy for a picnic on the beach or an in-room hotel feast. Food is sold by the pound, so watch how much you pile on your tray.

3

stuffed with asparagus or shiitake, are also on the menu. ⊠ *69 Pitts Bay Rd.* ☎ *441/295–2167* ⊙ *No lunch Sat.– Sun.*

$$$ ✕**Harbourfront.** When you dine at a table beside the enormous open win-
INTERNATIONAL dows, you might feel as though you are floating on the harbor yourself.
★ Nearly every seat in the house has beautiful views of the quiet waters. Few Bermuda restaurants have menus as varied as this busy spot, where sushi is served alongside international specialties. For lunch you might have a burger, a salad, or sushi. For dinner, start with salmon tartare and tuna carpaccio, followed by the roasted chicken, veal milanese, roasted duck breast, or mushroom risotto. Sushi devotees should come during sushi happy hour from 5 to 6:30 pm, Monday through Friday. ⊠ *Next to Bermuda Underwater Exploration Institute (BUEI), 40 Crow La.* ☎ *441/292–6122* ⊕ *www.harbourfront.bm* ⊙ *No lunch Sun.*

$$$ ✕**Harley's Restaurant.** Serene water views of Hamilton Harbour and
BERMUDIAN gracious service combine with top-notch continental and Bermudian
★ cuisine to make Harley's one of the best restaurants in Hamilton. Chefs prepare a wonderful Bermudian specialty: baked rockfish smothered in the local-favorite chili gombey jam. Dry-aged beef is always cooked to perfection, but if you prefer something vegetarian, try hand-rolled can-nelloni filled with ricotta cheese and grilled vegetables with a blackened-tomato coulis. The restaurant is bright and airy, and in summer has a large outside canopy. Eat-all-you-can Sunday brunch is $39. Compli-mentary wine tasting is available to diners on Wednesday evening and a barbecue on Tuesday evening. ⊠ *Fairmont Hamilton Princess Hotel, 76 Pitts Bay Rd.* ☎ *441/298–5779.*

$$$ ✕**Harry's.** This family-run restaurant has a modern feel, with dark wood
AMERICAN paneling, leather chairs, soft lighting, and brass fixtures. But its main draw remains its creative menu with plenty of organic ingredients. The beef here is aged for 21 days and flavored to taste; there's also plenty of fresh seafood on offer. The food is good, but expensive for the small portions. There's also a bar and an oceanside patio (with a huge marlin statue), but these areas get crowded and the noise travels into the restaurant when the workers pile in for their after-work cocktails. ⊠ *The Waterfront, 96 Pitt's Bay Rd.* ☎ *441/292–5533* ⊕ *www.harrys. bm* ⊙ *Closed Sun.*

$$ ✕**Heritage Court.** Classic and conservative, with a refined afternoon tea
BERMUDIAN service and piano music throughout the day, the Heritage Court is a calm, relaxing spot for any meal. Clinking china can be heard at break-fast and teatime, while lunch and dinner bring businesspeople, hotel guests, couples, and families for reliable Bermudian-continental fare and like-clockwork service. The Bermuda fish chowder, classic Caesar salad, and calamari are faultless. There's a late-night snack menu until 12:30 am, and on Saturday evenings a local band livens things up with sing-along favorites. Watch out for the hotel's Friday-night happy hour: the revelers tend to take over the restaurant area. ⊠ *Fairmont Hamilton Princess Hotel, 76 Pitts Bay Rd.* ☎ *441/298–5779.*

$$ ✕**Hog Penny Pub and Restaurant.** Veterans of London pub crawls may feel
BRITISH nostalgic at this dark, wood-filled watering hole off Front Street. Those
★ die-hard aficionados of old-style British comfort food will adore the Yorkshire pudding, shepherd's pie, steak-and-kidney pie, fish-and-chips,

and bangers and mash. You can work up an appetite just deciding from the impressive burger selection, and the British ale on tap will wash the food down nicely. This is Hamilton's oldest licensed establishment, opened in 1957. From May to December there's live music every night. ✉ *5 Burnaby St.* ☎ *441/292–2534* ⊕ *www.irg.bm.*

> **OK, RACHAEL RAY!**
>
> If you've got an eye for bargains, the Hog Penny in Hamilton has been showcased on the Food Network's "$40 a Day." Rachel Ray said it was the place to go in Bermuda for a value-priced meal.

3

$ ✕ **House of India.** Slightly off the beaten track, this authentic Indian restaurant is well worth the 10-minute walk or short cab ride from the town center. Start with vegetable *samosas* (small deep-fried turnovers), which are sure to whet your appetite. For your second course, you really can't go wrong with any entrée—meat, fish, or vegetarian. If you like spicy food, take on the chicken *chetanod*. It's hotter than a vindaloo, and not everyone has the palate for it. All the naan (a flat, doughy bread) is freshly made in the tandoor, and the *lassi* (sweetened yogurt) drinks, particularly the mango, are delicious and refreshing. A filling weekday lunch buffet is worth every dollar ($20). Even though the restaurant has recently doubled in size, it still remains busy, but if you can't get a table, you can opt for takeout. ✉ *58 North St.* ☎ *441/295–6450* ⊘ *No lunch Sat.–Sun.*

INDIAN

$ ✕ **Jamaican Grill.** Journey outside the familiar city limits to Court Street and you'll find Jamaican food at its best. The Thomas family is proud of their Jamaican heritage and want everyone to taste the Caribbean flavors with them at their restaurant. Classics like jerk and curry chicken, hot wings, rice and beans, dumplings, and meat and veggie patties adorn the menu. Be sure to order Jamaica's own Ting grapefruit drink to wash down the tasty homemade cakes and cookies. It's no-frills food, but the prices are good and the portions are huge. The take-out service makes for a great beach picnic. A firm favorite with the locals, there are three other branches scattered around the island. ✉ *32 Court St.* ☎ *441/296–6577* ⊘ *Closed Sun.*

JAMAICAN

$$ ✕ **La Trattoria.** Tucked away in a Hamilton alley, you can't go wrong with this no-nonsense trattoria, which is pleasant and unpretentious. Any of the pastas, such as lasagna, manicotti, and spaghetti with mixed seafood, can be served in smaller portions as appetizers. Fish fillets are generally panfried with olive oil, garlic, and herbs. La Trattoria's pizzas are cooked in Bermuda's only brick wood-burning pizza oven. About 20 inventive topping combinations (such as arugula and prosciutto) are on the menu, but the chef will mix and match whatever you like. ✉ *22 Washington La.* ☎ *441/295–1877* ⊕ *www.latrattoria.bm* ⊘ *No lunch Sun.*

ITALIAN
Fodor's Choice
★

$$ ✕ **Latin.** As one of Bermuda's newest and most contemporary restaurants, Latin offers something a little different. The Spanish-themed and cheerfully decorated eatery serves up paella, tapas, and plenty of fresh seafood. Exotic flavors and healthy portions make it well worth the stroll from the main restaurant strip. Fair warning: the place is small and tables are so close that people sitting next to you will hear every word you are saying. In addition to the restaurant there's a coffee shop

SPANISH

with patio seating and a rum bar and courtyard frequented by local salsa dancers. A DJ also comes in to spin the tunes every Friday and Saturday night. ✉ *29 Victoria St.* ☎ *441/296–5050* ⊕ *www.irg.bm.*

$$$ ✕ **Little Venice.** Little Venice is a little pricey and pretentious, but it has
ITALIAN fancy and flavorful Italian food. You can't go wrong with the fried calamari for starters, although the Caesar and Greek salads are hard to resist. For main courses, the ever-changing menu always has both contemporary and classic Italian dishes, including pasta, meat, and fish. Options include the lobster, crab, and shrimp casserole, veal parmigiano and braised beef. Bermuda's business elite fill the restaurant after work, making their way through the wine list that boasts 1,000 different wines from around the world. The less-than-filling average-size portions make the restaurant more suitable for clinching a business deal than enjoying a night out with the family. ✉ *32 Bermudiana Rd.* ☎ *441/295–3503* ⊕ *www.littlevenice.bm* ⌂ *Reservations essential* ☺ *No lunch Sat. Closed Sun.*

$$ ✕ **L'Oriental.** Above its sister restaurant, Little Venice, this Asian hot spot
ASIAN is a favorite among locals for its fresh sushi bar. Take the footbridge— over an indoor stream—to the raised seating at the lively teppanyaki table, where trained chefs stylishly slice, stir, and season your steak and veggies onto your plate. The menu includes traditional Asian soups and entrées and a variety of Indonesian and Thai dishes (don't miss the curries), as well as nightly specials. Choose from a selection of wines, sakes, and Japanese beers to wash it all down. The backdrop of colorful dragons and a handcrafted pagoda add to the Asian flavor. There's also an open kitchen, so you can see the chefs at work, complete with flames. L'Oriental's Take Out Express locations are on Church Street and Victoria Street. ✉ *32 Bermudiana Rd.* ☎ *441/296–4477* ⊕ *www. loriental.bm* ☺ *No lunch weekends.*

$$ ✕ **Lobster Pot.** Bermudians swear by this spot, where the maritime-
SEAFOOD theme dining room is filled with brass nautical gear, lobster traps,
☺ and sun-bleached rope. The fresh local lobster, available September through March, is most requested next to rockfish, snapper, wahoo, and mahimahi with bananas and almonds, all local favorites. The "Cup Match Special" is everything locals love about fried seafood dinners: crispy fish strips on a bun with a decent helping of coleslaw and fries. If you're looking for a good deal, there's also a limited-availability three-course set lunch for $21.75. ✉ *6 Bermudiana Rd.* ☎ *441/292–6898* ☺ *No lunch weekends.*

$$ ✕ **Maria's Ristorante.** Childhood memories of homecooked Italian food
ITALIAN inspired owner, Claudio Vigilante, to rename this restaurant after his
★ mom. It's a cozy place tucked away off Front Street, known for its simple Italian fare and low menu prices. Consider comfort food such as homemade pizzas, risottos, gnocchi, potato dumplings, and lemon-herb chicken. The restaurant was renovated to look like an Italian piazza, complete with overhead washing lines. Before or after dinner, you can swirl a glass of *rosso* (red wine) beneath the vaulted ceiling of the wine bar, which boasts Bermuda's largest selection of wines by the glass. There's also a patio area with huge sofas and an outside bar. ✉ *2 Chan-*

KNOW-HOW

RESERVATIONS

Reservations are always a good idea. We mention them only when they're essential or not accepted. Book as far ahead as you can and reconfirm when you arrive, especially in high season. Many restaurants close—or curtail hours, or days of service—in the off-season, so call ahead before setting out for lunch or dinner.

DRESS

Bermuda has had a reputation for strict sartorial standards, but most of the mid-price restaurants are much more casual these days. In many of the pubs and bars in town you would not be out of place in shorts and a T-shirt. It's a different story in more upscale restaurants, often attached to the hotels. Even when not required, a jacket for men is rarely out of place. In our restaurant reviews, we mention dress only when men are required to wear either a jacket or a jacket and tie.

PRICES

Much harder to swallow than a delicious Bermuda fish chowder are the prices of dining out. Bermuda has never sought a reputation for affordability, and restaurants are no exception. A few greasy spoons serve standard North American fare (and a few local favorites) at a decent price, but by and large you should prepare for a bit of sticker shock. Don't be surprised if dinner for two with wine at one of the very top places—Tom Moore's Tavern, for example—puts a $200–$300 dent in your pocket. A 17% service charge is almost always added to the bill "for your convenience."

cery Ln. ☎ 441/295–5058 ⊕ www.frescosgroup.bm ⚞ Reservations essential ⊘ Closed Sun. No lunch Sat.

$$
BERMUDIAN
☾

✕ **The Pickled Onion.** This former whiskey warehouse is now a lively restaurant serving creative, contemporary Bermudian cuisine, as well as a handful of Latin- and Asian-flavored dishes. Try the bow-tie chicken pasta, the panfried rockfish, or one of the many burgers, salads, or sandwiches. If it's beef you're after, they grill it to perfection. For those lazy weekends, they also do a great all-day Sunday brunch. For dessert, go straight for the Oreo-crusted cheesecake or brownie split. If you get there early enough, grab a table on the veranda overlooking Front Street and the harbor. A great martini list makes this a fabulous spot to hang out after dinner, too. There's live music seven nights a week from April to December and five nights a week in winter. ⊠ 53 Front St. ☎ 441/295–2263 ⊕ www.irg.bm.

$$$
SEAFOOD
Fodor's Choice
★

✕ **Port O' Call.** What was a small and intimate restaurant tripled in size with an extensive refurbishment. The two-level restaurant and sushi bar boasts a very modern look and elegant feel, and is one of the few ground-entry dining spots on Front Street, with an outdoor dining area reminiscent of a European sidewalk café. Fresh local fish—such as wahoo, tuna, grouper, and snapper—is cooked perfectly, and the preparations are creative. Don't miss the certified Angus rib-eye steaks, grilled lamb loin and pan-roasted chicken breast, and all the mouthwatering, homemade desserts. This is one of the island's most sophisticated

QUICK BITES

✕ **Buzz.** Cheap and cheerful Buzz, inside the Hamilton Pharmacy on Parliament Street, is a good spot for a filling sandwich. There are salads and some great fruit smoothies, too. ☎ 441/292–5160.

✕ **City Café.** This is the place to go to grab a quick lunch in town. It's close to City Hall and serves a great selection of sandwiches, salads, and cakes. ☎ 411/296–9462.

✕ **Delicious.** Inside the Washington Mall on Reid Street, Delicious offers a—you guessed it—delicious sandwich. ☎ 441/295–5890.

✕ **Kathy's Kaffee.** In the Emporium Building next to Bank of Butterfield on Front Street, Kathy's Kaffee serves robust breakfasts and satisfying lunches at reasonable prices. ☎ 441/295–5203.

✕ **Paradiso Café.** Watch your waistline with a tasty salad or sandwich from Paradiso Café on Reid Street. But be warned, this place is popular, and you'll probably have to wait for a table. ☎ 441/295–3263.

dining experiences. ✉ *87 Front St.* ☎ *441/295–5373* ⊕ *www.portocall. bm* ⊘ *No lunch Sat.–Sun.*

$$ ✕ **Portofino.** You'll be transported to Italy as you step inside Portofino,
ITALIAN with its shuttered windows and brick walls covered in pictures from
☾ the owner's family album. There's also an outside dining area for those
balmy evenings. Start with calamari or garlic bread, the two starters
for which the restaurant is renowned. Then move on to the pizzas (we
favor the pepperoni and artichoke variety). Why not try the tiramisu,
chocolate brownie, or rum cake for dessert? Prices and portions are
good. A separate take-out section with its own entrance means you
can get the good food while avoiding the crowds. ✉ *20 Bermudiana Rd.*
☎ *441/292–2375, 441/295–6090* ⊘ *No lunch Sat.–Sun.*

$$$ ✕ **The Red Carpet.** This tiny restaurant in the old Armoury is popular
CONTINENTAL at lunch, especially among local politicians and businesspeople. But
at dinner the dining room is usually uncrowded, and the pace relaxes
so that diners can take their time with the deliciously prepared food.
Among the culinary highlights are the grilled lamb chops with rosemary, grilled fresh Bermuda fish with fried banana and almonds, and
the seafood kettle (mussels, shrimp, fish, scallops, and lobster tail in
a creamy white-wine and curry sauce). ✉ *Armoury Bldg., 37 Reid St.*
☎ *441/292–6195* ⊘ *Closed Sun.*

$$ ✕ **Rosa's Cantina.** Take a stroll to the opposite end of Front Street from
MEXICAN the ferry terminal and you'll stumble across Bermuda's very own slice
of Mexico. With the walls covered in Mexican memorabilia, you'll
be reaching for the sombrero before you know it! If you like your
spicy food, you'll love the Mexican specialties such as big Texas steaks,
barbecue ribs, fajitas, and seafood combos. Don't miss the all-you-
can-eat ribs nights on Mondays and Thursdays for $25.95. There's
also a cocktail list, featuring about 10 different margaritas for you to
make your way through. ✉ *121 Front St.* ☎ *441/295–1912* ⊕ *www.
bermudarestaurants.com.*

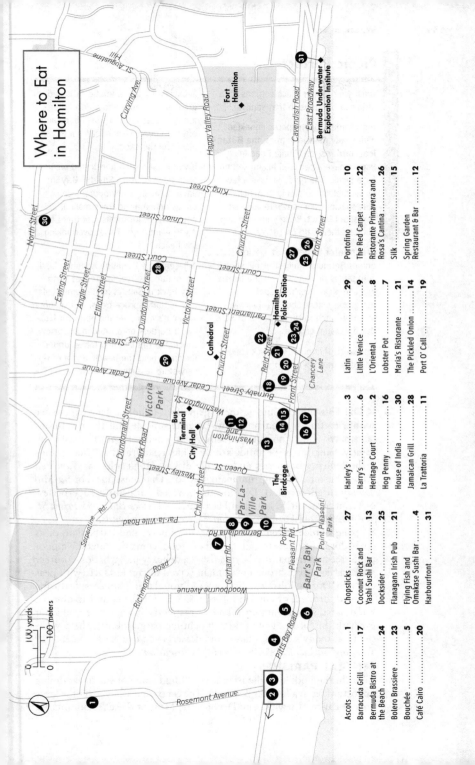

Where to Eat in Hamilton

Ascots **1**
Barracuda Grill **17**
Bermuda Bistro at the Beach **24**
Bolero Brassiere **23**
Bouchée **5**
Café Cairo **20**

Chopsticks **27**
Coconut Rock and Yashi Sushi Bar **13**
Docksider **25**
Flanagans Irish Pub **21**
Flying Fish and Omakase Sushi Bar ... **4**
Harbourfront **31**

Harley's **3**
Harry's **6**
Heritage Court **2**
Hog Penny **16**
House of India **30**
Jamaican Grill **28**
La Trattoria **11**

Latin **29**
Little Venice **9**
L'Oriental **8**
Lobster Pot **7**
Maria's Ristorante **21**
The Pickled Onion **14**
Port O' Call **19**

Portofino **10**
The Red Carpet **22**
Ristorante Primavera and Rosa's Cantina ... **26**
Silk **15**
Spring Garden Restaurant & Bar **12**

Picnic Perfect

Ditch your proper place settings for a little sea breeze with that sandwich.

With verdant open spaces sprinkled with shady poinciana trees, the **Botanical Gardens,** on Middle Road in Paget, make a peaceful inland setting for a picnic. The gardens have a few picnic tables and plenty of benches, plus spacious lawns where you can spread a blanket. Bring your own supplies, as there's no on-site café.

Clearwater Beach in St. David's is one of Bermuda's nicest picnic spots, with tables near to and on the beach. You can pick up picnic supplies at the grocery store about ¼-mi away or order lunch to go from one of St. David's casual eateries.

Just west of popular Warwick Long Bay, tiny, tranquil **Jobson Cove** beach is backed by the dramatic cliffs and greenery of South Shore Park. There are no tables and no snack bars, and often no people—perfect for a private picnic on the sand.

If you want a tried-and-tested picnic spot, head to **John Smith's Bay** in Smith's Parish. The wooden picnic tables beneath the trees make it a popular spot for locals. Get there early if you want a good spot overlooking the beach.

Adjacent to a Bermuda Audubon Society nature reserve, **Somerset Long Bay Park** in Sandys has a semicircular beach, fluffy spruce trees, and shallow water. It's also a terrific place for birding: it borders on an Audubon Society sanctuary. You can find tables under the trees near the beach, and a grocery store less than ½-mi away.

$$ ✕ **Silk.** This culinary and aesthetic gem offers a unique Thai experience
THAI with a picturesque harbor view. One step inside and the restaurant transports you to an authentically Asian environment. The colorful, trendy hangout is Bermuda's only Thai restaurant. Menu options include plenty of curries and noodle dishes. Don't miss the *Yam Ped Yang* (chicken or shrimp and mango salad), Thai roast duck, or *Ba-Miii Thalay* (fried noodles). Dine on the covered patio for a superb view of Front Street and Hamilton Harbour. ⊠ *Masters Bldg., 55 Front St.* ☎ *441/295–0449* ⊕ *www.silk.bm* ☉ *No lunch weekends.*

$ ✕ **Spring Garden Restaurant & Bar.** If you've never had Barbadian, or as
CARIBBEAN Barbados natives like to call it, "Bajan" food, come sit under the indoor palm tree and try panfried flying fish—a delicacy in Barbados. Another good choice is the broiled mahimahi served in creole sauce, with peas and rice. During lobster season, an additional menu appears, featuring steamed, broiled, or curried lobster ($38.50 for the complete dinner). For dessert, try coconut cream pie or raspberry-mango cheesecake. Or eat with the locals at the Friday lunchtime bargain buffet; help yourself to as many starters, mains, and desserts you can eat for $22. ⊠ *19 Washington La.* ☎ *441/295–7416* ☉ *Closed Sun.*

CENTRAL PARISHES

Right in the middle of the island, you'll find some of the finest dining opportunities available in Bermuda. The central parishes cover the large area of Paget, Warwick, and Devonshire. Most of these restaurants are located in luxury hotels and resorts, so you'll know to expect nothing but the best. The only downside is that these restaurants are in hard-to-reach places not always easily reachable by public transport. Therefore renting a scooter or taking a cab are your best options.

$$$$ ✗**Ascots.** In an elegant former man-
CONTINENTAL
Fodor's Choice
★
sion just outside downtown Hamilton, Ascots gives you a wonderful excuse to leave the city. The high standards of owners Angelo Armano and Edmund Smith result in creative and seasonal menu offerings that incorporate fresh ingredients from local farmers and fishermen. For something different, start off with the chilled banana soup with black rum—it's unusual but very popular. Main courses include the Bermuda fish cakes with citrus curry sauce and fruit chutney; caramelized tuna steak; and char-grilled 18-ounce rib-eye steak. Save room for dessert, as raspberry and white-chocolate crème brûlée are on the menu. An extensive wine list is available to complement your meal. You can relax on the sofas surrounding the handsome cedar bar before and after meals. ✉ *Royal Palms Hotel, 24 Rosemont Ave., Pembroke Parish* ☎ *441/295–9644* ⊕ *www.ascots.bm* ☾ *Closed Sun. No lunch Sat.*

$$$ ✗**Beau Rivage.** This upscale restaurant adds a touch of French flavor
FRENCH
to Bermuda's restaurant scene. It's an authentic French eatery with an extensive menu that's very ooh-la-la. The menu includes frogs' legs, lobster ravioli, and beef Wellington. The dessert menu is just as good, with French soufflé, chocolate fondant, and crème brûlée. Following the French theme, there's also a vast selection of wines available. The open-plan restaurant with alfresco patio dining provides great views of the city and the hotel's infinity pool. In addition, there's also a table in the heart of the chef's kitchen for eight to 16 people. ✉ *Newstead Belmont Hills Resort, 27 Harbour Rd., Paget Parish* ☎ *441/232–8686* ⊕ *www.newsteadbelmonthills.com* ☾ *No dinner Sun.*

$$ ✗**Blu Bar & Grill.** This is a great spot for dinner, with impressive views
AMERICAN
★
across the golf course and out to the sea. There's standard American cuisine, including steaks and ribs, but the eclectic chefs like to add bold flavors with lots of exotic herbs and spices. The wide variety of fresh seafood is your best bet. Follow up your fish chowder with lobster, yellowfin tuna, rockfish, snapper, or wahoo. ✉ *Newstead Belmont Hills Golf Course, 97 Middle Rd., Warwick Parish* ☎ *441/232–2323* ⊕ *www.blu.bm* ☾ *No lunch.*

$$$ ✗**Café Coco.** This ocean-side restaurant has a real European feel to it.
BERMUDIAN
You can sit in the dining room, which looks like a typical white Mediterranean villa, complete with archways and art depicting typical street

NOT-SO-FAST FOOD

If you think something may be missing from the horizon of Bermuda eateries, you are quite right. Apart from a lone KFC (which snuck in sometime during the 1970s), you won't find any fast-food chains on the island. The majority of Bermuda's residents strongly believe that allowing American franchises onto the island would dilute Bermuda's distinctive foreign (and rather upscale) appeal, eventually leading to the island's resembling Anyplace, USA. Adjust your eyes (and belly) to the absence of big golden double arches!

3

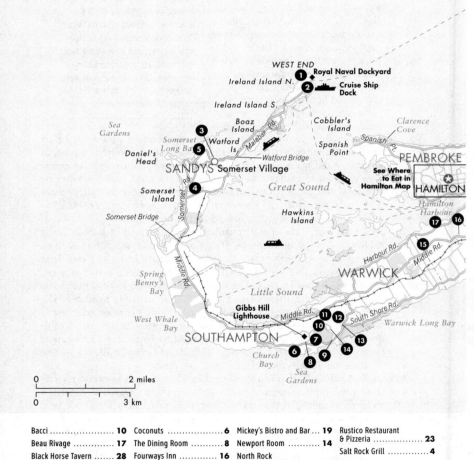

Where to Eat in the Parishes

ATLANTIC OCEAN

WEST END — Royal Naval Dockyard ❶
Ireland Island N. ❷ — Cruise Ship Dock
Ireland Island S.
Sea Gardens
Boaz Island
Cobbler's Island
Clarence Cove
Watford Is. — Malabar Rd.
Somerset Long Bay ❸
Spanish Point — Spanish Pt.
Daniel's Head ❺
PEMBROKE
Watford Bridge
SANDYS — Somerset Village
See Where to Eat in Hamilton Map
HAMILTON
Great Sound
Hamilton Harbour
Somerset Island ❹
Somerset Bridge
Hawkins Island
❶⑦
⑯
Somerset Rd.
Harbour Rd. — Middle Rd.
⑮
WARWICK
Spring Benny's Bay
Middle Rd.
Little Sound
West Whale Bay
Gibbs Hill Lighthouse — Middle Rd.
⑪⑫
South Shore Rd.
Warwick Long Bay
⑩
SOUTHAMPTON
⑦
⑬
Church Bay
❻ ⑨ ⑭
❽
Sea Gardens

0 — 2 miles
0 — 3 km

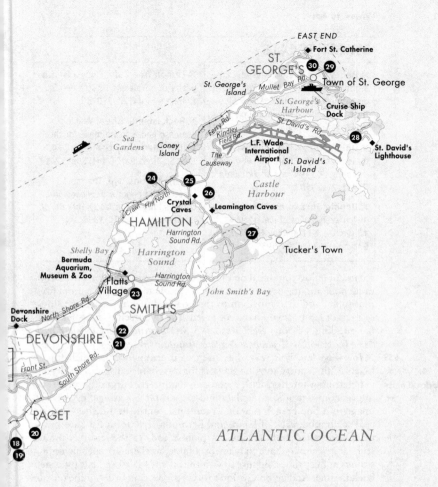

EAST END

ST. GEORGE'S

◆ Fort St. Catherine

30 29

St. George's Island

Mullet Bay Rd.

Town of St. George

St. George's Harbour

Cruise Ship Dock

Ferry Rd.

Kindley Field Rd.

St. David's Rd.

L.F. Wade International Airport

St. David's Island

28

■ St. David's Lighthouse

Sea Gardens

Coney Island

The Causeway

Castle Harbour

24

25

26 ♦ Crystal Caves

HAMILTON

◆ Leamington Caves

Harrington Sound Rd.

27 ○ Tucker's Town

Shelly Bay

Harrington Sound

Bermuda Aquarium, Museum & Zoo

Flatts Village

Harrington Sound Rd.

John Smith's Bay

23

Devonshire Dock

North Shore Rd.

SMITH'S

DEVONSHIRE

22

21

Front St.

South Shore Rd.

PAGET

20

18

19

ATLANTIC OCEAN

KEY

Cruise Ship

Ferry

Railway Trail

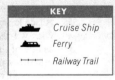

SWEET TREATS

✕ **Bailey's Ice Cream**. This remains a firm favorite with locals. You can't go wrong with any flavor! ⊠ *6 Blue Hole Hill, Bailey's Bay, Hamilton Parish* ☎ *441/293–8605.*

✕ **Double Dip**. A triple serving of Butter Pecan in a waffle bowl makes us happy. ⊠ *119 Front St., Hamilton* ☎ *441/292–3503.*

✕ **Double Dip Express**. Mix and match every flavor of ice cream imaginable. ⊠ *1 Kindley Field Rd., St. George's* ☎ *441/293–5959.*

✕ **Lemon Tree Cafe**. Enjoy a French pastry or a fruit tart. ⊠ *7 Queen St., Hamilton* ☎ *441/292–0235.*

✕ **Rock Island Coffee**. Vanilla espresso and a scone make for the perfect afternoon pick-me-up. ⊠ *48 Reid St., Hamilton* ☎ *441/296–5241.*

✕ **Temptations Two**. The most perfect little finger sandwiches and cookies for teatime. ⊠ *31 York St., St. George's* ☎ *441/297–1368.*

scenes, or enjoy your meal on the outside terrace overlooking the swimming pool and the ocean. Start with tropical crab salad or caramelized pineapple, and then move on to the poached wahoo, seared scallops, or rack of lamb. If you have room left, treat yourself to the sticky toffee pudding. ⊠ *Coco Reef Resort, 3 Stonington Circle Paget Parish* ☎ *441/236–5416* ⊕ *www.cocoreefbermuda.com.*

$$$
CONTINENTAL
Fodor's Choice
★

✕ **Fourways Inn**. Fourways has risen to preeminence as much for its lovely 17th-century surroundings as for its reliable cuisine. The elegant yet charming interior, with mahogany banisters, burgundy carpeting, impressionist prints, and silver-and-crystal table settings, evokes the image of a fine French manor. Traditional continental dishes, such as veal scaloppini, rack of lamb, and Bermuda-style fresh fish, are beautifully presented and delicious. A pianist adds to the leisurely dining style, but you may have to wait for a table, as there are specific dining sittings at busy times. Be sure to visit the on-site "Peg Leg" bar for a step back in time. And definitely don't forget to place an order at the on-site pastry shop, the chocolate-dipped strawberries are a must. This is one of the most popular places on the island to head to for Sunday brunch. ⊠ *1 Middle Rd., Paget Parish* ☎ *441/236–6517* ⊕ *www.fourwaysinn. com Jacket required* ⊙ *No lunch. No dinner Sun.*

$$$
MEDITERRANEAN
★

✕ **Lido Restaurant**. On the beachfront terrace at the Elbow Beach Resort, with waves breaking just below, the Lido Restaurant is often invoked as one of the island's most romantic settings. You could easily just stare out the window all evening. Food and service are top-notch to give you a truly memorable dining experience. Items to try: the Angus ribeye steak, Bermuda lobster, roasted halibut, lamb shank, and the New York strip loin. It's best to reserve a table, but regardless, the place gets crowded and sometimes feels like you're on top of the other diners. ⊠ *Elbow Beach Resort, 60 S. Shore Rd., Paget Parish* ☎ *441/236–9884* ⊕ *www.lido.bm* ♧ *Reservations essential* ⊙ *No lunch.*

$$$
MEDITERRANEAN

✕ **Mickey's Bistro & Bar**. This is the place to go for alfresco dining—you can dine right on the sand. The no-fuss bistro serves inexpensive continental and local dishes. It's the ultimate in relaxing dining with the

CLOSE UP

Dining with Kids

Kids are people, too, and very hungry little people on a regular basis. Little-big eaters are usually banished to a far-flung corner away from all the action (which they'll then have to find, leaving a spaghetti trail behind), or forced to dine in fast-food restaurants for fear they'll actually express themselves. Well, Bermuda has no fast-food chains, except for a lone KFC in Hamilton, but little diners and their big companions will have no trouble finding familiar foods in welcoming settings here.

Frog & Onion Pub. Let the kids build up an appetite in the game room at the Frog & Onion Pub. It's crammed full of games to keep children ages three and upward entertained—and their parents thankful for the peace and quiet. The pub also has a kids' menu containing all the tried and tested favorites. ☎ 441/234-2900.

Harbour Nights. Harbour Nights festival in Hamilton (Wednesday evenings May through September) lets kids eat on their feet. Choose fish sandwiches, patties, wraps, sweets, and more from booths and kiosks along Front Street.

Paraquet. Rather than just ordering a hamburger and fries, let your child watch it being cooked at the Paraquet. This American-style diner's low counter with stools is ideal for little ones to watch what's going on in the kitchen. The large selection of kids' food and the well-priced menu make this a great spot for families. ☎ 441/236-9742.

Pizza House. Youngsters love being creative and eating with their hands, so let them have the best of both worlds by creating their own pizza. Head here to see who can come up with the tastiest combination of pizza toppings. Kids also enjoy watching the minibike racing at the nearby race-track. ☎ 441/293-5700.

Shelly Bay. Bermuda has the ideal picnic venue to keep the younger set entertained all day long. Shelly Bay in Hamilton Parish has a huge children's play area right next to its sandy beach, so little ones won't have time to be bored. Grab a bite to eat from the beach snack bar or bring a picnic, and prepare for a fun—and probably tiring—day by the ocean.

Warwick Lanes. Let the kids knock 'em down with a family bowling challenge at Warwick Lanes. Winners get their pick off the menu at the on-site Last Pin restaurant. Kids' meals at the bowling alley in Middle Road, Warwick, include all the favorites: pizza, hamburgers, chicken nuggets, and french fries. ☎ 441/236-5290.

3

---

waves almost at your toes. The red snapper, seafood casserole, or a mixed grill seafood platter which includes prawns, salmon, and scallops are all worthy contenders. ⊠ *Elbow Beach Resort, 60 S. Shore Rd., Paget Parish* ☎ *441/236-9107* ⊕ *www.lido.bm* ⊘ *Closed Nov.–May.*

ST. GEORGE'S AND EASTERN PARISHES

ST. GEORGE'S

St. George's is a lovely dining spot, with many restaurants right by the water's edge. You can sit back and relax as you watch life at sea and even dip your toes to cool down. It's the perfect place to stop for dinner after you've built up an appetite walking around the Old Town's museums and historic buildings. The restaurants here are less crowded and more relaxed than those in Hamilton and Dockyard. You'll probably find yourself dining with some of the country's politicians without even realizing it.

$$

BERMUDIAN

✕ **Polaris Restaurant at The Carriage House.** Local food using Bermuda's finest ingredients is the specialty here. There's also plenty of variety on the menu, with a mix of fish and lobsters, steaks, and prime cuts of beef, as well as sushi—all at a reasonable price. Owner Abdul Amjath moved his business from the St. George's Dinghy Club in early 2011 and relocated at the former Carriage House restaurant in the heart of St. George's. Wednesday is barbecue night during the summer and there's a Friday happy hour from 5 pm to 9 pm. But Sunday is the busiest day of the week here, as staff serve up traditional Bermudian codfish breakfasts, an all-you-can-eat brunch, and in the evening it's movie night. Takeout is also available. ⊠ *22 Water St.* ☎ *441/297–0786, 441/297–1730* ⊕ *www.polarisrestaurant.net.*

$$$

BERMUDIAN

✕ **White Horse Pub & Restaurant.** Step back in time with the help of this restaurant's rustic 1600s feel. The former Merchant's Hall, the harbor-side building is overflowing with history. Try the sizzling shrimp or conch fritters for an appetizer, then the "Bermuda Triangle," which mixes up rockfish, snapper, and wahoo. If you're sitting on the terrace, watch out for the hungry fish waiting for food scraps. Tables get snapped up when the cruise ships are in. A roast dinner is also available all-day Sunday, complete with Yorkshire pudding and mashed potato. ⊠ *8 King's Sq.* ☎ *441/297–1838* ⊕ *www.whitehorsebermuda.com* ۵ *Closed Jan.–Mar.*

EASTERN PARISHES

The East of the island is best known for The Swizzle Inn. It's probably the one place that most people have heard of before they even arrive. Its reputation is legendary, and it doesn't disappoint. Other restaurants are quite spread out from Flatts Village to St. David's, but they will be well worth the trek. Your efforts will be rewarded with the freshest of ingredients (there's an abundance of fishermen at this end of the island) away from the crowds.

$$

BERMUDIAN

Fodor's Choice

★

✕ **Black Horse Tavern.** Way off the main tourist trail in a remote corner of St. David's, the Black Horse is a dark horse, or at least a well-kept local secret. Its beer garden overlooks a picturesque bay dotted with fishing boats and tiny islands. This is a great place for island originals: fish chowder and curried conch stew with rice are favorites, as are the straightforward renderings of

> **DID YOU KNOW?**
>
> An 80-foot harbor mural by Eurasian artist Gerard Henderson winds around the Point restaurant. Originally hung in the Pan Am offices in Manhattan, the impressive artwork brings a little piece of history to Bermuda.

amberjack, rockfish, shark, tuna, wahoo, and Bermuda lobster. Just about everything is deep-fried, so if that doesn't suit, request it be cooked the way you like. ✉ *101 St. David's Rd., St. George's Parish* ☎ *441/297–1991* ◷ *Closed Mon.*

$$ ✕ **Landfall Restaurant.** This is a lovely

BERMUDIAN little spot for that all-important view of the ocean. From your table you can see both ends of the horse-shoe-shape island and any passing cruise ships. Traditional Bermudian fare is offered, such as fresh fish and lobster when in season. The restaurant is housed in a historic building right on the water, and the restaurant's walls are covered in artwork by local artist Arthur Trott. ✉ *165 North Shore Rd., Hamilton Parish* ☎ *441/293–1322.*

IN THE KNOW

For the lowdown on where to eat in Bermuda, restaurant and menu guides are available at any Visitor Information Centre. The island's telephone directory also publishes a good selection of restaurant menus.

$$ ✕ **North Rock Brewing Company.** The copper and mahogany tones of the

BERMUDIAN handcrafted beers and ales are reflected in the warm interior of this English-type bar and restaurant, Bermuda's only brewpub. David Littlejohn runs North Rock, which has an extensive menu focusing on seafood and English pub favorites. Sit in the English style pub, the dining room, or outside on the breezy patio for fish-and-chips, bangers and mash, toad in the hole, steak and ale pie, codfish cakes, or prime rib. Daily specials are also available. ✉ *10 South Rd., near Collector's Hill, Smith's Parish* ☎ *441/236–6633* ⊕ *www.northrockbrewing.com.*

$$$ ✕ **The Point.** If you can have just one splurge in Bermuda, here's where to

BERMUDIAN do it. Swiss executive chef Serge Bottelli uses local produce in his flaw-

Fodor'sChoice lessly crafted entrées. Caramilized sea scallops or champagne risotto

★ can be followed with mushroom-crusted sea bass or grilled swordfish with shrimp. To save money you can request a smaller portion of any dish for about three-quarters of the price. There's also a set four-course dinner for $82 and five courses for $95. Sunday brunch is also available November through April. Adjoining the restaurant is a quaint English-style bar decorated with political cartoons and prints; the perfect stop for a pre- or post-dinner drink. ✉ *Rosewood Tucker's Point, 60 Tucker's Point Dr., Tucker's Town, Hamilton Parish* ☎ *441/298–4070* ⊕ *www.rosewoodtuckerspoint.com* ⌕ *Reservations essential. Jacket required.*

$$ ✕ **Rustico Restaurant & Pizzeria.** At Rustico you can eat and drink in the

ITALIAN quaint village of Flatts, across from the Bermuda Museum, Aquarium &

★ Zoo. It's won a number of awards and is regularly fully booked during summer. Bermudian favorites are on the menu along with Italian specialties; the seafood pasta, or pasta *pescatore,* is well worth a try. The restaurant's casual and friendly atmosphere extends to its outside dining patio. ✉ *8 N. Shore Rd., Flatts Village, Smith's Parish* ☎ *441/295–5212* ⊕ *www.bermuda-dining.com.*

$ ✕ **Speciality Inn.** You may have to wait a few minutes for a table, but it's

BERMUDIAN worth it. A favorite of locals and families, this south shore restaurant

☺ is cheerful and clean, with low prices, and always packed come dinnertime. The no-frills food is Bermudian with Italian and Portuguese accents. There's something for every diner, with a sushi bar, tasty soups, and pizza. Carnivores should try the meaty Bermudian pizza. ✉ *Collectors Hill, 4 S. Shore Rd., Smith's Parish* ☎ *441/236–3133* ☻ *Closed Sun.*

$$
BERMUDIAN
★
☻

✕ **Swizzle Inn.** No trip to Bermuda is complete without stopping off at the Swizzle. In fact, Swizzle Inn created one of Bermuda's most hallowed (and lethal) drinks—the Rum Swizzle (amber and black rum, triple sec, orange and pineapple juices, and bitters). This place is a Bermuda landmark, with a warm and welcoming atmosphere, friendly staff, and plenty of affordable pub fare. Try a "Swizzleburger" (a bacon cheeseburger), or a huge plate of nachos and chili, which will challenge even the biggest of appetites. Food is served until 10 pm, with a snack menu until midnight, so you won't go hungry. The Friday and Saturday barbecues with ribs, steaks, chicken, and seafood are a mouthwatering feast capable of satisfying any carnivore. With so many jugs of the island's national drink being consumed day and night, there's never a dull moment. It's also customary to leave your business card or scribble your name on the pub's colorful walls. A sister restaurant, The Swizzle South Shore, is in Warwick. ✉ *87 Blue Hole Hill, Bailey's Bay, Hamilton Parish* ☎ *441/293–1854* ⊕ *www.swizzleinn.com.*

$$$
BERMUDIAN
Fodor's Choice
★

✕ **Tom Moore's Tavern.** In a house that dates from 1652, Tom Moore's Tavern has a colorful past, thanks to the Irish poet for whom it's named. Tom Moore visited friends here frequently in 1804 and caused a scandal by writing odes to a local woman who was already married. Today fireplaces, casement windows, and shipbuilders' cedar joinery capture a sense of history that in no way interferes with the fresh, light, and innovative cuisine. Bermuda lobster (in season), and sautéed-then-broiled Bermuda fish with pine nuts stand out. Soufflés are always excellent, as is the chef's pastry. Both change daily. Eat in one of five cozy rooms; by special arrangement, groups may dine alfresco on a terrace that overlooks Walsingham Bay. ✉ *7 Walsingham La., Bailey's Bay, Hamilton Parish* ☎ *441/293–8020* ⊕ *www.tommoores.com* ☻ *Closed Jan. No lunch.*

DOCKYARD AND WESTERN PARISHES

There are plenty of restaurants on offer in the western parishes. Many of them are centered around the Royal Naval Dockyard, within easy reach of the cruise-ship piers. Many of the restaurants offer their own entertainment, such as salsa dancing, quiz nights, and live music. Another cluster of restaurants certainly worthy of a visit are those at the Fairmont Southampton Resort. At this hotel you can eat fresh seafood overlooking the beach, traditional Italian cuisine at the golf clubhouse, or grab a quick snack next to the swimming pool.

$$
ITALIAN

✕ **Bacci.** A winning combination of authentic Italian cuisine with fine dining is what you can find at Bacci, which translates as "quick and friendly kisses." Walk in and you feel like you've been adopted into the Italian family. On the upper floor of the golf clubhouse, the restaurant is decorated in bright and bold colors with impressive golf-course views. Bacci celebrates all that is great about Italy, and the chefs are not afraid to experiment with the latest cooking trends. Don't miss the antipasto buffet, the fettuccine alfredo, or the spaghetti carbonara. The menu isn't huge, but does a great job of combining traditional and modern Italian

The Dish on Local Dishes

Shark hash made of minced shark meat sautéed with spices may not sound too appetizing, but it's a popular Bermudian appetizer, usually served on toast.

Bermudians love **codfish cakes**—made of salted cod mashed with cooked potatoes and fresh thyme and parsley, then shaped into a patty and panfried. They taste great topped with a zesty fruit salsa and a side of mesclun salad.

The island's traditional weekend brunch is a huge plate of **boiled or steamed salt cod** with boiled potatoes, onions, and sliced bananas,

all topped with a hard-boiled egg or tomato sauce, and, sometimes, avocado slices.

Cassava pie—a savory blend of cassava, eggs, sugar, and either pork or chicken—is a rich, flavorful dish (formerly reserved for Christmas dinner) often offered as a special side. More common is **mussel pie**, made of shelled mussels, potatoes, and onions, baked and seasoned with thyme, parsley, and curry.

As for Bermudian desserts, **bananas** baked in rum and brown sugar are to die for, and **loquat or banana crumble** is sweet and rich.

recipes with different flavors from different regions of Italy. Make sure you leave room for dessert—but be warned, they are big enough for two or even three people to share. At night the lights are dimmed and candles are lighted to create a more romantic atmosphere, but there's little privacy, as the tables are so close together. ⊠ *Fairmont Southampton Resort, 101 S. Shore Rd., Southampton Parish* ☎ *441/239–6966* ⊕ *www.fairmont.com/southampton* ⌲ *Reservations essential.*

$$
BERMUDIAN
✕ **Bone Fish.** You can't miss this restaurant's huge patio right in front of the cruise-ship dock. Service isn't exactly speedy, but it's a favorite of both locals and tourists nonetheless. Choose from Bermuda-style catch of the day, fish-and-chips, rib-eye steaks, and homemade pasta, and look out for likeable Italian owner Livio Ferigo, who loves to mingle with diners. If you're famished, head over on a Sunday for the all-you-can-eat Texas barbecue. ⊠ *6 Dockyard Terr., Dockyard, Sandys Parish* ☎ *441/234–5151* ⊕ *www.bonefish.bm.*

$$
BERMUDIAN
✕ **Breezes.** This is what coming to Bermuda on vacation is all about. The food's not fancy, but the location is simply perfection. As the name suggests, you can feel the ocean breeze when you sit at this casual beach restaurant. For an alfresco lunch you can opt for sandwiches or salads, and steaks or seafood for dinner. Every Monday night, it's the place to be for a beach barbecue. ⊠ *Cambridge Beaches Resort, 30 Kings Point Rd., Somerset* ☎ *441/234–0331* ⊕ *www.cambridgebeaches.com* ⊙ *Closed Oct.–May.*

$$
BERMUDIAN
Fodor'sChoice
★
✕ **Coconuts.** Nuzzled between high cliff rocks and a pristine private beach on the southern coast, this outdoor restaurant is one of the best places to nab that table overlooking the ocean. The view is made even more dramatic at night by floodlights. The menu changes often, but you can always be sure of fresh, local produce, and fish prepared with a mix of contemporary Bermudian and Asian flair. On-beach dining is a fixed-price

menu of five courses and a glass of champagne for $125 (plus 17% gratuity). A dinner menu is available for those dining in the restaurant, and a simpler, less expensive lunch menu includes weekly specials, burgers, sandwiches, and salads. ⊠ *The Reefs, 56 S. Shore Rd., Southampton Parish* ☎ *441/238–0222* ⊕ *www.thereefs.com* ⚲ *Reservations essential* ⊗ *Closed Nov.-Apr.*

$$
CONTINENTAL
★

✕ **The Dining Room.** At the base of Gibbs Hill Lighthouse, in the old home of the former lighthouse keeper, this adorable little restaurant is the perfect place to rest after the climb up and down the tower's 185 spiraling steps. Lunch and dinner menus include everything you could ever want, from traditional fish and chicken dishes to pizzas, curries, and even black pudding. For that romantic dinner, ask for a table on the patio—you'll get an impressive view across the island. They also do a traditional Bermudian codfish breakfast on Sunday. ⊠ *68 St. Anne's Rd., Southampton Parish* ☎ *441/238–8679* ⊕ *www.primaverarestaurant.com* ⊗ *No lunch Mon.*

$$
BRITISH
☾

✕ **Frog & Onion Pub.** This is a pub lover's dream, with everything on the menu named after old English pubs. The food is good, as are the ale and the atmosphere. With its vaulted limestone ceilings and thick walls, the former Royal Naval Dockyard warehouse is a fitting place for this nautically decorated pub and its large game room. The food caters to every palate, from hearty English pub fare and light European dishes to a selection of fresh local fish plates. Fodors.com users love the bangers and mash, the Argus Bank fish sandwich, panfried local rockfish or tuna, and the Frog & Onion burger. There's also a gift shop where you can purchase your hot toddy mix. ⊠ *The Cooperage, 4 Freeport Rd., Dockyard* ☎ *441/234–2900* ⊕ *www.frogandonion.bm.*

$$
BRITISH
☾

✕ **Henry VIII.** As popular with locals as it is with vacationers from nearby Southampton resorts, the lively Henry VIII exudes an Old English charm that stops just short of "wench" waitresses and Tudor styling. It's a bit pricey for what you get, but you can find a mix of English and Bermudian menu favorites, including steak-and-kidney pie, rack of lamb, and fish chowder. Save room for the chocolate fudge cake. There's also a sushi bar and an eat-as-much-as-you-can Sunday brunch. For alfresco dining, sit on the patio overlooking the southern coast. Don't be surprised if you're serenaded as you eat—it's "The Strolling Minstrel," aka Duke Joell. After dinner, things start to get lively, as Henry's turns into a popular nightspot, especially on Sunday. Diners head to the dance floor as the live entertainment or DJs take over. ⊠ *69 S. Shore Rd., Southampton Parish* ☎ *441/238–0908* ⊕ *www.henrys.bm.*

$$$$
FRENCH
Fodor's Choice
★

✕ **Newport Room.** Glistening teak and models of victorious America's Cup yachts give this fine restaurant a nautical theme. Each dish is beautifully presented, matching the clientele, which is made up of Bermuda's elite. Known as one of Bermuda's best restaurants, it changes its menu

Where to Take Tea

When afternoon arrives, Bermuda, like Britain, pauses for tea. Usually, tea is served between 3 and 5, but teatime can mean anything from an urn or thermos and cookies sitting on a sideboard to the more formal stiff-pinkie-presentation of brewed-to-order tea in a porcelain or silver teapot, served with cream and sugar on a tray, and accompanied by finger sandwiches and scones with clotted cream and jam.

Fairmont Hamilton Princess. Have a posh afternoon tea at the Fairmont Hamilton Princess's Heritage Court, adjacent to the lobby and Japanese koi pond. Fine Eastern teas are

brought to your Italian linen–covered table in shining silver teapots and poured into delicate Belgian china. The cost is $34 for tea, miniature sandwiches, and cakes. Served 2:30–5 daily. Reservations are required. ⊠ *76 Pitts Bay Rd., Hamilton* ☎ *441/295–3000, 800/441–1414.*

Willowbank. The Willowbank tearoom features a slightly ersatz collection of Victorian memorabilia. High tea for two arrives on a triple-tiered china tray and costs $17; à la carte options are also available for $22.50. Served 12–2 and 4–4:30, Monday–Saturday. ⊠ *126 Somerset Rd., Sandys Parish* ☎ *441/234–1616.*

every season, and the chef works with as much local produce as possible. Appetizers of smoked salmon, carved tableside, or Hudson Valley foie gras with a port sauce will send the taste buds soaring. But it's the entrées that really shine. You might have velouté of fennel with roasted cod or dover sole meunière with citrus and caper beurre noisette. For dessert, try the soufflé of the day or the timeless lemon tart. ⊠ *Fairmont Southampton Resort, 101 S. Shore Rd., Southampton Parish* ☎ *441/239–6964* ⚖ *Reservations essential. Jacket required* ⊘ *Closed Sun. and Mon., and Jan.–Mar. No lunch.*

$$$
SEAFOOD
Fodor's Choice
★
✗ **Ocean Club.** From your table overlooking the crashing surf you can sometimes see fishing boats offshore, catching the seafood for this restaurant's next meal. Ocean Club is one of the top seafood restaurants on the island, serving only the freshest of fish delivered daily by local fishermen. Chefs go out of their way to blend Asian ingredients with European techniques. Try the miso-marinated butterfish, prepared with baby bok choy and yuzu citrus sauce, or Georges Bank yellowtail sole with soy butter sauce. If you prefer landside fare, go for your favorite steak smothered in an Asian-infused sauce. Desserts, such as the coconut-and-chocolate-brownie sundae, are unforgettable. ⊠ *Fairmont Southampton Resort, 101 S. Shore Rd., Southampton Parish* ☎ *441/239–6968* ⊕ *www.fairmont.com/southampton* ⊘ *Closed Nov.–May. No lunch.*

$$
BERMUDIAN
✗ **Salt Rock Grill.** This restaurant is a little off the beaten track, but it's well worth the trek "out west." It's a friendly local place where diners are made to feel welcome. The menu changes daily, but lots of fish, meat, and pasta dishes are guaranteed. There's also a sushi bar. Some dishes are a little pricey for what you get on your plate, but the huge terrace and lovely garden make up for it. The three-course early-bird special for $26.75 is a deal. ⊠ *27 Mangrove Bay Rd., Sandys*

Parish ☎ *441/234–4502* ⊕ *www.*
saltrockgrillbda.com.

$ ✕**Somerset Country Squire.** Over-
BRITISH   looking Mangrove Bay, this typi-
☾   cally English tavern is all dark
wood and good cheer, with a great
deal of malt and hops in between.
Much of the food isn't good enough
to warrant a special trip across the
island, but some of it is: Bermuda
fish chowder, panfried mahimahi,

and steak-and-kidney pie are all delicious. The in-house nightly specials are another draw. Watch out for steak-and-chips, and beer-bat-
tered fish-and-chips for $12 on Monday and Wednesday, and the Fish
Friday deals, where you can get wahoo, tuna, mahimahi, or rockfish
for approximately $17. There's usually live entertainment on Saturday
night, too. ⊠ *10 Mangrove Bay Rd., Somerset* ☎ *441/234–0105* ⊗ *No
lunch Mon., Nov.–Mar.*

$$ ✕**Tio Pepe.** You don't have to spend much money for healthy portions
ITALIAN   of home-style cooking at this Italian restaurant with a Mexican name.
☾   The easygoing atmosphere makes it an ideal stop for bathers returning
from a day at nearby Horseshoe Bay—just grab a seat at one of the
plastic tables on the porch and get ready to chow down. The pizzas
are delicious (they're freshly made with superb sauces), and there's an
extensive list of comforting, classic Italian dishes, including lasagna,
fettuccine, ravioli, and spaghetti. ⊠ *117 S. Shore Rd., Southampton
Parish* ☎ *441/238–1897, 441/238–0572.*

$$$$ ✕**Waterlot Inn.** This graceful, two-story manor house, which dates from
BERMUDIAN   1670 and once functioned as a bed-and-breakfast, now holds one of
Fodor's Choice   Bermuda's most elegant and elaborate steak restaurants. The service is
★   impeccable, with waiters that have just enough island exuberance to
take the edge off their European-style training. Nestled in Jew's Bay, the
restaurant also offers breathtaking sunset views. The Bermudian–con-
tinental menu changes every season, but always offers an excellent fish
chowder. If steak isn't your thing, grilled fish-of-the-day over a plate of
local, colorful vegetables makes a perfect main course. Decadent des-
serts, like sticky toffee pudding, round off an extremely satisfying meal.
The restaurant is also known for its fine wine list and its cigar selection.
⊠ *Fairmont Southampton Resort, 101 S. Shore Rd., Southampton Par-
ish* ☎ *441/238–8000* ⊗ *No lunch.*

$$ ✕**Wickets.** Simple but satisfying American fare and prompt service make
AMERICAN   this cricket-theme restaurant a great spot for families. You can find all
☾   the classics: salads, burgers, sandwiches, pastas, and pizza as well as
good fish-and-chips, chicken cacciatore, and grilled steak. End your
meal on a sweet note with delicious German chocolate cake or Belgian
waffles. The casual restaurant offers all-day dining (11 am–4 pm) with
great pool and ocean views. ⊠ *Fairmont Southampton Resort, 101 S.
Shore Rd., Southampton Parish* ☎ *441/238–2555* ⊕ *www.fairmont.
com/southampton* ⊗ *Closed Nov.–May.*

Where to Stay

WORD OF MOUTH

"If you want a basic room, pool, in town, look at the Rosemont—that's where we put the in-laws when they came to visit. No frills but friendly and the kitchens saved tons on dining out."

—txgirlinbda

"Try the listings on www.bermudarentals.com and www.bermudagetaway.com. Many of the properties are reviewed on Trip Advisor. These rentals represent a substantial savings over the hotel prices and are every bit as lovely, but without the bells and whistles the hotels offer."

—cmcfong

Updated by
Sirkka Huish

Few places in the world boast the charm of Bermuda's curvaceous, colorful shoreline. It's a boon, then, that the lagoons, coves, coasts, as well as its inland sanctuaries are filled with equally colorful, alluring places to stay. But wherever you opt to stay, you are never far away from picture-perfect water views.

The quintessential accommodation on the island is a pink cottage amid manicured gardens and coral-stone pathways. Terraced whitewashed roofs (designed to capture rainwater) sit atop walls of pinks, peaches, and pastels, looking like cakes of ice cream in pink-wafer sand. Add a waterfront setting, and voilà—the lure of Bermuda.

If you find yourself craving a beachfront resort, and you can afford it, several places in this chapter offer quality right-on-the-sand stays; another handful are a stone's throw away from the beach. The island is blessed with clean, well-maintained public beaches that are easily reached by bus and aren't far from any point on the island.

Hamilton has many sophisticated lodging choices, but vacationers who are looking for beachfront relaxation will be disappointed in the beach-less capital city. In fact, all noteworthy beaches are on the southern side of the island. With only a couple of exceptions, beachfront lodging choices are along a 7-mi stretch of coast that runs along the central to western tail of the island, west from Paget to Warwick, Southampton, and Sandys. Lodging choices on the north coast of the island often are on glittering Hamilton Harbour or have deepwater access to the Atlantic, but not beaches.

With the closure of hotels such as Waterloo House and Horizons, some regular visitors are bemoaning the end of elegance on the island (excluding the still-posh Cambridge Beaches and Pink Sands). A new wave of luxury, however, is on the way. Among others, a Jumeirah is in the developmental stages and the revival of Lantana as a deluxe property is being discussed. The first of the new luxury hotels debuted in spring 2009: the Rosewood Tucker's Point now occupies the old Castle Harbour site, bringing new life to the island's East End.

WHAT IT COSTS IN U.S. DOLLARS				
	¢	$	$$	$$$	$$$$
Hotels	under $110	$110–$200	$201–$300	$301–$400	over $400

Prices are for two people in a standard double room in high season, excluding 7.25% tax and 10% service charge.

HOTEL REVIEWS

Listed alphabetically within region. The following reviews have been condensed for this book. Please go to Fodors.com for full reviews.

HAMILTON AND CENTRAL PARISHES

HAMILTON

Stay in the heart of the city for added convenience. You won't need to worry about paying for a rental bike because everything you could need, such as stores, restaurants and attractions, is right on your doorstep. This location will prove particularly useful to the business travelers who need to be close to Hamilton's financial sector. However, it's not the best of locations for families or beach bums.

$$ **Edgehill Manor.** The breakfasts alone will make you feel right at home at this comfortable colonial-style 20th-century guesthouse within walking distance of the restaurants, stores, and attractions of Hamilton. **Pros:** nice pool; well maintained; mouthwatering breakfast. **Cons:** not a leisure destination; no beach. ⊠ *36 Rosemont Ave., Hamilton* ☎ *441/295–7124* ⊕ *www.bermuda.com/edgehill* ➡ *14 rooms* ⚐ *In-room: a/c, safe, kitchen, Wi-Fi. In-hotel: pool* ⊙ *Breakfast.*

$$$ **The Fairmont Hamilton Princess.** The reigning royalty of Bermuda lodging, the Princess boasts some of the most comfortable rooms on the island and caters to its mainly business guests like no one else. **Pros:** reliable first-rate rooms; only full-service resort in the capital; attractive harbor-front location. **Cons:** mainly corporate guests; ferry or cab necessary to reach beaches. ⊠ *76 Pitts Bay Rd., Hamilton* ☎ *441/295–3000, 800/441–1414* ⊕ *www.fairmont.com/hamilton* ➡ *368 rooms, 42 suites* ⚐ *In-room: a/c, safe, Internet, Wi-Fi. In-hotel: restaurant, bar, pool, gym, spa, water sports, business center, some pets allowed* ⊙ *Breakfast.*

$$ **The Oxford House.** The Oxford House is the only true bed-and-breakfast in Hamilton, and one imagines that even if it had competition, it would still be the best. **Pros:** friendly and attentive service; clean and updated rooms; right in Hamilton. **Cons:** rooms more executive than cozy; no beach; no pool. ⊠ *20 Woodbourne Ave., Hamilton* ☎ *441/295–0503* ⊕ *www.oxfordhouse.bm* ➡ *12 rooms* ⚐ *In-room: a/c, kitchen, Internet, Wi-Fi* ⊙ *Breakfast.*

$$ **Rosedon Hotel.** Expect a tranquil, refined environment and friendly service from longtime staff at this bright, blue-shuttered, white manor house in the center of Hamilton town. **Pros:** hotel pays cab fare to

---

TOP 5 LODGING

■ Meet a living legend of eccentric hospitality: Salt Kettle House matriarch Hazel Lowe (and her cats and ducks!).

■ Get away from it all and pretend you have the island to yourself at Rosewood Tucker's Point.

■ Dine right on the beach at The Reefs, decidedly marvelous.

■ Meander from beach to pool to tea to croquet at cottage colony Cambridge Beaches.

■ Live the fantasy of a Bermuda beachfront home at Pink Beach Club.

KNOW-HOW

Bermuda is a land of cottage colonies, cliff-top apartments, and beachfront resort hotels. Hidden along small parish roads, however, you can also find family-run, flower-filled guesthouses and simple, inexpensive efficiencies. The lodgings we list are the cream of the crop in each price category.

FACILITIES AND SERVICES

Considering Bermuda hotel rates, it might come as a surprise that perks like 24-hour room service and same-day laundry service are rare. Fortunately, however, personalized attention, exceptionally comfortable rooms, and trim, scenic surroundings are not. The number and quality of facilities vary greatly according to the size and rates of the property. Resort hotels are the best equipped, with restaurants, pools, beach clubs, gyms, and (in the case of Fairmont Southampton) a golf course. Cottage colonies also typically have a clubhouse with a restaurant and bar, plus a pool or private beach, and perhaps a golf course. Each cottage has a kitchen, and housekeeping services are provided. Small hotels usually have a pool, and some have a restaurant or guest-only dining room, but few have fitness facilities or in-room extras like minibars. Efficiencies or housekeeping apartments almost always come with a kitchen or kitchenette. Some properties have pools, but you may have to take the bus or a scooter to get to the beach. Even the smallest property can arrange sailing, snorkeling, scuba, and deep-sea fishing excursions, as well as sightseeing.

All lodgings listed are equipped with private bathrooms and air-conditioning. In each review, we list the facilities that are available, but we don't specify whether they cost extra; when pricing accommodations, always ask what's included. Most lodgings offer a choice of meal plans, several with "dine-around" privileges at other island restaurants.

PRICES

Rates at Bermuda's luxury resorts are comparable to those at posh hotels in New York, London, and Paris. A 7.25% government occupancy tax is tacked on to all hotel bills, and a service charge is levied. Some hotels calculate the service charge as 10% of the bill, whereas others charge a per-diem amount. Virtually every hotel on the island offers at least one vacation package—frequently some kind of honeymoon special—and many of these are extraordinarily good deals.

You can shave about 40% off your hotel bill by visiting Bermuda in low or shoulder seasons. Because temperatures rarely dip below 60°F in winter, the low season (November through March) is ideal for tennis, golf, and shopping.

beach; nice gardens; complimentary tea service; central Hamilton location. **Cons:** no beach, old-fashioned decor. ⊠ *61 Pitts Bay Rd., Hamilton* ☎ *441/295–1640, 800/742–5008 in U.S. and Canada* ⊕ *www. rosedon.com* ↪ *40 rooms* ᗢ *In-room: a/c, safe, Wi-Fi. In-hotel: bar, pool, business center* ❑*Breakfast.*

CENTRAL PARISHES

If you can't decide whether to opt for the city or the beach, your best bet is to position yourself between the two. In the Central Parishes you are close enough to enjoy the South Shore beaches by day and Hamilton by night. Paget, Warwick, and Devonshire parishes have plenty of hotels to choose from, as this is one of the most picturesque areas of the island.

> **KNOW THIS**
>
> Americans accustomed to resorts with big private beaches steps from guest rooms will find their expectations best met at Elbow Beach. The Fairmont Southampton is the island's other large-scale beach resort, but its sand is a five-minute walk across the huge property and the street. Willowbank, Cambridge Beaches, Pink Beach, Pompano, and The Reefs offer smaller resorts but equally nice beaches.

$
Fodor's Choice
★
Clairfont Apartments. Probably the island's best buy if you're on a budget; although it's not exactly fancy, it's spotlessly clean and the beach is just a five-minute stroll away. **Pros:** cheap; very clean and well maintained; large units. **Cons:** basic furnishings; not beachfront. ⊠ *6 Warwickshire Rd., Warwick Parish* ⊠ *Box WK 85, Warwick Parish* ☎ *441/238–3577* ⊕ *www.clairfontapartments. bm* ➷ *8 apartments* ⚛ *In-room: a/c, kitchen, Internet. In-hotel: pool* ⦿ *No meals.*

$$$
Coco Reef Resort. In the prime location of the highly desirable Elbow Beach, this hotel is tired and in need of an update, but you'll probably be too busy admiring the gorgeous views to let it bother you. **Pros:** close to the beach; impressive pool; steps from restaurants at Elbow Beach Resort. **Cons:** improvements needed; expensive for what you get. ⊠ *3 Stonington Circle, off S. Shore Rd., Paget Parish* ☎ *441/236–5416* ⊕ *www.cocoreefbermuda.com* ➷ *64 rooms* ⚛ *In-room: a/c, safe. In-hotel: restaurant, bar, pool, tennis court, beach* ⦿ *Multiple meal plans.*

$$$$
☾
★
Elbow Beach. Some Mandarin Oriental properties are exercises in orchestrated perfection; this one trails far behind any such level of finesse, yet many highly appealing components still make Elbow Beach worth a stay. **Pros:** great beach; kids' activities; many restaurants to entertain. **Cons:** somewhat generic; very expensive; huge property can mean a lot of walking. ⊠ *60 S. Shore Rd., Paget Parish* ☎ *441/236–3535, 800/223–7434 in U.S. and Canada* ⊕ *www.mandarinoriental. com/bermuda* ➷ *89 rooms, 9 suites* ⚛ *In-room: a/c, safe, Internet, Wi-Fi. In-hotel: restaurant, bar, pool, tennis court, gym, spa, beach, water sports, children's programs* ⦿ *Breakfast.*

$$
Fourways Inn. With a top-notch restaurant on-site, this pleasant cottage colony comes to life at meal times, but for the rest of the day you have to entertain yourself, as you're in the middle of the island with limited facilities. **Pros:** great dining; can walk to beaches. **Cons:** middle of the island; little in the immediate area. ⊠ *1 Middle Rd., Paget Parish* ☎ *441/236–6517, 800/962–7654 in U.S.* ⊕ *www.fourwaysinn.com* ➷ *6 rooms, 5 suites* ⚛ *In-room: kitchen, Wi-Fi. In-hotel: restaurant, bar, pool* ⦿ *Multiple meal plans.*

$
Fodor's Choice
★
Granaway Guest House. A 1734 manor house with villa-like lawn and gardens, Granaway is an affordable accommodation option for

4

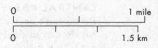

Where to Stay in Hamilton and Central Parishes

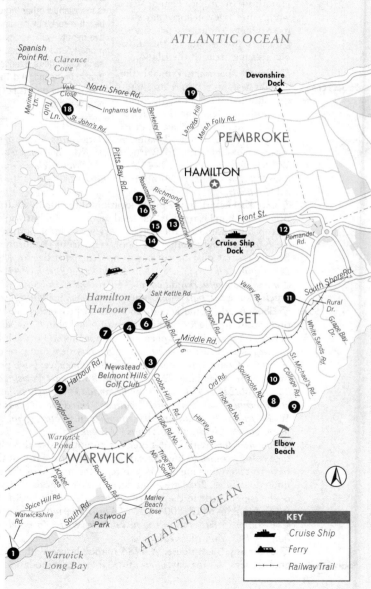

KEY

Cruise Ship

Ferry

Railway Trail

those who do not need to be on the beach. **Pros:** garden terrace; relaxing lawn and pool area; historic property. **Cons:** not waterfront or easy walk to beaches; only continental breakfast. ⊠ *1 Longford Rd., off Harbour Rd., Warwick* ☏ *441/236–3747* ⊕ *www.granaway.com* ↩ *4 rooms, 1 cottage* ⚹ *In-room: kitchen, Wi-Fi. In-hotel: pool, business center* ⋔ *Breakfast.*

$ ▦ **Greenbank Guesthouse & Cottages.** Greenbank has been family-run for 57 years, and this is what Bermuda vacations were like back then: by way of entertainment you had a due-west pier with chairs to watch the sunset. **Pros:** close to ferry; secluded neighborhood; relaxed place. **Cons:** no pool or beach. ⊠ *17 Salt Kettle Rd., Paget Parish* ☏ *441/236–3615* ⊕ *www.greenbankbermuda.com* ↩ *7 cottages, 4 rooms* ⚹ *In-room: a/c, kitchen, no TV, Wi-Fi* ⋔ *Breakfast.*

$ ▦ **Little Pomander Guest House.** This lovely, welcoming guesthouse with lush gardens is in the perfect location, not right in town but close enough to walk. **Pros:** inexpensive; residential area makes you feel like part of a community; nice waterfront views of Hamilton; 10-minute walk to Hamilton or beaches. **Cons:** no beach; rooms slightly aging; linens clean but not contemporary. ⊠ *16 Pomander Rd., Paget Parish* ☏ *441/236–7635* ↩ *6 rooms* ⚹ *In-room: a/c, Wi-Fi* ⋔ *Breakfast.*

$ ▦ **Mazarine by the Sea.** You get the best of both worlds at this cozy, ⟳ well-hidden guest cottage, as it is right on the water's edge, yet just a mile from the city of Hamilton. **Pros:** waterfront property; swimming galore. **Cons:** no hotel-style services; residential area; a bus ride from Hamilton. ⊠ *91 N. Shore Rd., Pembroke Parish* ☏ *441/292–1690* ↩ *7 apartments* ⚹ *In-room: a/c, kitchen. In-hotel: pool* ⋔ *No meals.*

$$$$ ▦ **Newstead Belmont Hills.** This hotel, linked to a private golf course, is the place to be seen with some of the sleekest rooms in Bermuda and a gorgeous infinity pool right on the edge of the harbor. **Pros:** harbor views; new facility; stylish contemporary amenities. **Cons:** golf course not on premises; no beach; odd location for a very expensive hotel. ⊠ *27 Harbour Rd., Paget* ☏ *441/236–6060* ⊕ *www.newsteadbelmonthills.com* ↩ *60 suites* ⚹ *In-room: safe, kitchen, Wi-Fi. In-hotel: restaurant, bar, golf course, pool, tennis court, gym, spa* ⋔ *Multiple meal plans.*

$ ▦ **Paraquet Tourist Apartments.** For those not picky about the room they stay in, Paraquet (pronounced "parakeet") provides a centrally located, motel-like, no-frills stay. **Pros:** convenient diner; affordable; close to the beach. **Cons:** no views; no pool; no amenities. ⊠ *72 South Rd.,*

4

Spaaaah Resorts

Befitting their lovely island location, the best of Bermuda's hotel spas are spectacular in appearance, with white columns, marble floors, flowing linens, and burbling fountains. Bermuda has three full-service spas, located at the Fairmont Southampton, Elbow Beach, and Cambridge Beaches. Day spas are available at Pompano Beach and the Fairmont Princess.

Sunlight dapples the indoor swimming pools at the **Cambridge Beaches Ocean Spa,** inside a traditional Bermudian cottage with pink-stucco walls and a ridged roof. The glass dome that covers the pools is opened in warm weather, allowing salt-tinged ocean breezes to drift into the villa. The treatments offered here are hard to find outside Europe. Both full-day and half-day packages include lunch on a bayside terrace.

The Fairmont Southampton's Willow Stream Spa is the island's largest facility. Besides a complete health club, including personal trainers, there's a garden-enclosed indoor pool, a sundeck overlooking the ocean, two Jacuzzis, three lounges, steam rooms, inhalation rooms, and 15 treatment rooms.

Specially designed lengthy treatments combine baths, wraps, and massage conducted with the utmost skill.

The **Inverurie Day Spa at the Fairmont Hamilton Princess** offers a full array of body treatments, massages, and salon services.

Serenity Spa at Pompano Beach Club offers a full range of individual and couples treatments, including baths, scrubs, and massages from its three treatment rooms, two of which face the ocean.

The **Spa at Elbow Beach** is the most pampering of Bermuda's spas, with personal and couples spa suites overlooking the Atlantic. The suites include personal showers, vanity area, granite bath, and daybeds on private balconies outside the suite. Treatments are based on ayurvedic principles and use ESPA products. While not the largest, this is the most lavish, personal, private, and relaxing spa on the island.

The **Rosewood Tucker's Point Hotel's Spa** is the island's most luxurious, with 12 treatment rooms and 14,000 square feet.

Paget Parish ☎ *441/236–5842* ⊕ *www.paraquetapartments.com* ⇔ *18 rooms* ᐸ *In-room: a/c, kitchen. In-hotel: restaurant, laundry facilities* ❘○❘ *No meals.*

$ ⊞ **Robin's Nest.** This well-maintained valley property is a tad off the beaten path, in a quiet residential neighborhood about a mile north of Hamilton and within walking distance of a secluded beach cove. **Pros:** well-kept rooms and grounds; pool. **Cons:** out-of-the-way location; difficult to locate. ✉ *37 Mount View, Pembroke* ☎ *441/292–4347* ⊕ *www. robinsnestbda.com* ⇔ *8 studio apartments* ᐸ *In-room: a/c, kitchen, Wi-Fi. In-hotel: pool* ❘○❘ *No meals.*

$$$ ⊞ **The Royal Palms.** The Royal Palms is a winner for having high stan-
Fodor's Choice   dards, great service, and a welcoming touch with fresh-from-the-garden
★   flowers to celebrate your arrival. **Pros:** beautiful gardens; wonderful breakfast; terrific service; great restaurant. **Cons:** no beach; 10-minute

LODGING ALTERNATIVES

APARTMENT AND VILLA RENTALS

If you want a home base that's roomy enough for a family, consider renting a private house or apartment. Furnished rentals can save you money, especially if you're traveling with a group.

⚏ **BermudaGetaway.** BermudaGetaway lists a selection of high-standard properties but does not accept reservations. ⊕ *www.bermudagetaway.com.*

⚏ **Bermuda Rentals.** Bermuda Rentals maintains an up-to-the-minute listing of available properties all over the island *and* makes reservations. ⊕ *www.bermudarentals.com.*

⚏ **Coldwell Banker JW Bermuda Realty.** Coldwell Banker JW Bermuda Realty requires you to register with the company before an agent will help you find a property that meets your requirements. ☎ *441/292–1793* ⊕ *www.bermudarealty.com.*

BED-AND-BREAKFASTS

Bed-and-breakfasts in Bermuda range from grand, converted Victorians to a couple of rooms with shared bath in a small home. Breakfasts, too, run the gamut, though light continental breakfasts with fresh fruit are more common than hearty bacon-and-eggs meals. Sometimes there is a pool on the property, but to get to the beach you usually have to travel by bus or scooter.

⚏ **Bermuda Accommodations.** Bermuda Accommodations lists and takes reservations for rooms available in bed-and-breakfasts. ⊕ *www.bermudarentals.com.*

HOME EXCHANGES

If you would like to exchange your home for someone else's, join a home-exchange organization, which will send you its updated listings of available exchanges for a year and will include your own listing in at least one of them. It's up to you to make specific arrangements.

walk to Hamilton. ⊠ *24 Rosemont Ave., Pembroke Parish* ☎ *441/292–1854, 800/678–0783 in U.S. and Canada* ⊕ *www.royalpalms.bm* ➽ *32 rooms* ☖ *In-room: a/c, safe, kitchen, Internet, Wi-Fi. In-hotel: restaurant, bar, pool* ⍾ *Breakfast.*

$
Fodor'sChoice ★

⚏ **Salt Kettle House.** Innkeeper Hazel Lowe has the warmth and personality that bed-and-breakfast aficionados dream about; she will go out of her way to make sure your stay at her pristine home is extraordinary. **Pros:** steps from ferry; wonderful private setting; beautiful gardens; great hospitality. **Cons:** no beach; no pool. ⊠ *10 Salt Kettle Rd., Paget Parish* ☎ *441/236–0407* ➽ *3 rooms, 4 cottages* ☖ *In-room: a/c, safe, kitchen, no TV, Wi-Fi* ⊟ *No credit cards* ⍾ *Breakfast.*

$
⚏ **Serendipity Guest Apartments.** You'd never stumble across these two studio apartments in residential Paget unless you were looking, but it's a lovely spot for budget travelers. **Pros:** clean; private; friendly; spacious; cheap. **Cons:** have to walk to beach; no hotel-style services; a little hard to locate. ⊠ *6 Rural Dr., Paget Parish* ☎ *441/236–1192* ➽ *2*

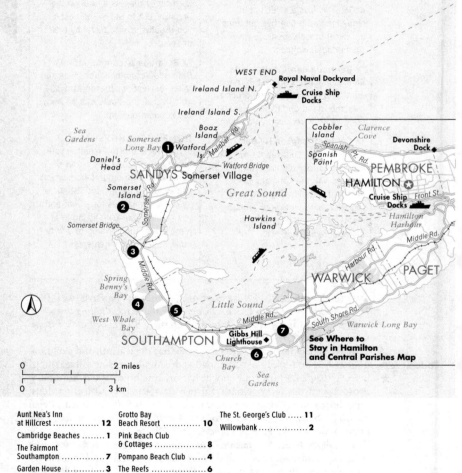

Where to Stay in the East and West Ends

ATLANTIC OCEAN

WEST END Royal Naval Dockyard
Ireland Island N. Cruise Ship Docks
Ireland Island S.

Sea Gardens

Boaz Island

Somerset Long Bay **1** Watford Is. Watford

Daniel's Head

Malabar Rd.

SANDYS Watford Bridge
Somerset Village

Great Sound

Somerset Island **2**

Somerset Rd.

Somerset Bridge **3**

Hawkins Island

Spring Benny's Bay

Middle Rd.

4 **5**

Little Sound

West Whale Bay

Middle Rd.

Gibbs Hill Lighthouse **7**

SOUTHAMPTON **6**

Church Bay

Sea Gardens

Cobbler Island Clarence Cove
Spanish Pt. Rd. Devonshire Dock
Spanish Point

PEMBROKE

HAMILTON ⭐

Cruise Ship Docks Front St.

Hamilton Harbour

Middle Rd.

Harbour Rd.

WARWICK PAGET

South Shore Rd.

Warwick Long Bay

See Where to Stay in Hamilton and Central Parishes Map

0 ___ 2 miles
0 ___ 3 km

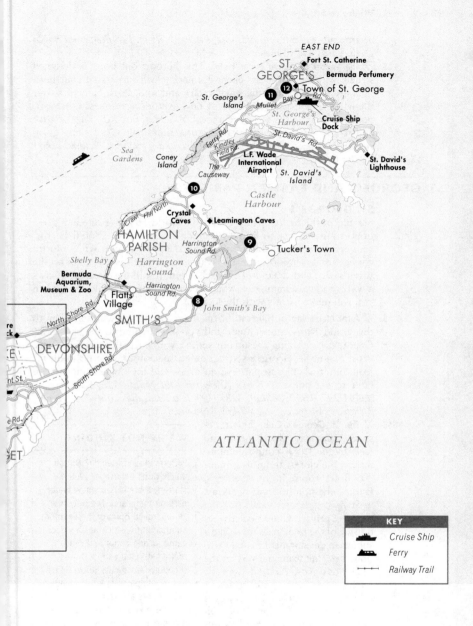

EAST END

ST. GEORGE'S

● Fort St. Catherine

● Bermuda Perfumery

St. George's Island

11 Mullet Bay *St. George's Rd.*

12 ○ Town of St. George

St. George's Harbour

Cruise Ship Dock

Ferry Rd.

Kindley Field Rd.

St. David's Rd.

Sea Gardens

Coney Island

The Causeway

L.F. Wade International Airport

St. David's Island

● **St. David's Lighthouse**

Castle Harbour

10

◆ **Crystal Caves**

◆ **Leamington Caves**

HAMILTON PARISH

Harrington Sound Rd.

9 ○ Tucker's Town

Crawl Hill North

Harrington Sound

Shelly Bay

Bermuda Aquarium, Museum & Zoo

◆ ○ **Flatts Village**

Harrington Sound Rd.

SMITH'S

8

John Smith's Bay

North Shore Rd.

DEVONSHIRE

South Shore Rd.

nt St.

e Rd.

GET

ATLANTIC OCEAN

KEY	
⛴	*Cruise Ship*
⛴	*Ferry*
┝━┿━┥	*Railway Trail*

apartments ⬩ *In-room: a/c, safe, kitchen, Wi-Fi. In-hotel: pool* 🛏 *No credit cards* 🍴 *No meals.*

$$ ⚏ **The Wharf Executive Suites Hotel.** This harborfront hotel is designed strictly with the corporate client in mind; it will surpass all your business needs but it's lacking in character and soul. **Pros:** balconies over the harbor; next to ferry service. **Cons:** overpriced business hotel; carpet is raggedy; lacks welcome appeal. ✉ *1 Harbour Rd., Paget Parish* ☎ *441/232–5700* ⊕ *www.wharfexecutivesuites.com* ⤙ *15 suites* ⬩ *In-room: a/c, safe, kitchen, Wi-Fi. In-hotel: laundry facilities, business center* 🍴 *Breakfast.*

ST. GEORGE'S AND EASTERN PARISHES

ST. GEORGE'S

Staying in the heart of this UNESCO World Heritage Site is a great opportunity to get to know Bermuda's rich history. You'll be surrounded by some of the prettiest streets on the island, with colorful cottages and scores of little alleyways. St. George's is also right on the water's edge with a handful of beaches within walking distance. There's a warm and welcoming feel to St. George's, so stay a couple of days and you will make friends with the locals.

$ ⚏ **Aunt Nea's Inn at Hillcrest.** Stroll down a narrow winding alley to this grand 18th-century home and you'll be treated to the best of St. George's, combining the quaint setting with several home comforts. **Pros:** quaint St. George's setting; quiet; spacious. **Cons:** no pool; far from other island destinations; no meals and no kitchens means you have to eat out. ✉ *1 Nea's Alley, off Old Maid's La., St. George's* ☎ *441/297–1630, 888/392–7829* ⊕ *www.1neasalley.com* ⤙ *12 rooms, 2 suites* ⬩ *In-room: a/c, Wi-Fi* 🍴 *No meals.*

$$$ ⚏ **The St. George's Club.** This time-share complex, which looks and feels like a 1990s condo community, is the closest thing to a modern hotel room in St. George's. **Pros:** only non-bed-and-breakfast in St. George's; nice views walking to town; private. **Cons:** no activities outside of the pool; feels more like a suburban development than a vacation spot; far from the rest of the island. ✉ *6 Rose Hill, St. George's Parish* ☎ *441/297–1200* ⊕ *www.stgeorgesclub.bm* ⤙ *71 cottages* ⬩ *In-room: safe, kitchen, Wi-Fi. In-hotel: restaurant, bar, pool, tennis court, gym, laundry facilities, business center* 🍴 *Breakfast.*

> ### WE'RE NOT KIDDING
>
> Is Bermuda kid-friendly? Not so much. Don't believe it? Well, for starters, there isn't a single water park on the island. The only true kid-approved hotel is The Fairmont Southampton, which has a video-game arcade and a real year-round kids' club with activities scheduled each day. Elbow Beach has less impressive kids' activities, but it offers a kids' room; Grotto Bay has a kids' club during summer months. Pompano Beach Club has an arcade room, and Pink Beach Club and Willowbank have playgrounds. Luckily, the beach is fun for all ages—but don't forget the pails and shovels!

EASTERN PARISHES

This is the perfect hideaway spot that's off the beaten track. One of the sparsest areas of the island, it really isn't geared towards tourists, but the hotels are in the lovely Castle Harbour area, which offers great water views and water sports opportunities. If you opt for this location you're in for a peaceful and relaxing getaway.

$$ ⊡ **Grotto Bay Beach Resort.** The ocean is never far from sight at this popular resort best known for its two on-site caves; you can treat yourself to a spa treatment in one, then go for a relaxing swim in the other. **Pros:** kids' program in summer; on-site aquatic activities; caves. **Cons:** small beach; big complex; doesn't feel much like Bermuda; rooms unexciting. ⊠ *11 Blue Hole Hill, Bailey's Bay, Hamilton Parish* ☎ *441/293–8333, 800/582–3190* ⊕ *www.grottobay.com* ⋗ *198 rooms, 3 suites* ⌂ *In-room: a/c, safe, Wi-Fi. In-hotel: restaurant, bar, pool, tennis court, gym, beach, water sports, children's programs, business center* ⏐◎⏐ *Multiple meal plans.*

$$$$ ⊡ **Pink Beach Club & Cottages.** Step back in time for a total getaway at this first-class cottage colony which is one of the classiest places on the island to unwind, especially if you are a golfer. **Pros:** near Mid Ocean and Tucker's Point golf courses and the airport; classic cottage colony; very formal and private; two private beaches. **Cons:** isolated from populated parts of island and other vacationers; a little on the stuffy side; no TV. ⊠ *116 S. Shore Rd., Tucker's Town, Smith's Parish* ☎ *441/293–1666, 800/355–6161 in U.S. and Canada* ⊕ *www. pinkbeach.com* ⋗ *94 suites* ⌂ *In-room: safe, no TV, Wi-Fi. In-hotel: restaurant, bar, pool, tennis court, gym, beach, water sports, business center* ⏐◎⏐ *Multiple meal plans.*

$$$$
Fodor's Choice
★ ⊡ **Rosewood Tucker's Point.** If you're looking for a chic place to get away from it all, you can't go wrong with Bermuda's newest boutique hotel, which has become synonymous with luxury since opening in 2009. **Pros:** top-notch service; all sporting options covered; amazing ocean views. **Cons:** hotel is a substantial distance from its own beach club; in secluded area of the island. ⊠ *60 Tucker's Point Dr., Hamilton Parish* ☎ *441/298–4000, 888/767–3966* ⊕ *www.rosewoodtuckerspoint.com* ⋗ *88 rooms* ⌂ *In-room: a/c, safe, Wi-Fi. In-hotel: restaurant, bar, golf course, pool, tennis court, gym, spa, beach, water sports, business center* ⏐◎⏐ *Multiple meal plans.*

DOCKYARD AND WESTERN PARISHES

$$$$
Fodor's Choice
★ ⊡ **Cambridge Beaches Resort and Spa.** Cambridge Beaches has a coat of arms that reads "Prima Et Optima", or First and Best. **Pros:** private; gamut of activities and beaches to choose from; beautiful grounds and beaches. **Cons:** far removed from rest of island; very expensive. ⊠ *30 King's Point Rd., Somerset, Sandys Parish* ☎ *441/234–0331, 800/468–7300 in U.S.* ⊕ *www.cambridgebeaches.com* ⋗ *66 rooms, 25 suites, 3*

4

Think Pink

Long before Bermuda's tourism heyday, when only British aristocrats, Hollywood stars, and blue bloods from America's East Coast could afford to come to the island and disappear for a while, Bermuda's would-be hoteliers were sowing the seeds of one of the island's most important future economy bases. The beautiful people, with their well-lined pockets, were transforming Bermuda into a chic getaway destination, and this exclusive clientele would want seclusion, colonial sophistication, and traditional Bermudian hospitality. And so the cottage colony was born: a purpose-built resort that left no comfort unexplored, no luxury ignored—a plush home-away-from-home for those who could afford it.

The Bermuda Department of Tourism recognizes the following properties as cottage colonies: Cambridge Beaches, Fourways Inn, Mid Ocean Golf Club, Pink Beach Club, the St. George's Club, and Willowbank. Despite the tourism department's demarcation, you might well be baffled by the island's numerous lodgings that have the word cottage in their names or descriptions, and that's before realizing that there are even more cottages (often private homes) that have been converted into lodgings, and which *might not* have the word cottage in their title.

Confused? The definitive line over what does and does not qualify to earn the title continues to blur, but generally speaking it describes a purpose-built beachfront collection of Bermudian cottages, separated from a main building that often houses the front desk, restaurants, bars, and lounge areas. Often twisting walkways connect the cottages to the main building and lead down to

the beach, over to the tennis courts, and elsewhere on the property. Many of the cottages are pink (Bermuda's trademark color) or other pastel shades, and most have either stunning water views or lush, tropical garden settings. Traditionally, the cottages have Bermudian white stair-step roofs, terraces or balconies, cedar-beamed ceilings and furniture, and British country-style fabrics and ornaments. Newer complexes, however, may have much larger cottages of more modern design, divided into suites, or they may have attached apartments. Some may not even have kitchens—a staple of the traditional cottages.

Whatever a cottage colony is, it certainly isn't basic or budget. Bermuda's homegrown accommodations are some of the island's most exceptional—and expensive—and while many offer a unique holiday experience, they won't suit everyone. The emphasis is on peace and quiet, and they provide this admirably. Entertainment, children's programs, and other activities are not emphasized in many complexes, so they may not be ideal for those seeking a lively, fun-packed vacation.

Although the concept and reality of cottage colonies continues to evolve, the unabashed romance of these magical oases is alive and well. The pursuit of authentic Bermudian living, with a distinct British colonial tradition, still remains to transport guests into gracious lifestyle rather than simply a hotel room.

—Vivienne Sheath

CLOSE UP

Bermudian Architecture

The typical Bermudian building is built of limestone block, usually painted white or a pastel shade, with a prominent chimney and a tiered, white-painted roof that Mark Twain likened to "icing on the cake." More than just picturesque, these features are proof that "necessity" really is "the mother of invention." Limestone, for instance, was a widely available building material—and far better able to withstand hurricane-force winds than the old English-style "wattle and daub."

The distinctive roof, similarly, was not developed for aesthetic reasons. It's part of a system that allows Bermudians to collect rainwater and store it in large tanks beneath their houses. The special white roof paint even contains a purifying agent. If your visit includes some rainy days, you may hear the expression, "Good day for the tank!" This is rooted in the fact that Bermuda has no freshwater. It relies on rain for drinking, bathing, and cooking water, as well as golf-course and farmland irrigation. So residents are careful not to waste the precious liquid. The island has never run out of water, though the supply was stretched during World War II,

when thousands of U.S. soldiers were stationed in Bermuda.

"Moongates" are another interesting Bermudian structural feature, usually found in gardens and walkways around the island. These Chinese-inspired freestanding stone arches, popular since the late 18th century, are still often incorporated into new construction. Thought to bring luck, the ring-shaped gates are favored as backdrops for wedding photos.

Other architectural details you may notice are "welcoming arms" stairways, with banisters that seem to reach out to embrace you as you approach the first step, and "eyebrows" over window openings. Also look for "butteries": tiny, steep-roofed cupboards, separate from the house, and originally built to keep dairy products cool in summer. If you wonder why, in this warm climate, so many houses have fireplaces in addition to air-conditioners, come in January, when the dampness makes it warmer outside than in.

—revised by Susan MacCallum-Whitcomb

4

---

cottages ☆ *In-room: a/c, safe, Internet. In-hotel: restaurant, bar, pool, tennis court, gym, spa, beach, water sports, business center, some age restrictions* ⍩ *Multiple meal plans.*

$$$ ⊞ **The Fairmont Southampton Resort.** This is the island's most inclusive ☺ resort, with the best restaurants, the best kids' club, the biggest spa, ★ the best hotel golf course, lobby, shops—and so on. **Pros:** all-year kids' camp with arcade; full-service resort with golf course; great selection of restaurants; private beach. **Cons:** hotel building is unattractive and older; slightly long walk to beach. ⊠ *101 S. Shore Rd., Southampton Parish* ☎ *441/238–8000, 800/441–1414* ⊕ *www.fairmont.com/ southampton* ⛵ *593 rooms, 37 suites* ☆ *In-room: a/c, safe, Internet. In-hotel: restaurants, bar, golf course, pool, tennis court, gym, spa, beach, water sports, children's programs, business center, some pets allowed* ⍩ *Breakfast.*

$ ⚐ **Garden House.** Eccentric owner Rosanne Galloway is the most memorable aspect of this tucked-away hideout, which has more space than you'll know what to do with. **Pros:** inexpensive cottages and rooms; quiet; interesting corner of the island to explore; edgy hostess. **Cons:** few services; not beachfront. ✉ *4 Middle Rd., Somerset Bridge, Sandys Parish* ☎ *441/234–1435* 🖷 *441/234–3006* 🖙 *2 apartments, 2 cottages* 🛁 *In-room: a/c, safe, kitchen. In-hotel: pool, laundry facilities* ▬ *No credit cards* ⊘ *Closed Dec.–Feb.* ⊠ *No meals.*

$ ⚐ **The Greene's Guest House.** Avoid the crowds and head west to this spacious home where you'll be treated to beautiful views of the Great Sound from the huge front and backyards. **Pros:** airy views; open spaces; quiet; bottom-dollar. **Cons:** feels like you're in a stranger's big weird house; away from island action. ✉ *71 Middle Rd., Jennings Bay, Southampton Parish* ☎ *441/238–0834* ⊕ *www.thegreenesguesthouse. com* 🖙 *6 rooms* 🛁 *In-room: a/c, Wi-Fi. In-hotel: pool, business center* ▬ *No credit cards* ⊠ *Breakfast.*

$$$$ ⚐ **Pompano Beach Club.** Pompano, which is passionately run by an American family, understands its customers—and those customers return year after year for the casual atmosphere and beachfront location. **Pros:** private and intimate resort; three hot tubs; three bars. **Cons:** rooms lack a designer's style; rooms vary in quality. ✉ *36 Pompano Beach Rd., Southampton Parish* ☎ *441/234–0222, 800/343–4155 in U.S.* ⊕ *www. pompanobeachclub.com* 🖙 *75 rooms* 🛁 *In-room: a/c, safe, Wi-Fi. In-hotel: restaurant, bar, pool, gym, spa, beach, water sports, business center* ⊠ *Multiple meal plans.*

$$$$ ⚐ **The Reefs.** This is an upscale cliff-side property that remains a popular ★ wedding and honeymoon getaway, as it's so private and serene, but the look of the once small resort has changed dramatically as 19 time-share units have now sprung up where you'd least expect them. **Pros:** intimate resort that caters to couples; small but satisying beach; spacious rooms with mod cons. **Cons:** too serious for families seeking fun; new additions are too upscale and formal. ✉ *56 South Rd., Southampton Parish* ☎ *441/238–0222, 800/742–2008 in U.S. and Canada* ⊕ *www. thereefs.com* 🖙 *45 rooms, 4 suites, 8 junior suites, 8 cottage suites, 19 time-share units* 🛁 *In-room: a/c, safe, Internet. In-hotel: restaurant, bar, pool, tennis court, gym, spa, beach, business center* ⊠ *Some meals.*

$ ⚐ **Willowbank.** Willowbank is simply a serene and restful alternative to glitzier resorts, with 6 acres of wonderful views and marvelous beaches. **Pros:** serene, quiet setting; two beaches; expansive grounds. **Cons:** religious environment might make some uncomfortable; rooms in back of the main facility have poor views. ✉ *126 Somerset Rd., Sandys Parish* ☎ *441/234–1616, 800/752–8444* ⊕ *www.willowbank.bm* 🖙 *70 rooms* 🛁 *In-room: a/c, Internet, Wi-Fi. In-hotel: restaurant, pool, tennis court, beach* ⊠ *Multiple meal plans.*

Nightlife and the Arts

WORD OF MOUTH

"There are some nightclubs, mostly geared towards a 20s to 30s crowd. There are a few jazz/music wine bars, Hamilton Princess has a good Friday happy hour and the Lemon Tree does as well."
—txgirlinbda

"If you are looking for lots to do in the evening, I would suggest you get closer to Hamilton."
—cmcfong

Updated by
Sirkka Huish

Bermudians love to drink. That's the title of a popular local song, and it hits the nail right on the head. Yes, the island that gave the world the Dark 'n Stormy and the Rum Swizzle might not have the largest selection of hot spots in which to party the night away, but what Bermuda lacks in venues it makes up for in attitude.

Tourists, expats, and locals all mix together to create a melting-pot social scene, especially on Friday nights—the unofficial party day for just about everyone living on the Rock. The vibe is civilized but still fun and friendly, and if you're not sure where you want to go, just ask around; people will be more than happy to give you their thoughts—they might even buy you a drink!

If you prefer your nightlife to have more culture than rum concoctions, there's still plenty to do. City Hall provides a venue for visiting artists on an ad hoc basis. Dramatic productions take place across a variety of venues—anywhere from a hotel auditorium to the back of a Front Street pub.

For a rundown of what's hot and happening in Bermuda, pick up the Bermuda Calendar of Events brochure at any Visitor Information Centre. The free monthly *Bermuda.com* guide also lists upcoming island events and can be accessed online at ⊕ *www.bermuda.com*. *The Bermudian* ($6.30), a quarterly magazine, has a calendar of events, as does *RG* magazine, which is included free in the *Royal Gazette* newspaper every two months. *This Week in Bermuda,* another free magazine, describes arts and nightlife venues. The *Bermuda Sun* newspaper has a "Scene" section on Friday, which includes an events calendar (⊕ *www. bermudasun.bm*). It's also a good idea to check ⊕ *www.bdatix.com* or ⊕ *www.premierticketsglobal.com* for upcoming show information. And to prove there's plenty to do in Bermuda (if you know where to look), the Nothing To Do In Bermuda Web site is updated regularly (⊕ *www. nothingtodoinbermuda.com*).

For recorded event information, dial ☎ 974. Because the arts scene in Bermuda is so casual, many events and performers operate on a seasonal or part-time basis. Bulletin boards are also good places to check for upcoming events.

NIGHTLIFE

Hamilton is the island's central nightlife hub, with a smattering of decent bars and clubs, featuring live music and drink promotions. Outside the city there's a thriving nightlife scene within the hotels. In summer, weekly cruises and beach bashes add to the party scene.

Don't overlook the work of local musicians: Bermuda has a long tradition of producing superb jazz artists, you just have to make sure you know where they are playing. As a general rule, both men and women tend to dress smart-casual for clubs. This means you may not want to wear T-shirts, ratty jeans, or running shoes. Pubs and clubs begin to fill up around 10 or 11.

HAMILTON AND CENTRAL PARISHES

Follow the crowd and enjoy a night out in Hamilton. This is where you'll find most of the island's bars and clubs—and all the people to go with them. You can find a good mix of wine bars, sports bars, dance clubs, and live music venues to suit your mood. Most of the music is reggae, hip-hop, R&B, and Top 40. Most bars serve light pub fare to keep you going through the night. The busiest night of the week in Hamilton is typically Friday, when everyone heads to the happy hours straight from work. Entrance fees are rare, but you can expect to wait in line outside of venues for up to 10 minutes.

BARS AND LOUNGES

Bermuda Bistro at the Beach. A cross between a café and a sports bar, the Bermuda Bistro at the Beach is clean and relatively cheap, with large television screens showing live sports during the day. At night it operates somewhere between a bar and a nightclub, attracting a mixed crowd of tourists and locals. There's usually a DJ, and sometimes bands play. Wednesday night is quiz night during the winter months. It's open until 3 am nightly and there's a covered seating area outside. ⊠ *103 Front St., Hamilton* ☎ *441/292–0219* ⊕ *www.thebeachbermuda.com.*

Fodor's Choice ★ **Cafe Cairo.** Egyptian-theme Cafe Cairo is one of the most popular Hamilton nightspots. Decorated with North African furnishings, it's a great place for an early-evening meal. Eating later may lead to indigestion, as after 10 pm it transforms into a jumping nightclub that's often packed with both locals and tourists. Food and drink are served until 3 am, and there's a covered outside area where the adventurous can try smoking the fruit tobacco pipe. There's a DJ who plays mostly R&B, but you may have trouble finding a space on the dance floor since this is where everyone ends up at the end of the night. ⊠ *93 Front St., Hamilton* ☎ *441/295–5155.*

Coconut Rock. With a trendy Bermudian restaurant in front and an even trendier sushi bar called Yashi in the back, Coconut Rock has a relaxed and friendly buzz. This is more of a locals' hangout, probably because it's hard to find, tucked away underneath Hamilton's main shopping street. Locals sit at the bar hooked to the huge TV screens, which show music videos

5

TOP 5 NIGHTLIFE

■ Enjoy a jug of Rum Swizzle, some fine barbecued food, and decent live music at the Swizzle Inn.

■ Take in an enchanting Gombey dance performance at Hamilton Harbour Nights.

■ Have happy hour in the grand gardens of the Fairmont Hamilton Princess Hotel, and admire the yachts in the harbor.

■ Enjoy the very best of local talent at the Bermuda Folk Club.

■ Stomp the boards at Café Cairo after a few too many Dark 'n Stormys.

and sports. Don't confuse this place with Coconuts, the upscale restaurant at the Reefs resort in Southampton. ✉ *Williams House, downstairs, 20 Reid St., Hamilton* ☎ *441/292–1043.*

Docksider. Commonly known as Dockies, this bar attracts a mixed crowd, and since it has 15 big-screen TVs it's the place to watch the weekend's games. It's a no-frills bar with a good party atmosphere, a decent jukebox, and reasonably priced pub food. There's sometimes a cover charge for the back room's various theme parties, live bands, and tie-ins with local sports events, organized at irregular intervals. Docksider is open until 1 am Sunday through Thursday and 2 am on Friday and Saturday. ✉ *121 Front St., Hamilton* ☎ *441/296–3333* ⊕ *www.dockies.com.*

★ **Fairmont Hamilton Princess Hotel.** During the high season from May through October, the hotel's happy hour is the place to be seen on Friday nights from 5 to 9. You'll find an outdoor barbecue, special drink prices, and live bands. The magnificent lawns of the famous hotel are packed with locals and tourists who equally enjoy a cold drink and an ogle at the elegant yachts in the harbor. The vibe is trendy, so save your most stylish duds for this night. ✉ *76 Pitts Bay Rd., Hamilton* ☎ *441/295–3000.*

Flanagan's Irish Pub. Flanagan's has a real homely feel and remains a firm favorite for folks who like to dance and talk over drinks. Lots of exotic, fun beverages, like frozen mudslides, are served up and there's often live music or a DJ on weekends. The pub underwent a complete renovation in 2010 to give it a much more modern and welcoming look. Adjoining the Irish pub is its sister bar, Outback Sports Bar, at the same address. Giant screens flicker with live sports action and walls are plastered with photographs of Bermuda's sporting heroes. The bars are open from 11 am to 1 am. ✉ *Emporium Building, 69 Front St., 2nd fl., Hamilton* ☎ *441/295–8299* ⊕ *www.flanagans.bm.*

★ **Fresco's Wine Bar.** Fresco's has the largest selection of wines by the glass in Bermuda, plus desserts to die for. Its huge, comfy sofas make it one of the most popular places to start a Friday evening out. It attracts a faithful straight-from-work crowd who are sophisticated but buttoned down. If the weather's nice, try the outdoor bar, where you can sip away and chat with your friends under the stars. Dinner (from the menu of adjoining Maria's Ristorante) is served at the bar until 10. ✉ *2 Chancery La., off Front St., Hamilton* ☎ *441/295–5058.*

Hog Penny. Small, cozy Hog Penny, aka the *Cheers* bar, was the inspiration for the Bull & Finch Pub in Boston. With dark-wood paneling and pub fare like steak-and-kidney pie and bangers and mash, the Hog Penny will likely remind you more of an English country pub than a Boston hangout. Popular musician Will Black plays most nights in the summer, and the floor is cleared for dancing. It's open nightly until 1, and it can be very busy. ✉ *5 Burnaby St., Hamilton* ☎ *441/292–2534.*

Lemon Tree Café. This is a popular happy-hour spot on Friday nights from around 9 pm to midnight, especially during high season from April through November It's a good place to continue the party after Hamilton Princess's happy hour. Lemon Tree caters to a mixed crowd of expats, locals, and tourists who come either to dance to the DJ's disco-style tunes or to sit and chat in the outside area overlooking Par-La-Ville Park. ⊠ *7 Queen St., Hamilton* ☎ *441/292–0235.*

Opus. A café by day, wine bar by night, Opus is one of the newest additions to Hamilton's burgeoning nightlife scene. It's relaxed and modern with lounge-style music. A DJ plays on the weekend, when it's usually standing-room only. ⊠ *4 Bermudiana Rd., Hamilton* ☎ *441/292–3500.*

Pickled Onion. The Pickled Onion is a restaurant and bar that caters to a well-heeled crowd of locals and visitors. A refurbishment has glammed up the place and given it a cleaner, more sophisticated feel. Live music— usually chart and pop—plays nightly from about 10 to 2 in the summer and about five nights a week in the winter. The dance floor is packed every Friday and Saturday night. ⊠ *53 Front St., Hamilton* ☎ *441/295–2263.*

Port O' Call. The serious, dark-wood Port O' Call at the island's oldest cottage colony, has live music nightly in summer and a lovely outdoor terrace. You'll mostly mingle with hotel guests at this secluded West End resort. ⊠ *Cambridge Beaches, 30 King's Point Rd., Sandys Parish* ☎ *441/234–0331.*

Robin Hood. Casual, friendly Robin Hood is popular for inexpensive pub fare, pizza, and beer served on the patio under the stars. There's almost always something sports-related on the TV, and a late-night snack menu is served until 11 pm. There's a quiz competition on Tuesday nights with general knowledge and entertainment themes on alternating weeks. Wednesday is college game night; there's usually live music on Fridays and Saturdays. ⊠ *25 Richmond Rd., Hamilton* ☎ *441/295–3314.*

Seabreeze. Seabreeze and **Mickey's Beach Bar** look better than ever on a hot summer night. With intimate dining areas and expansive bars, both establishments overlook the cool blue waters just beyond the south shore's Elbow Beach. This complex is perfect for a quiet evening for two. Come for the popular salsa dancing social nights; you'll get the chance to learn a few steps. ⊠ *Elbow Beach Hotel, 60 S. Shore Rd., Paget Parish* ☎ *441/236–9884.*

MUSIC AND DANCE CLUBS

Bermuda Folk Club. The Bermuda Folk Club hosts monthly get-togethers, which usually take place at 8:30 on the first Saturday of the month. Note that musicians might perform any number of musical styles besides folk. Drinks are often served at happy-hour prices, and the cover is $10 but can rise to more than $20 for off-island acts. It's worth calling to inquire about nights other than first Saturdays, too, as unpublicized

SAY CHEESE!

During your wanderings through Hamilton's nightlife scene, don't be surprised to bump into the odd photographer asking if you want your picture taken. Bermuda has two party Web sites, **Bermynet** (⊕ *www.bermynet.com*) and **Black and Coke** (⊕ *www.blackandcoke. com*), which take hundreds of snaps of partying people in the island's bars every weekend. Be sure you're striking your best pose on the dance floor!

5

gigs and events sometimes pop up. ✉ *Spanish Point Boat Club, 1 Spanish Point Rd., Pembroke Parish* ☎ *441/291–2070* ⊕ *www.folkclub.bm.*

Fodor's Choice **The Loft at Hubie's.** The Loft at Hubie's books the best jazz bands on the
★ island for weekly sessions on Friday from 7 to 10. Other kinds of live
music might be on the schedule other nights—whatever it is, it's bound
to be good. There's a $10 cover, which includes a drink. The area is a
bit dodgy, so it's best to take a cab to and from the bar. ✉ *10 Angle St.,
Hamilton* ☎ *441/336–6372.*

Moon Nightclub. This looks and feels like a European-style dance club,
with the dance floor in an open-air courtyard. The club fills up on Friday and Saturday nights, but usually with a younger crowd. The mostly
dance and techno music keeps the party going until 3 am nightly. ✉ *Bermuda House La., off Front St., Hamilton* ☎ *441/595–6666.*

LV's Piano Jazz Lounge. LV's Piano Jazz Lounge targets an upscale crowd
with drink prices to match. The all-white decor, including sumptuous
leather sofas, looks the part, and there are large dance floors on both
levels. It's worth a look in, but unless it's a special event, this place
doesn't seem to attract much of a crowd. Security staff are strict about
who gets in: the dress code is smart. ✉ *12 Bermudiana Rd., Hamilton*
☎ *441/296–3330.*

Shine's. Saxophone player and music teacher Wendell "Shine" Hayward
has set up his own business to boost the live music scene in Bermuda.
Something different is offered every night, but whatever music you
encounter here will be Bermuda at its finest. You'll get to hear mainly
jazz and R&B, but on Wednesdays there's a chance to show off your
own talents with karaoke night. This is also one of the best spots to
meet locals. There's $10 cover on some nights. ✉ *91 Reid St., Hamilton*
☎ *441/292–7356.*

ST. GEORGE'S AND EASTERN PARISHES

The East End is the quietest corner of the island, but that isn't to say you
won't find anything going on. You may just have to look a little harder.
The bars in St. George's can get lively in the summer, with offerings
such as quiz nights, live bands, and themed nights. But your best bet is
to head to The Swizzle Inn for a rowdy night of singing with strangers
and making new friends. The nightly entertainers are more than happy
to welcome people to the stage.

BARS AND LOUNGES

North Rock Brewing Company. As well as being a relaxed and traditional
pub and restaurant, the North Rock Brewing Company is one of only
two places on the island to get a genuine Bermuda-brewed ale. Try a
sampler for a taste of all six of North Rock's famous beers—ranging
from the sharp St. David's Light Ale to the head-spinning Whale of
Wheat. You might want to book a taxi back to your hotel. ✉ *10 S.
Shore Rd., Smith's Parish* ☎ *441/236–6633.*

Fodor's Choice **Swizzle Inn.** Swizzle Inn has business cards from all over the world tacked
★ on the walls, ceilings, and doors. "Swizzle Inn, swagger out" is the
motto. As the name suggests, it's the best place on the island for a

jug of Rum Swizzle. Entertainment in the summer includes live bands, pub quizzes, and barbecues. This Bailey's Bay venue proved so successful that the owners have set up a sister bar close to the south-shore beaches in Warwick. ✉ *3 Blue Hole Hill, Bailey's Bay, Hamilton Parish* ☎ *441/293–1854.*

Tavern by the Sea. The yachting crowd gathers at Tavern by the Sea for Rum Swizzles, moderately priced pub fare, and nautical talk. ✉ *14 Water St., St. George's* ☎ *441/297–3305.*

★ **White Horse.** White Horse is great for an afternoon pint on the wooden terrace overlooking the water, where swarms of fish fight for scraps thrown from the tables. There are large-screen TVs for sports fans; sometimes there's nightly entertainment for everyone else. ✉ *8 King Sq., St. George's* ☎ *441/297–1838.*

DOCKYARD AND WESTERN PARISHES

5

There are a handful of nightspots to keep you entertained in Dockyard. Most are bars with live entertainment. You should head to Snorkel Park Beach if you want to party until the early hours. Some of the island's best nightlife takes place at hotel bars in the western parishes. Bermuda's musicians are often found in the less obvious places, so check the live music listings. The Cellar at the Fairmont Southampton Resort is a popular late-night venue for locals and hotel guests.

BARS AND LOUNGES

Frog and Onion Pub. Frog and Onion Pub serves a splendid variety of down-to-earth pub fare in a dark-wood, barnlike setting. If you're spending the day at Dockyard, it's a great place to recharge your batteries. It's also one of only two places on the island where you can buy Bermudian-brewed beer. There's a weekly quiz night, and you may be able to catch the odd DJ or live band if you're lucky. ✉ *The Cooperage, Dockyard, Sandys Parish* ☎ *441/234–2900.*

Henry VIII. Henry VIII is a popular restaurant and bar with rich oak paneling, polished brass, and a good program of local or visiting entertainment almost every night. There's a grand piano in the bar, and local entertainers often perform sing-along sessions. Follow the locals on Sunday nights as the crowds head from Henry VIII to the nearby Fairmont Southampton's The Cellar. ✉ *69 S. Shore Rd., Southampton Parish* ☎ *441/238–0908* ⊕ *www.henrys.bm.*

★ **Jasmine Lounge.** Jasmine Lounge draws the smartly dressed to its lounge and dance floor. Definitely check out the Joe Wylie Trio in season. This is the place to go to hear the sweet sound of jazz. Sandwiches, salads, and other light fare are served until 12:30 am. ✉ *Fairmont Southampton Resort, 101 S. Shore Rd., Southampton Parish* ☎ *441/238–8000.*

Salt Rock Grill. Salt Rock Grill keeps locals and visitors alike coming back for more, with its fine cuisine (which includes sushi), water views, and reasonable prices. The cheap happy-hour drinks will lure you in, but the friendly staff and intimate dance floor will keep you there all night. ✉ *27 Mangrove Bay Rd., Sandys Parish* ☎ *441/234–4502.*

Somerset Country Squire. Somerset Country Squire is an unpretentious bar adorned with Nascar flags and other memorabilia, and great views of the water. It's a decent spot for a quiet pint in the West End and its sizable beer garden and pub menu make it particularly popular in summer. ✉ *10 Mangrove Bay, Somerset* ☎ *441/234–0105.*

MUSIC AND DANCE CLUBS

The Cellar. The Cellar is a nightclub and sports bar at the Fairmont Southampton Resort. It's an authentic stone cellar with a decent-size dance floor that vibrates to the sound of live music and DJs on a nightly basis throughout the summer until 3 am. There are also a couple of pool tables. The place is particularly popular on Sunday and draws a mixed crowd of locals and hotel guests. ✉ *Fairmont Southampton Resort, 101 S. Shore Rd., Southampton Parish* ☎ *441/238–8000.*

Snorkel Park Beach. If you really want to feel like you are on vacation, head to this club that's right on the beach. You can dance on the sand; if you're a cruise passenger, you won't have far to get to your bed, since it's just a stone's throw from the cruise-ship pier at Dockyard. This place caters to cruise-ship passengers, with the party continuing until 3 am. On Monday, Wednesday, and Thursday there's an Island BBQ Beach Party with dinner and a two-hour show, including limbo and fire dancers, drinking competitions, and a huge conga line. The music is mainstream hits, and entrance is usually $10, more if it's a special event. ✉ *7 Maritime La., Dockyard, Sandys Parish* ☎ *441/234–2809* ⊕ *www.snorkelparkbeach.com.*

THE ARTS

Bermuda's arts scene is concentrated in a number of art galleries—Masterworks in the Botanical Gardens, City Hall in Hamilton, and the Arts Centre in Dockyard are the best known—a handful of performance venues, and a few gathering spots, like Rock Island Coffee on Reid Street. For dramatic and musical performances, the City Hall Theatre, the Mid-Ocean Amphitheatre at the Fairmont Southampton Resort, and the Ruth Seaton James Auditorium at CedarBridge Academy host the country's best, including Bermuda Festival events.

DANCE

Bermuda Civic Ballet. The Bermuda Civic Ballet performs classical ballet, as well as modern dance, at various venues during the academic year. The company's most important performances of the year are in August, when internationally known artists sometimes appear as guests. Visitors are also welcome to attend one-off dance lessons at Pembroke Sunday School. ☎ *441/293–4147* ⊕ *www.balletbermuda.bm.*

Bermuda School of Russian Ballet. The Bermuda School of Russian Ballet has been around for half a century and presents unique ballet and modern-dance performances. Showtimes and venues vary, so call for details. ☎ *441/293–4147* ⊕ *www.balletbermuda.bm.*

CLOSE UP

Gombey Dancers

The Gombey dancer is one of the island's most enduring and uniquely Bermudian cultural icons. The Gombey (pronounced *gum*-bay) tradition here dates from at least the mid-18th century, when enslaved Africans and Native Americans covertly practiced a unique form of dance incorporating West Indian, British, and biblical influences. Nowadays, Gombeys mainly perform on major holidays. The Gombey name originates from a West African word, which means rustic drum. The masked, exclusively male dancers move to the accompaniment of Congolese-style drums and the shrill, whistle-blown commands of the troupe's captain. The dancers' colorful costumes include tall headdresses decorated with peacock feathers, and capes covered with intricate embroidery, ribbons, and tiny mirrors.

The Gombey tradition is passed from father to son (some of the dancers are as young as 10 years old) and many of the same families have been involved in Bermuda's troupes for generations. Bermudians are extremely proud of their musical heritage, and the sight of the colorful Gombey troupe's ducking and twirling to the mesmerizing rhythm of the rapid drumbeat is one of the most enchanting spectacles on the island. The Gombeys appear at all major events on the island and are the central element of the Bermuda Day parade. It's traditional for crowds to toss money at the dancers' feet. Gombeys are also regularly on display at the Bermuda Harbour Nights event on Front Street in Hamilton. Consult the Visitor Information Centre for other locations.

5

National Dance Foundation of Bermuda. The National Dance Foundation of Bermuda funds workshops and develops local talent as well as attracting international dancers and putting on shows and fund-raisers. It draws support from all over the island and enjoys the patronage of Bermuda's most famous resident, Catherine Zeta-Jones. ☎ *441/236–3319* ⊕ *www.dancebermuda.org.*

Sabor Dance School. Feel the Latin beat with group classes in salsa, cha cha, Argentine tango, and Merengue. Bermuda has a thriving salsa scene, with classes open to all levels; no experiences is necessary. Dancers also show off their fancy footwork at a series of social dancing events across the island, including at BoneFish Bar & Grill at Dockyard every Sunday afternoon. The Mambo Nights show, featuring international dancers, is held at the Fairmont Southampton Resort in August. ⊠ *Old Berkeley School, Corner of Berkeley and St. John's Rd., Pembroke* ☎ *441/799–6616* ⊕ *www.bermudasalsa.com.*

United Dance Productions. Every style of dance is taught to adults and children at this popular dance school. Performances are held throughout the year, with its annual recital show usually in June. Shows include ballet, modern, hip-hop, and also musical theater. ⊠ *Alexandrina Hall, 75 Court St., Hamilton* ☎ *441/295–9933.*

FILM

🕭 **Bermuda National Library.** Kids love Movie Day at the Youth Branch of the Bermuda National Library. ⊠ *74 Church St., Hamilton* ☎ *441/295–0487.*

Liberty Theatre. Liberty Theatre is a 270-seat cinema with three daily showtimes, including a matinee. The area immediately outside the theater is safe during the day, but you should not linger in this neighborhood after dark. ⊠ *Union and Victoria Sts., Hamilton* ☎ *441/292–7296* ⊕ *www.libertytheatre.bm.*

Neptune Cinema. Neptune Cinema is a 118-seat cinema that typically shows feature films twice nightly, with matinees only on Saturday and Sunday. Get there early if you are going to showings of popular movies, as this small cinema often sells out. ⊠ *The Cooperage, Dockyard* ☎ *441/234–2923* ⊕ *www.libertytheatre.bm/neptune.*

Southside Cinema. Southside Cinema, the island's largest theater, is on the former U.S. military base near the airport. Showtime is usually 7:30. Make sure you have enough cash on you, as this cinema doesn't accept credit cards. It's also the most expensive place to watch a movie at up to $15 per showing. ⊠ *Southside Rd., St. David's* ☎ *441/297–2821.*

Specialty Cinema and Grill. The Specialty Cinema is a 173-seater across the street from City Hall. There are usually three showtimes per day. This cinema has a great café selling all the hot food and snacks, so you can eat during the movie. Lots of 3-D movies are shown here. ⊠ *11 Church St., Hamilton* ☎ *441/292–2135* ⊕ *www.specialitycinema.bm.*

MUSIC

Bermuda Folk Club. The Bermuda Folk Club hosts monthly get-togethers, which usually take place at 8:30 pm on the first Saturday of the month. Note that musicians might perform any number of musical styles besides folk. Drinks are often served at happy-hour prices, and the cover is $10, but can rise to more than $20 for off-island acts. It's worth calling to inquire about nights other than first Saturdays, too, as unpublicized gigs and events sometimes pop up. Venues vary; check the Web site for details. ⊠ *Spanish Point Boat Club, 1 Spanish Point Rd., Pembroke Parish* ☎ *441/291–2070* ⊕ *www.folkclub.bm.*

Bermuda School of Music. The Bermuda School of Music was formed when the country's two leading music schools merged in 2001. Concerts are presented periodically at various venues. There's a guitar festival in May and various other events throughout the year. ☎ *441/296–5100* ⊕ *www.musicschool.bm.*

READINGS AND TALKS

Bermuda National Gallery. The Bermuda National Gallery often hosts a series of lunchtime lectures on art and film. You can stop by or call the gallery for a schedule. ⊠ *City Hall, 17 Church St., Hamilton* ☎ *441/295–9428* ⊕ *www.bermudanationalgallery.com.*

CLOSE UP

Very Fine Arts Festivals

Bermuda Festival of the Performing Arts. In January and February, the Bermuda Festival brings internationally renowned artists to the island. The two-month program includes theater, as well as classical and jazz concerts. Most shows take place in City Hall and CedarBridge Academy. ☎ 441/295–1291 ⊕ www.bermudafestival.org.

Bermuda International Film Festival. This top-notch festival is a celebration of independent films from all over the world. There are screenings during a full week in mid-March at the cinemas in Hamilton. Tickets are sold for individual films as well as for workshops and seminars. Festival parties are also popular, as Hamilton mimics—for a few days at least—the glamour of Sundance, minus the fancy cars. ☎ 441/293–3456 ⊕ www.biff.bm.

Harbour Nights, a street festival featuring Bermudian artists, crafts, Gombey dancers, face painting, and the like, takes place every Wednesday night in summer on Front Street in the City of Hamilton.

5

★ **Chewstick.** To showcase your talents, whether it be through music, spoken word, or dance, stop by headquarters of The Chewstick Foundation on Sunday (every other in winter) for Chewstick, Bermuda's most popular open mike, between 8 pm and midnight. Admission is free before 8 and $10 thereafter. Full bar service is available. With a usually full house, Chewstick is a great place to mingle with locals and witness raw Bermudian talent. ⊠ *28 Elliot St., at Court St., Hamilton* ☎ *441/292–2439* ⊕ *www.chewstick.org.*

THEATER

Bermuda Musical & Dramatic Society. The Bermuda Musical & Dramatic Society has some good amateur actors on its roster. Formed in 1944, this active theater society stages performances year-round at their Daylesford headquarters, one block north of City Hall. The Christmas pantomime is always a sellout, as are most other performances. Visit or call the box office at Daylesford, on Dundonald Street, for reservations and information. Tickets are about $25. ⊠ *Daylesford Theatre, 11 Washington St., Hamilton* ☎ *441/292–0848, 441/295–5584* ⊕ *www.bmds.bm.*

Gilbert & Sullivan Society. The "G & S" holds big-name theater shows and musicals once or twice a year at City Hall. Bermuda may be a small island, but the talent is amazing, with past productions including *The Full Monty, Jesus Christ Superstar, Oliver!,* and *Animal Farm.* Check out what's on the calendar during March and October. ☎ *441/295–3218* ✍ *www.gands.bm.*

Hasty Pudding Theatricals. Bermuda is the only place outside the United States where Harvard University's Hasty Pudding Theatricals perform. For almost 30 years this satirical troupe has entertained the island during March or April. Each of these Bermuda-based shows incorporates political and social issues of the past year. They're all staged at the

City Hall Theatre. Tickets are about $25. ⊠ *City Hall, 17 Church St., Hamilton* ☎ *441/295–1727.*

VENUES AND SOCIETIES

Bermuda Society of Arts. The Bermuda Society of Arts has outstanding gallery space in City Hall, and it's a good place to meet local painters and see some of their work. ⊠ *City Hall, 17 Church St., Hamilton* ☎ *441/292–3824* ⊕ *www.bsoa.bm.*

City Hall Theatre. City Hall Theatre is the major venue for top-quality cultural events each year. ⊠ *City Hall, 17 Church St., Hamilton* ☎ *441/295–1727.*

★ **Rock Island Coffee Café.** Rock Island Coffee Café is a good place to stop and ask what's going on. Not only is it the unofficial watering hole for Bermuda's eclectic group of artists—it also doubles as an informal art space. ⊠ *48 Reid St., Hamilton* ☎ *441/296–5241.*

Beaches, Sports, and the Outdoors

WORD OF MOUTH

"We like to go later in the season because the water is warmer then and we love to swim in the ocean. It is one of the few places that I will swim in the ocean; the water is warm, crystal clear (as long as there are no storms out to sea), and beautiful!"

—luvsun

"We decided to head to Horseshoe Bay for the day. The drive along the South Shore is beautiful and when the beaches come into sight from the cliff—it is a breathtaking sight."

—Tanya

Updated by
Sirkka Huish

Long before your plane touches down in Bermuda, the island's greatest asset becomes breathtakingly obvious—the crystal-clear, aquamarine water that frames the tiny, hook-shape atoll.

So clear are Bermuda's waters that, in 1994, the government nixed a local scuba-diving group's plan to create a unique dive site by sinking an abandoned American warplane in 30 feet of water off the island's East End, fairly close to the end of the airport's runway. The government feared that the plane would be easily visible from above—to arriving passengers—and could cause undue distress. It's the incredible clarity of the water that makes Bermuda one of the world's greatest places for exploratory scuba diving and snorkeling, especially among the age-old shipwrecks off the island. The presence of these sunken ships is actually one of Bermuda's ironies—as translucent as the water is, it wasn't quite clear enough to make Bermuda's treacherous reefs visible to the hundreds of ship captains who have smashed their vessels on them through the centuries.

Thanks to Bermuda's position near the Gulf Stream, the water stays warm year-round. In summer the ocean is usually above 80°F, and it's even warmer in the shallows between the reefs and shore. In winter the water temperature only occasionally drops below 70°F, but it seems cooler because the air temperature is usually in the mid-60s. There's less call for water sports December through March, not because of a drop in water temperature, but because of windy conditions. The wind causes rough water, which in turn creates problems for fishing and diving boats, and underwater visibility is often clouded by sand and debris.

In high season, mid-April through mid-October, fishing, diving, and yacht charters fill up quickly. Three major water-sports outfitters on the island—Blue Hole Watersports, Somerset Bridge Watersports, and H20 Sports—provide most of the rentals. Many boats carry fewer than 20 passengers, so it's advisable to sign up as soon as you arrive on the island. During the "golf and spa season," December through February, many operators close to make repairs and perform routine maintenance.

Bermudians take their onshore sports seriously, too. Cricket and soccer are the national sports, but road running, golf, field hockey, rugby, and a host of other activities get their share of love. Bermudian soccer stars, such as former Manchester City striker Shaun Goater, have delighted crowds in British and U.S. leagues through the years, and Bermudian sailors hold their own in world competition, as do runners, equestrians, and swimmers. Bermuda catapulted onto the squash world stage after holding the Bermuda Masters in 2005, and the World Championships in 2008. Tennis is quite a big deal here, too, and with 70 courts packed into these 21.6 square mi, it's hard to believe there's room left for horseback riding, cycling, running, and golf.

BEACHES

Bermuda's south-shore beaches are more scenic than those on the north side, with fine, pinkish sand, and limestone dunes topped with summer flowers and Bermuda crabgrass. The water on the south shore does get a little rougher when the winds are from the south and southwest, but mainly the pale-blue waves break at the barrier reefs offshore and roll gently onto the sandy shoreline. Because the barrier reefs break up the waves, surfing has not really taken off in Bermuda, though many locals—especially children—love to bodysurf at Horseshoe Bay. Kite surfing is also becoming increasingly popular. Most Bermudian beaches are relatively small compared with ocean beaches in the United States, ranging from about 15 yards to half a mile or so in length. In winter, when the weather is more severe, beaches may erode—even disappear—only to be replenished as the wind subsides in spring.

The Public Transportation Board publishes *Bermuda's Guide to Beaches and Transportation,* available free in all visitor information centers and most hotels. A combination map and bus-and-ferry schedule, the guide shows beach locations and how to reach them. The Bermuda telephone directory, available in hotels, also has maps and public-transportation schedules, plus many other tips for how to get around and what to see.

Few Bermudian beaches offer shade, but some have palm trees and thatched shelters. The sun can be intense, so bring a hat and plenty of sunscreen. You can rent umbrellas at some beaches, but food and drink are rare, so pack snacks and lots of water.

HAMILTON AND CENTRAL PARISHES

Astwood Cove and Park. On weekends you can find lots of children and families at this popular beach. The Astwood Park area is shady and grassy, which makes it popular among locals for birthday parties, family picnics, and weddings. **Pros:** shady park area; great ocean views; lots of lush greenery. **Cons:** steep climb from the park down to the beach area; beach has suffered hurricane damage; steep cliff drops not suitable for young children. ⊠ *Off S. Shore Rd., Warwick Parish* Ⓜ *Bus 7 from Hamilton.*

☺ ★ **Elbow Beach.** Swimming and body-surfing are great at this beach, which is bordered by the prime strand of sand reserved for guests of the Elbow Beach Hotel on the left, and the ultra-exclusive Coral Beach Club beach area on the right. It's a pleasant setting for a late-evening stroll, with the lights from nearby hotels dancing on the water, but the romance dissipates in daylight, when the beach is noisy and crowded. Groups also gather here to play football and volleyball.

TOP 5 OUTDOORS

- Marvel at the sea life on the ocean floor aboard a glass-bottom boat.

- Feel the wind whip through your hair on a rented Jet Ski.

- Sit on the top deck of the public ferry and cruise from Hamilton to Dockyard.

- Rent a Boston Whaler and tour the island.

- Swim with the turtles at Turtle Beach.

Beaches

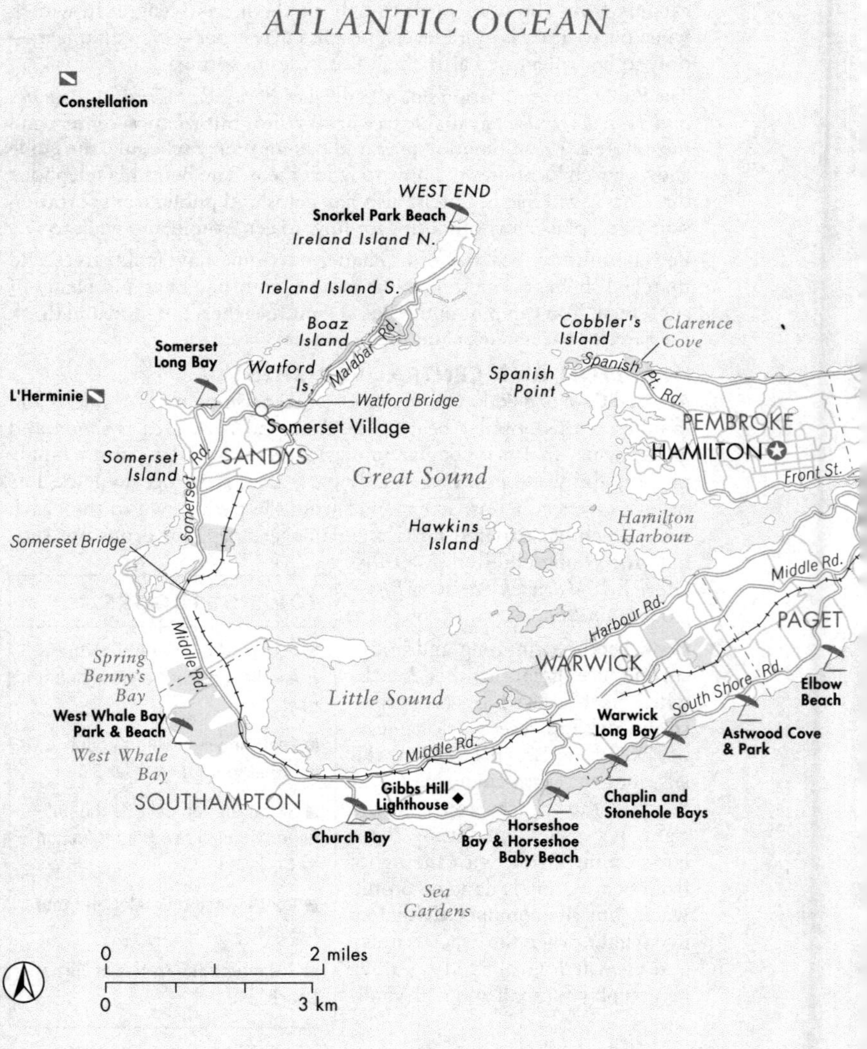

ATLANTIC OCEAN

◥ Constellation

WEST END

⛱ Snorkel Park Beach
Ireland Island N.

Ireland Island S.

Boaz
Island
⛱ Somerset   Watford   Malabar Rd.
Long Bay   Is.
────── Watford Bridge

Cobbler's   Clarence
Island   Cove

Spanish   Spanish Pt. Rd.
Point

L'Herminie ◥

Somerset Village

PEMBROKE

Somerset
Island   SANDYS   Great Sound

HAMILTON ✪

Front St.

Hamilton
Harbour

Somerset Bridge

Hawkins
Island

Middle Rd.

Spring
Benny's
Bay

Middle Rd.

Little Sound

Harbour Rd.

WARWICK

PAGET

⛱ West Whale Bay
Park & Beach

West Whale
Bay

SOUTHAMPTON

Middle Rd.

South Shore Rd.

Warwick
Long Bay ⛱

⛱ Elbow
Beach

Astwood Cove
& Park

Gibbs Hill
Lighthouse ◆

Church Bay

Horseshoe
Bay & Horseshoe
Baby Beach

⛱ Chaplin and
Stonehole Bays

Sea
Gardens

0 ──────── 2 miles
0 ──────── 3 km

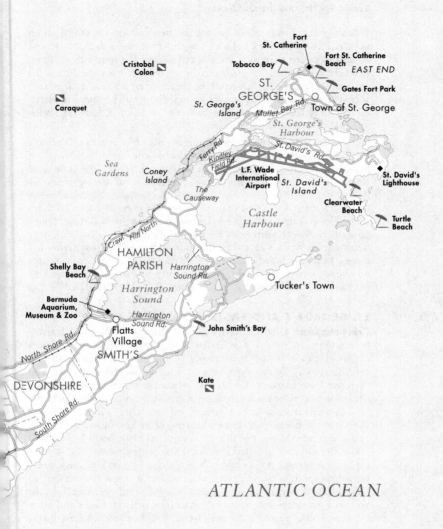

Fort
St. Catherine

Tobacco Bay

Fort St. Catherine
Beach

EAST END

Cristobal
Colon

Gates Fort Park

**ST.
GEORGE'S**

*St. George's
Island*

Town of St. George

Caraquet

Mullet Bay Rd.

*St. George's
Harbour*

St. David's Rd.

Ferry Rd.

*Sea
Gardens*

Coney
Island

*Kindley
Field Rd.*

St. David's
Lighthouse

L.F. Wade
International
Airport

*St. David's
Island*

*The
Causeway*

Clearwater
Beach

*Castle
Harbour*

Turtle
Beach

Crawl Hill North

**HAMILTON
PARISH**

*Harrington
Sound Rd.*

Shelly Bay
Beach

*Harrington
Sound*

Tucker's Town

Bermuda
Aquarium,
Museum & Zoo

*Harrington
Sound Rd.*

Flatts
Village

John Smith's Bay

SMITH'S

North Shore Rd.

DEVONSHIRE

Kate

South Shore Rd.

ATLANTIC OCEAN

Hermos

Protective coral reefs make the waters the safest on the island and a good choice for families. A lunch wagon sometimes sells fast food and cold drinks during the day, and Mickey's Beach Bar (part of the Elbow Beach Hotel) is open for lunch and dinner, though it may be difficult to get a table. **Pros:** beautiful stretch of beach; safest waters on the island; snorkel rental shop. **Cons:** busy; parking fills up quickly; need to watch out for stray footballs and volleyballs. ⊠ *Off South Rd., Paget Parish* Ⓜ *Bus 2 or 7 from Hamilton.*

Warwick Long Bay. Different from the covelike bay beaches, Warwick Long Bay has about a ½-mi stretch of sand—the longest of any beach here. Its backdrop is a combination of steep cliffs and low grass- and brush-covered hills. The beach is exposed to some strong southerly winds, but the waves are usually moderate because the inner reef is close to shore. A 20-foot coral outcrop less than 200 feet offshore looks like a sculpted boulder balancing on the water's surface. South Shore Park, which surrounds the bay, is often empty, a fact that only heightens the beach's appealing isolation and serenity. **Pros:** Bermuda's longest beach; secluded location; nature trail walks. **Cons:** strong southerly winds in winter months; small parking area; steep uphill walk to get back to South Shore Rd. ⊠ *Off South Rd., Warwick Parish* Ⓜ *Bus 7 from Hamilton.*

ST. GEORGE'S AND EASTERN PARISHES

Ⓒ **Clearwater Beach.** On the eastern tip of the island in St. David's, Clearwater is a long sandy strip of beach that's popular with serious swimmers and triathletes who use it as a training ground. But don't be intimidated, the young and old also flock here to wade in the shallow water, and there are buoy markers that identify where the beach becomes deeper. Clearwater is one of the few beaches in Bermuda with an adjoining café, serving kids' favorites such as burgers and fries. There's also an in-house bar when the five-o'clock-somewhere mood strikes. Beach bathrooms and lifeguards during the tourist season (April through September) make this a great choice for families. **Pros:** nearby paved road is great for evening strolls; small children's playground keeps kids busy; great beach for spotting turtles; picnic area. **Cons:** it's near the airport, so there's lots of aircraft noise, popuar spot for family get-togethers, so you need to reserve your spot early; bathrooms can be stinky and often run out of toilet paper. ⊠ *Cooper's Island Rd., St. David's Island* Ⓜ *Bus 6 from St. George's.*

★ **Fort St. Catherine Beach.** Fort St. Catherine is one of the larger north-shore beaches, and the water's deep enough for a serious swim. There are also beach rentals and a snack bar. If and when you get beach-bummed out, head over to the military fort next door, for which this beach is named. Nearby Blackbeard's Hideout is a great place for a refueling meal. **Pros:** beach snack shop and nearby restaurant are convenient; great views of the fort, and fort tours are great for a beach break. **Cons:** beach is far from nearest bus stop and has very little shade. ⊠ *Coot Pond Rd., St. George's Parish* Ⓜ *Bus 10 or 11 from Hamilton.*

Ⓒ **Gates Fort Park.** Also named after its neighboring military fort, Gates has a very small beach that is popular with local families. The park is off Barry Road, not far from Alexandra Battery, a favorite diving spot of St. George's children. **Pros:** historic fort nearby; great for family picnics. **Cons:** tiny. ⊠ *Coot Pond Rd., St. George's Parish* Ⓜ *Bus 1, 3, 10, or 11 from Hamilton.*

↻ **John Smith's Bay.** This beach consists of a pretty strand of long, flat, open sand. The presence of a lifeguard in summer makes it an ideal place to bring children. The only public beach in Smith's Parish, John Smith's Bay is also popular with locals. Groups of young folk like to gather in the park area surrounding the beach for parties, especially on weekends and holidays, so if you're not in the mood for a festive bunch with loud radios, this may not be the place for you. There are toilet and changing facilities on-site, as well as scooter parking. **Pros:** grassy picnic area; right next to bus stop; serene beach in the evening. **Cons:** rough waves at high tide; can get busy at weekends. ⊠ *S. Shore Rd., Smith's Parish* Ⓜ *Bus 1 from Hamilton.*

↻ **Shelly Bay Beach.** Known for its sandy bottom and shallow water, Shelly Bay is a good place to take small children. It also has shade trees, a rarity at Bermudian beaches. A playground behind the beach attracts hordes of youngsters on weekends and during school holidays. A nearby soccer and cricket practice field and a public basketball court are handy when you want to blow off some steam. **Pros:** shallow beach and adjoining playground for kids; on-site Jamaican food eatery. **Cons:** noisy street traffic; lots of kids during summer camps; good swimming spots are hard to find during low tide. ⊠ *N. Shore Rd., Hamilton Parish* Ⓜ *Bus 10 or 11 from Hamilton.*

Tobacco Bay. The most popular beach near St. George's—about 15 minutes northwest of the town on foot—this small north-shore strand is huddled in a coral cove. Its beach house has a snack bar, equipment rentals, toilets, showers, changing rooms, and ample parking. It's a 10-minute hike from the bus stop in the town of St. George's, or you can flag down a St. George's Minibus Service van and ask for a lift ($2 per person). In high season the beach is busy, especially midweek, when the cruise ships are docked. **Pros:** beautiful rock formations in the water; great snorkeling. **Cons:** so popular it becomes overcrowded; no bus stops nearby. ⊠ *Coot Pond Rd., St. George's Parish* ☎ *441/297–2756* Ⓜ *Bus 10 or 11 from Hamilton.*

★ **Turtle Beach.** Down a stretch from Clearwater Beach, Turtle Beach offers the same tranquillity, but with a bit less traffic. The water's also a deeper turquoise color here. If you're lucky, you might even spot a turtle. There's also a lifeguard station with a guard on duty. When your tummy grumbles, it's a short walk to Gombey's Restaurant. **Pros:** quiet beach; popular for turtle sightings. **Cons:** little parking; moped traffic. ⊠ *Cooper's Island Rd., St. David's Island* Ⓜ *Bus 6 from St. George's.*

DOCKYARD AND WESTERN PARISHES

Chaplin and Stonehole Bays. In a secluded area east along the dunes from Horseshoe Bay, these tiny adjacent beaches almost disappear at high tide. An unusual high coral wall reaches across the beach to the water, perforated by a 10-foot-high, arrowhead-shape hole. Like Horseshoe Bay, the beach fronts South Shore Park. Wander farther along the dunes and you can find several other tiny, peaceful beaches before you eventually reach Warwick Long Bay. **Pros:** low-key atmosphere; you could be the only one on these beaches during the winter months; adjoining beaches. **Cons:** beach shoes needed; uneven beach; strong surf. ⊠ *Off South Rd., Southampton Parish* Ⓜ *Bus 7 from Hamilton.*

Ⓒ **Horseshoe Bay.** When locals say they're going to "the beach," they're
Fodor's Choice generally referring to Horseshoe Bay, the island's most popular spot.
★ With clear water, a 0.3-mi crescent of pink sand, a vibrant social scene, and the uncluttered backdrop of South Shore Park, Horseshoe Bay has everything you could ask of a Bermudian beach. A snack bar, changing rooms, beach-rental facilities, and lifeguards add to its appeal. The Good Friday Annual Kite Festival also takes place here. The undertow can be strong, especially on the main beach. A better place for children is **Horseshoe Baby Beach.** Before 2003's Hurricane Fabian, this beach was reached by climbing a trail over the dunes at the western end of Horseshoe Bay. Fabian's storm surge ploughed right through those dunes, creating a wide walkway for eager little beachgoers. Sheltered from the ocean by a ring of rocks, this cove is shallow and almost perfectly calm. In summer, toddlers can find lots of playmates. **Pros:** adjoining beach is perfect for small children; snack bar with outdoor seating. **Cons:** the bus stop is a long walk up a huge hill; gets very crowded; busiest beach on the island. ⊠ *Off South Rd., Southampton Parish* ☎ *441/238–2651* Ⓜ *Bus 7 from Hamilton.*

Ⓒ **Snorkel Park Beach.** This is a popular spot among local families who like to treat their children to a sandy white beach and pristine views of the water. Food and bar amenities are on-site with beach equipment rentals for the kids as well as parents. If your cruise ship docks in Dockyard, Snorkel Park Beach is a short walk from the cruise terminal. A children's playground is just outside the park. Before you leave, be sure to stop in the Clocktower Mall and the Craft Market. Also nearby are the Bone Fish Bar & Grill, the Frog & Onion Pub, and an ATM. **Pros:** park is perfect for children; popular water-sports spot; nearby shopping area and restaurants. **Cons:** entrance fee; can be busy with summer children's camps; turns into an outdoor nightclub early evening. ⊠ *7 Maritime La., Dockyard* ☎ *441/234–6989* 🎟 *$5* ☉ *Daily May–Oct.* Ⓜ *Bus 7 or 8 from Hamilton.*

Somerset Long Bay. Popular with Somerset locals, this beach is on the quiet northwestern end of the island, far from the bustle of Hamilton and major tourist hubs. In keeping with the area's rural atmosphere, the beach is low-key. Undeveloped parkland shields the beach from the light traffic on Cambridge Road. The main beach is long by Bermudian standards—nearly ¼ mi from end to end. Although exposed to northerly storm winds, the bay water is normally calm and shallow—ideal for children. The bottom, however, is rocky and uneven, so it's a good idea to put on water shoes before wading. **Pros:** low-key. **Cons:** rocky bottom. ⊠ *Cambridge Rd., Sandys Parish* Ⓜ *Bus 7 or 8 to Dockyard from Hamilton.*

★ **West Whale Bay.** This beach can be a secluded oasis if you go at the right time: sunset. To get to the beach, you need to cross a huge field and walk down a natural rock formation path. **Pros:** romantic. **Cons:** a bit of a walk from the parking area. ⊠ *Off Whale Bay and Middle Rds., Southampton Parish* Ⓜ *Bus 7 or 8 from Hamilton.*

SPORTS AND THE OUTDOORS

BICYCLING

The best and sometimes only way to explore Bermuda's nooks and crannies—its little hidden coves and 18th-century tribe roads—is by bicycle or motor scooter. Arriving at the small shore roads and hill trails, however, means first navigating Bermuda's rather treacherous main roads. They are narrow, with no shoulders, and often congested with traffic (especially near Hamilton during rush hours). Fortunately, there's another, safer option for biking in Bermuda: the Railway Trail, a dedicated cycle path blissfully free of cars.

PEDAL POINTER

You can pick up the Bermuda Handy Reference Map for free at Visitor Information Centres for Bermuda's bike routes, but it's not as detailed or clear as the Bermuda Islands map, available at the Bermuda Bookstore in Hamilton. You won't be lost without a map, as bike-rental shops and hotel clerks can recommend bike routes, too, but serious cyclists may find them worth examining.

Despite the traffic, bicycle racing is a popular sport in Bermuda, and club groups regularly whir around the island on evening and weekend training rides. Be prepared for some tough climbs—the roads running north and south across the island are particularly steep and winding—and the wind can sap even the strongest rider's strength, especially along South Shore Road in Warwick and Southampton parishes. Island roads are no place for novice riders. Helmets are strongly recommended on pedal bikes (it's illegal to ride without them on a motor scooter), and parents should think twice before allowing preteens to bike here.

Information on local races or on how to meet up with fellow cyclists for regular group rides is available at ⊕ *www.bermudabicycle.org.* The Winner's Edge bike shop on Front Street in Hamilton is also a good source of information about the local cycling scene.

BIKE PATHS

★ **The Railway Trail.** Running intermittently the length of the old Bermuda Railway (old "Rattle 'n' Shake"), this trail is scenic, and restricted to pedestrian and bicycle traffic. You can enter and exit the trail at several clearly-signposted points. One especially lovely route starts at Somerset Bridge and ends 2½ mi later near the Somerset Country Squire pub. You can take your bike onto the ferry for a pleasant ride from Hamilton or St. George's to the Somerset Bridge stop. From there, bike to the bridge on the main road, turn right, and ride uphill for about 50 yards until you reach the sign announcing "Railway Trail". Turning onto the trail, you find yourself along a course with spectacular views of the Great Sound. Along the way you pass old Fort Scaur, several schools, and the large pink Somerset Cricket Club. Toward the end of the trail segment, you'll find yourself on Beacon Hill Road opposite the bus depot. Here you can turn around and head back to Somerset Bridge, or, for refreshment, turn left and ride to the main road (you can see Somerset Police Station), and make a sharp right turn to find Mangrove Bay and the Somerset Country Squire pub and restaurant. ■ TIP➔ **Because the Railway Trail is somewhat isolated and not lighted, you should avoid it after dark.**

> ## ROAD RASH
>
> The Bermudian slang dictionary *Bermewjan Vurds* defines "road rash" (grazes received from sliding along Bermuda's roads in an accident) as "a skin disease common amongst tourists brave enough to rent mopeds."

South Shore Road. This main island road covers almost the full length of the Island and passes absolutely gorgeous ocean views. South Shore Road—also known as South Road—is well paved and, for the most part, wider than Middle Road, North Shore Road, and Harbour Road, with relatively few hills. However, it's one of Bermuda's windiest and most heavily traveled thoroughfares. Highlights are through Warwick and Southampton, looking down on the popular south shore beaches.

Tribe Road 3. Tribe roads are small, often unpaved side roads, some of which date to the earliest settlement of Bermuda. They make for good exploring, though many are quite short and lead to dead ends. Beginning at Oleander Cycles in Southampton, Tribe Road 3 steeply climbs the hillside just below Gibbs Hill Lighthouse, with views of the south shore below. It eventually leads to a point from where you can see both the north and south shores.

BIKE RENTALS

In Bermuda bicycles are called pedal or push bikes to distinguish them from the more common motorized two-wheelers, which are also called bikes. Some of the cycle liveries around the island rent both, so make sure to specify whether you want a pedal or motor bike. If you're sure you want to bicycle while you're in Bermuda, try to reserve rental bikes a few days in advance. Rates are around $30 a day, though the longer you rent, the more economical your daily rate. You may be charged an additional $15 for a repair waiver and for a refundable deposit.

Riding a motor scooter for the first time can be disconcerting, wherever you are. Here you have the added confusion that Bermudians drive on the left, and though the posted speed limit is 35 kph, the unofficial speed limit is actually closer to 50 kph (while many locals actually travel faster than that). At most rental shops, lessons on how to ride a motor scooter are perfunctory at best—practice as much as you can before going on to the main road. Though many tourists can and do rent motor scooters, the public transportation system (ferries and buses) is excellent and should not be ruled out.

Eve Cycle. With three convenient locations around the island, Eve's has moved its head office to Dockyard, just a few yards from the cruise terminal. It's about the only bike shop to still rent out adult mountain bikes, as well as motor scooters, including your mandatory helmet.

The staff readily supplies advice on where to ride, and you'll have to pay an extra $20 for third-party insurance. Other branches are in St. George's and Paget, and if these are a bit of a walk from your accommodation, a shuttle service is offered. ⊠ *10 Dockyard Terr., Dockyard* ☎ *441/236–6247* ⊕ *www.evecycles.com.*

WORD OF MOUTH

"My husband and I have been to Bermuda quite a few times and have rented scooters each time. We have rented from Oleander and they have been great. They give you a trial run in a parking lot to make sure you check out and are comfortable." —Shopinful

Oleander Cycles. Known primarily for its selection of motorbikes and scooters for rent and sale. Single and double bikes are available and a $30 damage waiver is charged. Oleander Cycles' main store is in Paget, but its Southampton location is convenient for Pompano Beach resort guests since it's next door to the resort. There are also small branches at the St. George's Club, the Reefs, and Cambridge Beaches. ⊠ *6 Valley Rd., off Middle Rd., Paget* ☎ *441/236–5235* ⊠ *8 Middle Rd., west of fire station, Southampton Parish* ☎ *441/234–0629* ⊠ *Maritime La., Dockyard* ☎ *441/234–2764* ⊠ *26 York St., St. George's* ☎ *441/297–0478.*

Smatt's Cycle Livery. Smatt's has three locations—one in Hamilton, next to the Fairmont Hamilton Princess Hotel, one in the West End at the Fairmont Southampton Resort, and the newest branch at the Rosewood Tucker's Point Hotel & Spa. The shop offers standard moped rentals with helmets. Smatt's has the cheapest daily rate at $50, plus the $30 damage waiver fee. Before a moped is rented, you'll be asked to take a riding test for your safety. ⊠ *74 Pitts Bay Rd., Hamilton* ☎ *441/295–1180* ⊠ *Fairmont Southampton Resort, 101 S. Shore Rd., Southampton Parish* ☎ *441/238–7800.*

Wheels Cycles. Peugeot single- and double-seat scooters are available to rent by the day, week, or month. These are some of the best-quality and best-looking rental bikes on the island. A quick riding test and safety tips are given before you ride off. If you're staying at Grotto Bay Beach Resort, you'll also find a Wheels Cycles on site. ⊠ *74 Front St., near the docks, Hamilton* ☎ *441/292–2245* ⊕ *www.wheelscycles.com.*

BIKE TOURS

★ **Fantasea Bermuda.** This comprehensive recreational company offers a 3½- hour bike tour along the Railway Trail. Your tour will start from Dockyard with a short boat cruise to the trail, where you can pick up your bikes. After the ride, finish with a cool-off swim and a drink at a beach in the Somerset area. The total trip, including the cruise and biking, costs $75 per person and includes equipment and drinks. There is a $5 administration fee per reservation. ⊠ *5 Point Pleasant Rd., Albuoy's Point, Hamilton* ☎ *441/236–1300* ⊕ *www.fantasea.bm.*

BIRD-WATCHING

Forty species of warblers have been spotted in Bermuda, especially in the casuarina trees along the south shore and West End. Other omnipresent species include kiskadee, swifts, cuckoos, flycatchers, swallows, thrushes, kingbirds, and orioles. Bird conservation is a big deal in Bermuda. You can see bluebird boxes on every island golf course, which act as safe nesting sites for this jeopardized species, threatened by development and the invasive sparrow.

The largest variety of birds can be spotted during fall migration, when thousands of birds pass overhead, stop for a rest on their way south, or spend the winter on the island. You might spot the rare American avocet or the curlew sandpiper. In spring look for brightly colored Central and South American birds migrating north. The white-tail tropic bird, a beautiful white bird with black markings and a 12- to 17-inch-long tail (locals call it a "longtail"), is one of the first to arrive. Summer is the quietest season for bird-watching in Bermuda. Late migrants, like the barn swallow and chimney swift pass by, and if you check the ponds you may see the occasional shorebird.

Bermuda Audubon Society. The society has an excellent book called *A Birdwatching Guide to Bermuda,* by president Andrew Dobson, published by the Arlequin Press. In it are maps, illustrations, and descriptions of birds and their habitats. Several birding events are organized throughout the year, including the Christmas Bird Count—Bermuda averages 74 species per count, although 200 species have been recorded. You can find a listing of the Audubon Society's events on their Web site as well as a bird-watching checklist. Birders may also be interested in David Wingate's successful efforts to repopulate the native cahow bird population via artificial burrows on Nonsuch Island. ☎ *441/238–8628* ⊕ *www.audubon.bm.*

Seymour's Pond Nature Reserve. Seymour's Pond is smaller than Warwick and Spittal Ponds, but it has the advantage of being a bit farther inland, and therefore better protected. Twenty-eight species of duck are recorded in Bermuda, and you're quite likely to see many of them here. ✉ *Middle Rd., near Barnes Corner, Southampton Parish.*

Spittal Pond Nature Reserve. Stretching placidly within a 60-acre nature reserve, Spittal Pond is an excellent place to view wildlife, especially birds. As long as the water level is not too high, some 30 species of shorebird can be present on the margins of the pond. On a good day in September you might see more than 100 birds. Semipalmated sandpipers are perhaps the most abundant. In winter, herons and egrets roost serenely in the shallow water. You can tour the reserve unaccompanied or take a scheduled tour with a park ranger. ■TIP➡ **Don't forget your camera if you take one of the great coastal nature trails.** ✉ *South Rd., Smith's Parish* ☎ *441/236–5902.*

Warwick Pond. In a well-kept inland nature preserve, Bermuda's only natural freshwater pond is prime bird territory. Shorebirds and herons gather around its edges in fall and winter. ■TIP➡ **In the heat of summer, the stagnant water lets off a rather putrid smell.** ✉ *Middle Rd., near Ettrick Animal Hospital, Warwick Parish.*

CLOSE UP

Good, Cheap Fun!

Bermuda is notoriously expensive, but if you've blown most of your inheritance getting here you needn't splash the rest of it on having a good time.

Walking Along the South-Shore Beaches. There's a 2-mi stretch from Horseshoe Bay in Southampton right down to Warwick Long Bay, which with a bit of clambering and the odd paddle in the ocean you can comfortably negotiate. The quiet secluded spots along the rocks are great for bird-watching and there are a number of tiny coves where you can stop for a picnic.

Cup Match. If you want a real Bermuda experience, come to the island during the annual Cup Match holiday—either the last weekend in July or the first weekend in August. It's essentially the all-star cricket game between the best of the west and the best of the east, but you don't have to like cricket to enjoy the atmosphere. Half the island trots through the ground at some stage during the two-day holiday to listen to the sound of the drums, sample the fried chicken, and wave a flag for Somerset or St. George's. It's also the one time of year when gambling is legal and thousands pack the Crown & Anchor tents to roll the dice for Bermuda's own unique version of the casino favorite—craps. Entry is $20.

Snorkeling at Tobacco Bay. You don't have to rent a boat or even swim very far offshore to get a close-up look at some of Bermuda's wonderful marine life. Tobacco Bay in St. George's is a favorite spot, where colorful sergeant majors, parrot fish, and clown fish can be seen in the crystal-clear water close to the rocks. John Smith's Bay in Smith's Parish, where shoals of tiny fish cast large, dark shadows across the bay, is another great spot.

Wildlife Photography. From a patient day's vigil with an ultralong lens, waiting for a shot of a humpback whale, to a frantic pursuit of a pair of longtails dancing in the summer sky, Bermuda is an amateur photographer's dream.

Rent a Bike. On an island where the speed limit is 20 mph there's no need to worry about renting a car. Bermuda's strict traffic control rules mean you're not allowed to anyway. A bike is the best way to discover for yourself the hidden nooks and crannies and secret beaches that the bus routes and the tourist cabs just won't take you to. It costs about $55 a day.

6

BOATING

Bermuda is gorgeous by land, but you should take to the water to fully appreciate its beauty. You can either rent your own boat (⇨ see *Aquatic Adventures*) or charter one with a skipper. There are literally scores of options to suit all tastes, from champagne cruises at sunset to cruise and kayak ecotours.

CHARTER BOATS

More than 20 large power cruisers and sailing vessels, piloted by local skippers, are available for charter. Primarily 30 to 60 feet long, most charter sailboats can carry up to 30 passengers, sometimes overnight. Meals and drinks can be included on request, and a few skippers offer dinner cruises for the romantically inclined. Rates generally range from $400 to $550 for a three-hour cruise, or $650 to $1,500 for a full-day cruise, with additional per-person charges for large groups. Where you go and what you do—exploring, swimming, snorkeling, cruising—is usually up to you and your

> **GOOD TO KNOW**
>
> If you rent a motorboat, be sure to ask for directions to Castle Island Nature Reserve, one of the most secluded and beautiful spots on the island.

skipper. Generally, however, cruises travel to and around the islands of the Great Sound. Several charter skippers advertise year-round operations, but the off-season schedule can be haphazard. Skippers devote periods of the off-season to maintenance and repairs or close altogether if bookings lag. Be sure to book well in advance; in the high season do so before you arrive on the island.

Ana Luna Adventures. The *Ana Luna* is a 45-foot catamaran, which offers snorkeling cruises, scuba diving trips, and sunset tours as well as a host of other marine adventures from $60. Captain Nathan will tailor his tours to your requirements. ⊠ *Grotto Bay Beach Resort, 11 Blue Hole Hill, Bailey's Bay, Hamilton Parish* ☎ *441/504–3780* ⊕ *www. analunaadventures.com.*

★ **Charter Bermuda.** The *Rising Son II* is a beautiful, 60-foot, 80-passenger catamaran with a full bar, and *The Aristocrat* is a 55-foot sailing-catamaran for up to 50 people. Besides offering sailing, swimming, and snorkeling trips, Captain William "Beez" Evans and the accommodating crews can arrange for you to spend part of the day on Jet Skis, in kayaks, or with a parasailing outfitter. Rates start at $550 for the first hour. You can also book one of the popular cruises, such as the Ultimate Catamaran Sail and Snorkel, which anchors off a quiet sandy bay for snorkeling and kayaking. Turtles are often spotted. The price is $69 a head. Shipwreck snorkeling is offered for $50. ⊠ *King's Wharf, Dockyard* ☎ *441/232–5789* ⊕ *www.charterbermuda.com.*

Restless Native Tours. Fresh batches of cookies baked on board at every sailing and washed down with lemonade or rum swizzles are the delicious trademark of this family-owned and -operated charter company. Restless Native is also unique in its educational approach to chartering—they offer a crash course on Bermuda's fish and a guided snorkeling trip. The 50- by 30-foot boat is excellent for dinner charters, evening cocktail cruises, birthday parties, and weddings. The owners can pick you up at any wharf on the island. ☎ *441/531–8149* ⊕ *www. restlessnative.bm.*

Tam-Marina. Founded in 1967, Tam-Marina has a reputation for lively dinner and cocktail cruises on a fleet of elegant white motor yachts. *Lady Charlotte* and *Lady Tamara* often accommodate large private parties on the Great Sound, whereas *Boss Lady* is smaller and more intimate. But luxury comes with a hefty price tag; the two larger yachts will set you back $1,390 for the minimum 1.5 hour cruise and Boss Lady is $400 for 1.5 hours. You can book online. ⊠ *61 Harbour Rd., Paget Parish* ☎ *441/236–0127* ⊕ *www.ladyboats.com.*

Wind Sail Charters. You can rent a 41-, 51-, or 60-foot Morgan yacht, including snorkeling equipment, from Wind Sail. Captain Mike or his daughter, Captain Melissa, will sail to your location and take you for a spin. The rates for six people are $475 to $575, depending on the boat, for three hours, making this the most affordable ride on the island. You can also "join a group" for the bargain price of $50, or just $30 each if there are six or more of you. Lunch catering is available for an extra charge. ☎ *441/734–8547* ⊕ *www.bermudawindsailcharters. com.*

WHALE-WATCHING

During March and April the majestic humpback whales pass Bermuda as they migrate north to summer feeding grounds. Watching these giant animals as they leap out of the ocean is an awe-inspiring spectacle. You can see them from Elbow Beach or West Whale Bay on a clear day, if you're prepared to wait. But if you want to get a close-up view you can book a tour with an operator like Fantasea Bermuda.

CRICKET

6

Cricket is one of the favorite pastimes on this sports-mad island, a fact that was seen with the national celebrations that followed Bermuda's qualification for the Cricket World Cup in 2007. Bermuda is the smallest country ever to make the finals of the competition, and its cricketeers are treated as heroes in their homeland. The island's cricket season runs from April through September.

Bermuda Cricket Board. Look at the Board's Web site for more information about events throughout the year. ☎ *441/292–8958* ⊕ *www. bermudacricketboard.com*

Fodor's Choice ★ **Cup Match.** Among Bermuda cricket aficionados, Cup Match in late July or early August is *the* summer sporting event, played over two days. The top players from around the island compete in two teams: the East End team and the West End team. Although the match is taken very seriously, the event itself is a real festival, complete with plenty of Bermudian food and music. Cup Match coincides with two national holidays, Emancipation Day and Somers' Day. Emancipation Day is the celebration of the passing of the Slavery Abolition Act in 1834, which freed Bermuda's slaves, and Somers' Day celebrates Admiral Sir George Somers's discovery of Bermuda, which led to its settlement in 1609. Cup Match is Bermuda's only venue for legal gambling, the Crown & Anchor tent is pitched at the field each year. Thousands of picnickers and partyers show up during the two-day match. Although the players wear only white, fans wear colors to support their team—blue on blue represents the East End and navy on red represents the West End. A $20 entry fee is charged per day.

For Love of Cricket

The Oval and Lords are names of English cricket grounds that evoke memories of Britain long ago, a time of cucumber sandwiches and tea poured from china pots—but the cricket scene in Bermuda is definitely Caribbean. The thwack of leather on willow is the same, but overcast skies and frequent breaks as the ground staff move quickly to put the rain covers in place are not for these players. The fans, gathered on grassy knolls and open terraces, are also far removed from those back in England, where the game originated. Polite clapping and hearty hurrahs are not to be heard here. Instead the air is filled with chanting, and the grandstands reverberate to the sound of music. Allegiances are clearly defined, though few miles separate the opposing factions—mothers, fathers, sons, and daughters all cheering on their favorites. As the match comes to a conclusion, the setting sun falls low behind the clubhouse and players and fans mingle to await the dawn of another day of runs, catches, and cries of "Howzat."

FISHING

Bermuda's proximity to the deep ocean makes it one of the best places in the world for deep-sea fishing. Many of the International Fishing Association's world-record catches were hauled in a few miles off the Bermuda coastline. July and August is marlin season, and anglers from all over the world come to the island in a bid to try and hook monster blue marlin in excess of 1,000 pounds. Deep-sea fishing is not just for the experts, though. Most charter companies are happy to teach amateurs how to hook and reel in a catch—whether it's tuna, wahoo, or even marlin. Some of the charter fishermen let you keep your catch but they're not obliged to do so. Many of the fishermen rely on sales to restaurants to bolster their businesses, so unless it's a good day they might not give much away. And don't be surprised to find fish you pulled out of the ocean that day on the menu in one of Bermuda's many restaurants that evening. As well as deep-sea fishing, shore fishing is also popular, while some fishermen trawl inside the reefs. If you've got the cash there's no substitute for the thrill of the open ocean. Scores of operators are on the island, about 20 of which are regularly out on the water. A full list is available at ⊕ *www.gotobermuda.com*. Prices vary depending on the size and quality of the boat.

REEF AND OFFSHORE FISHING

Three major reef bands lie at various distances from the island. The first is anywhere from ½ to 5 mi offshore. The second, the Challenger Bank, is about 12 mi offshore. The third, the Argus Bank, is about 30 mi offshore. As a rule, the farther out you go, the larger the fish—and the more expensive the charter.

Most charter-fishing captains go to the reefs and deep water to the southwest and northwest of the island, where the fishing is best. Catches over the reefs include snapper, amberjack, grouper, and barracuda. Of the most sought-after deepwater fish—marlin, tuna, wahoo, and dolphinfish—wahoo is the most common, dolphinfish the least. Trawling is the usual method of deepwater fishing, and charter-boat operators offer various tackle setups, with test-line weights ranging from 20 pounds to 130 pounds. The boats, which range from 31 feet to 55 feet long, are fitted with gear and electronics to track fish, including depth sounders, global-positioning systems, loran systems, video fish finders, radar, and computer scanners.

Half-day and full-day charters are offered by most operators, but full-day trips offer the best chance for a big catch because the boat has time to reach waters that are less often fished. Rates are about $900 per boat for half a day (four hours), $1,300 per day (eight hours). For more information about chartering a fishing boat, you can request or pick up a copy of *What to Do: Information and Prices* at the Bermuda Department of Tourism.

★ **Atlantic Spray Charters.** Half-day and full-day year-round charters are available on Atlantic's 40-foot *Tenacious*. Rates are $850 for the four-hour half day, $1,050 for six hours, and $1,250 for the eight-hour full day, including all the equipment you need, soda and water, and, most important, the knowledge you need to catch the big fish. ⊠ *St. George's* ☎ *441/735–9444.*

Fish Bermuda. Allen DeSilva is one of Bermuda's most knowledgeable skippers. His Web site is a great source of information on fishing conditions in Bermuda, and he guarantees a fun day out for beginners or serious anglers on his Mako boat, based out of Mill's Creek near Hamilton. It costs $2,000 to charter the boat for nine hours and $1,700 for six hours. ■TIP➔ Check out DeSilva's Web site for yummy recipes on how to cook up your local catch. ⊠ *11 Abri La., Spanish Point, Pembroke* ☎ *441/295–0835* ⊕ *www.fishbermuda.com.*

Messaround Charters. With charters of varying lengths available from Messaround Charters, it's easy to get to some of the prime offshore fishing grounds. Skipper Willard "Joe" Kelly can show you the ropes. The cost is $650 for four hours, $850 for six hours, and $1,050 for eight hours. ☎ *441/297–8093, 441/334–8953* ⊕ *www.fishandfun.bm.*

Overproof. Skipper Peter Rans is a regular in the big-game classic and a master at hooking monster marlin. He can take you to the best spots and help you reel in whatever game fish is in season. His rates vary from $900 for half a day to $1,300 for eight hours of serious marlin hunting. ⊠ *136 Somerset Rd., Somerset* ☎ *441/238–5663, 441/335–9850* ⊕ *www.overprooffishing.com.*

Playmate Fishing Charters. Kevin Winter has more than 30 years experience fishing Bermuda's waters, so you won't be stuck for experience on a Playmate charter. Rates go from $900 for half a day to $1,300 for the full day, with extra costs for tournament fishing. ⊠ *4 Mills Point La., Pembroke* ☎ *441/292–7131* ⊕ *www.playmatefishing.com.*

SHORE FISHING

The principal catches for shore fishers are pompano, bonefish, and snapper. Excellent sport for saltwater fly-fishing is the wily and strong bonefish, which hovers in coves, harbors, and bays. Among the more popular

One Fish, Two Fish, Red Fish, World Cup Fish

Bermuda's angling competitions attract top fishermen from all over the world. The Bermuda Blast tournament over the July 4 weekend coincides with the World Cup—where anglers across the globe compete to land the largest fish on the planet between 8 am and 4:30 pm. Each year more and more boats descend on Bermuda over the holiday weekend, the winners having been pulled out of the island's waters three times since 2002. The biggest local tournament is the Bermuda Big Game Classic, with many of the World Cup fishermen sticking around to take part in the three-day festival. The dates vary depending on when the weekend falls, but it's usually around July 15. The lure of monster marlin in excess of 1,000 pounds keeps them coming for the third leg of the Bermuda Triple Crown, the Seahorse Anglers Club tournament, the following week. Marlin season is what a lot of Bermuda's sport fishermen live for. "It's the biggest, baddest fish in the ocean—there's no feeling like landing a marlin," explains Sloane Wakefield of Atlantic Spray Charters. The **Bermuda Sport Fishing Association** (☎ 441/295–2370) is a good source of information about tournaments.

spots for bonefish are West Whale Bay and Spring Benny's Bay, which have large expanses of clear, shallow water protected by reefs close to shore. Good fishing holes are plentiful along the south shore, too. Fishing in the Great Sound and St. George's Harbour can be rewarding, but enclosed Harrington Sound is less promising. Ask at local tackle shops about the latest hot spots and the best baits. You can also make rental arrangements through your hotel or contact H2O Sports.

H2O Sports. Fishing rods and reels rent for $20 for a 24-hour period (credit card required to secure the rental). Squid bait and weights are also sold here, and it's open seven days a week. ⊠ *Cambridge Beaches Resort, 30 Kings Point Rd., Sandys Parish* ☎ *441/234–3082* ⊕ *www.h2osportsbermuda.com.*

Outcast. If you're not quite sure about your sea legs, this is the ideal fishing trip for beginners. Skipper Peter Rans will teach you inshore fishing on his 21-foot bay-boat *Outcast.* You'll more than likely catch bonefish, hogfish, and barracuda. It's also much more affordable than offshore fishing at $450 for half a day and $700 for the full day. ⊠ *16 Somerset Rd., Sandys Parish* ☎ *441/238–5663.*

GOLF

For descriptions of and information about Bermuda's nine golf courses, see Chapter 7.

HELMET DIVING

A different, less technical type of diving popular in Bermuda is helmet diving, offered between April and mid-November. Although helmet-diving cruises last three hours or more, the actual time underwater is about 25 minutes, when underwater explorers walk along the sandy bottom in about 10 to 12 feet of water (depending on the tide), wearing helmets that receive air through hoses leading to the surface. Underwater portraits are available for an extra charge. A morning or afternoon tour costs about $85 for adults and includes wet suits when the water temperature is below 80°F.

Hartley's Under Sea Adventures. The Hartleys schedule two diving trips per day, usually at 10 and 1:30, six days per week, in high season. Dives cost $85 for adults and $60 for children. Nondivers are not allowed to snorkel or swim in the same area as the divers, the theory being that fish that are used to helmet divers and approach them for food may endanger themselves by becoming used to snorkelers, swimmers, and eventually fisherfolk. ⊠ *Heritage Wharf, at cruise ship terminal, Dockyard, Sandys Parish* ☎ *441/234–2861* ⊕ *www.hartleybermuda.com.*

PARASAILING

The island's only parasailing outfitter operates in the Great Sound and in Castle Harbour from July through October. The cost is about $98 per person for an eight-minute flight.

KS Watersports. This is the one and only place to go for parasailing in Bermuda. Its Dockyard location, right next to the ferry stop, is open all year round, while its location in King's Square, St. George's, opens only for the summer months. The whole experience takes more than an hour out on the water, but you only get a maximum of 10 minutes in the air. The cost is $98 per person, and two people can go up together. Jet Ski tours also run from here, starting from $145. ⊠ *Dockyard Terr., Dockyard, Sandys* ☎ *441/297–4155* ⊕ *www.kswatersports.com.*

RUGBY

Bermuda's rugby season runs from September to April.

World Rugby Classic. The World Rugby Classic, in November, brings erstwhile top players, now retired, to the island for a week of play and parties—it's a hugely popular event among Bermuda's expatriate community. A game pass for the week is $100, daily admission is $25. The Classic can provide information about other matches as well. ☎ *441/295–6574* ⊕ *www.worldrugby.bm.*

RUNNING AND WALKING

Top runners flock to the island in January for the Bermuda International Race Weekend, which includes a marathon and 10-km races. Many of the difficulties that cyclists face in Bermuda—hills, traffic, and wind— also confront runners. Be careful of traffic when walking or running along Bermuda's narrow roads—most don't have shoulders.

Runners who favor firm pavement are happiest along the **Railway Trail** *(see ⇨ Bicycling, above)*, a former train route, one of the most peaceful stretches of road in Bermuda.

Wreck Diving

If you've heard the stories of the Bermuda Triangle then you won't be surprised to hear that there are more than 20 ships wrecked off the island. Actually it's got more to do with the craggy reefs that surround the island than that old myth, but each wreck has a story, and most dive operators here know it. Graham Maddocks, a 20-year veteran of Bermuda's waters and owner of Triangle Diving, gave us a history lesson on five of Bermuda's most interesting wrecks.

Constellation. Jaws author Peter Benchley based his follow-up novel *The Deep,* set in Bermuda, around the *Constellation* wreck. A cargo ship bound for Venezuela during World War II, she was carrying building materials, morphine, and 700 bottles of whiskey when her hull was broken apart on the reef. Some of the building materials remain, but the rest of her cargo is long gone.

The Cristobel Colon. This massive Spanish cruise liner is the biggest of Bermuda's shipwrecks, at 499 feet long. It crashed into the reefs off the North Shore in 1936 after its captain mistook an offshore communications tower for the Gibbs Hill Lighthouse. It was crewed by Spanish dissidents from the civil war in Puerto Rico. (They were eventually rounded up and hanged for treason in Spain.) The *Cristobel* sat in Bermuda's waters for several years and many of its furnishings can be found in Bermudian homes today. The British eventually sank its empty shell by using it for target practice during World War II.

The Hermes. Probably the most popular wreck dive in Bermuda, the *Hermes* remains fully intact sitting in 80 feet of water off the south shore.

It's one of the few wrecks that you can actually get inside and explore. It arrived in Bermuda with engine trouble and was ultimately abandoned by its crew. The Bermuda Government took possession of the 165-foot steel-hulled ship and sank it as a dive site in the early 1980s.

The Pelinaion. This 385-foot Greek cargo steamer was another victim of World War II. The British had blacked out the lighthouse in a bid to stop the Germans from spying on Bermuda. The captain had a perfect record, had sailed past Bermuda many times, and was months away from retirement when he made this journey from West Africa to Baltimore in 1940, carrying a cargo of iron ore. Without the lighthouse to guide him he couldn't find the island until he struck the reef off St. David's. You can still see the ship's steam boiler and engine as well as some of the cargo of iron ore.

The Xing Da. A modern-day pirate ship, the *Xing Da* was carrying a "cargo" of Chinese immigrants to be smuggled into the United States in 1996. Crewed by members of the Chinese mafia, the Triads, it had arranged to meet a smaller boat 145 mi off Bermuda for the immigrants to be transferred and taken into the States. Instead, they found themselves surrounded by the U.S. Marines. The boat was given to the government as a dive site in 1997.

If you like running on sand, head for the **south-shore beaches** *(see ⇨ Beaches, above)*. The trails through the South Shore Park are relatively firm. A large number of serious runners can be seen on Horseshoe Bay and Elbow Beach early in the morning and after 5 pm. Another good beach for running is half-mile-long Warwick Long Bay, the island's longest uninterrupted stretch of sand. The sand is softer here than at Horseshoe and Elbow, so it's difficult to get good footing, particularly at high tide. By using South Shore Park trails to skirt the coral bluffs, you can create a route that connects several beaches. Note that the trails can be winding and uneven in places.

Bermuda Half Marathon Derby. Held on Bermuda Day (May 24), a public holiday, the race brings thousands of locals and visitors, who line the edges of the 13.1-mi course. This race has recently been opened to tourists, but even if you aren't a runner, it's great fun to watch. There's a cycling race before and a carnival parade after. ⊕ *www.bermudamarathon.bm.*

Bermuda Triathlons. The Bermuda Triathlon Association holds these sporting events about once a month from April to October. The events combine a swim, a cycling leg, and a run. Many of the events take place on public holidays at Clearwater Beach, St. David's. ☎ *441/293–2765* ⊕ *www.bermudatriathlon.com.*

International Race Weekend. Held in mid-January, there's some serious competition for winning these races; they attract world-class distance runners from several countries, but they're open to everyone. The weekend event usually sees the Front Street mile race on Friday night, a 10k walk and run on Saturday, and the marathon on Sunday. It is the aim of many to get three medals in three days. ☎ *441/296–0951* ⊕ *www.bermudaraceweekend.com.*

Mid-Atlantic Athletic Club Fun Runs. These 2-mi sprints are held Tuesday evening April through October. Runs begin at 6 near the Berry Hill Road entrance to the Botanical Gardens. There's no fee. This popular recreational running club also holds Wednesday night track running at the National Stadium in the winter months. ☎ *441/239–4803* ⊕ *www.maac.bm.*

SAILING AND YACHTING

Bermuda has a worldwide reputation as a yacht-racing center. The sight of the racing fleet, with brightly colored spinnakers flying, is striking even if it's difficult to follow the intricacies of the race. The racing season runs from March to November. Most races are held on weekends in the Great Sound, and several classes of boats usually compete. You can watch from Spanish Point and along the Somerset shoreline. Anyone who wants to get a real sense of the action should be on board a boat near the racecourse. The Gold Cup race is held in October, and International Race Week is held at the end of April. In June in alternating years, Bermuda serves as the finish point for oceangoing yachts in three major races starting in the United States.

6

RACES AND EVENTS

Argo Group Gold Cup. This is the event of choice if you're more interested in racing than gawking at expensive yachts. Managed by the Royal Bermuda Yacht Club, the October tournament hosts many of the world's top sailors— some of whom are America's Cup skippers—and includes the elite among Bermudians in a lucrative chase for thousands in prize money. ⊠ *Royal Bermuda Yacht Club, 15 Point Pleasant Rd., Hamilton* ☎ *441/295–2214* ⊕ *www. bermudagoldcup.com.*

> ### ON A ROLL
>
> **Olde Town Railway.** Step back in time and give your feet a little rest by hopping onboard a trolley (in the form of an old-fashioned train) to take a rolling tour around St. George's. You get an hour's narrated tour, departing from York Street, for $25 for adults and $12 for children. The trolley tours operate with a minimum of two people. ⊠ *37 York St., St. George's* ☎ *441/297–4299.*

Bermuda Ocean Race. This race, sponsored by the St. George's Dinghy and Sports Club—setting out from Annapolis, Maryland, to Bermuda— takes place every other year in June, in even-numbered years. ⊠ *St. George's Dinghy and Sports Club, 24 Cut Rd., St. George's* ☎ *441/297– 1612* ⊕ *www.stgdsc.bm.*

Marion (MA)-to-Bermuda Cruising Yacht Race. Only slightly smaller in scale than the Newport-to-Bermuda, this race is held in June of odd-numbered years. Contact the Royal Hamilton Amateur Dinghy Club for information on where to watch it. ⊠ *Royal Hamilton Amateur Dinghy Club, 26 Pomander Rd., Paget* ☎ *441/236–2250* ⊕ *www.rhadc.bm.*

Newport (RI)-to-Bermuda Ocean Yacht Race. Powerhouse yachtsmen flock to this event in June. The race takes place every two years, in even-numbered years. Be sure to attend the after-race party—it's open to the public and is always extremely well attended. Contact the Royal Bermuda Yacht Club for more information. ⊠ *Royal Bermuda Yacht Club, 15 Point Pleasant Rd., Hamilton* ☎ *241/295–2214* ⊕ *www.rbyc.bm.*

Non-Mariners Race. Though not as prestigious as other Bermuda sailing yacht races, this annual race, which takes place in July or August during Cup Match weekend (the annual cricket holiday), is one of the highlights of the year. Held at the Sandys Boat Club at Mangrove Bay, the goal of this race is simple: to see whose boat (constructed on the beach minutes before) can make it out of the harbor without sinking. Easy to watch, as the boats never get very far from land, this race sets the stage for an afternoon of music, barbecue, local political satire, and merry-making. Legend has it that someone even tried to float an old bus one year. A good viewpoint from which to watch the race is the Somerset Country Square Pub (see ⇨ *Chapter 2, Where to Eat*). ⊠ *Sandys Boat Club, 8 Mangrove Bay Rd., Mangrove Bay, Somerset* ☎ *441/234–2248* ⊕ *www.sandysboatclub.com.*

RENTALS

Outfitters like **Blue Hole Watersports** and H20 Sports (*see* ⇨ *Aquatic Adventures*) have a range of craft to rent and also offer lessons for beginners.

Royal Hamilton Amateur Dinghy Club. If you're a sailor, it's worth checking out Royal Hamilton Amateur Dinghy Club, which is the main center for sailors in Hamilton and offers lessons for beginners. If you know what you're doing and fancy taking part in some amateur racing, this is the place to be on a Wednesday evening. Just turn up at the dock from about 5.30 pm —skippers are always looking for willing crew members. There's also a club barbecue afterwards and everyone is welcome. ⊠ *25 Pomander Rd., Paget* ☎ *441/236–2250* ⊕ *www.rhadc.com.*

SCUBA DIVING

Bermuda has all the ingredients for classic scuba diving—reefs, wrecks, underwater caves, a variety of coral and marine life, and clear, warm water. Although you can dive year-round (you will have to bring your own gear in winter, when dive shops are closed), the best months are May through October, when the water is calmest and warmest. No prior certification is necessary. Novices can learn the basics and dive in water up to 25 feet deep on the same day. Three-hour resort courses (about $200) teach the basics in a pool, on the beach, or off a dive boat, and culminate in a reef or wreck dive.

6

The easiest day trips involve exploring the south-shore reefs that lie inshore. These reefs may be the most dramatic in Bermuda. The ocean-side drop-off exceeds 60 feet in some places, and the coral is so honey-combed with caves, ledges, and holes that opportunities for discovery are pretty much infinite. Despite concerns about dying coral and dwindling fish populations, most of Bermuda's reefs are still in good health. No one eager to swim with multicolor schools of fish or the occasional barracuda will be disappointed. ⚠ **In the interest of preservation, the removal of coral is illegal and subject to hefty fines.**

Dive shops around Bermuda prominently display a map of the outlying reef system and its wreck sites. Only 38 of the wrecks from the past three centuries are marked. They're the larger wrecks that are still in good condition. The nautical carnage includes some 300 wreck sites—an astonishing number—many of which are well preserved. As a general rule, the more recent the wreck or the more deeply submerged it is, the better its condition. Most of the well-preserved wrecks are to the north and east, and dive depths range between 25 feet and 80 feet. Several wrecks off the western end of the island are in relatively shallow water, 30 feet or less, making them accessible to novice divers and even snorkelers.

Blue Water Divers and Watersports. The major operator for wrecks on the western side of the island, Blue Water Divers offers lessons, tours, and rentals. The lesson-and-dive package for first-time divers, including equipment, costs $135 for one tank or $185 for two tanks. From the Elbow Beach Hotel location, you can ride a diver-propulsion vehicle (DPV), which is like an underwater scooter, past a wreck and through caves and canyons. A one-tank dive for experienced divers costs $80, and a two-tank dive is $120. With two tanks—the more commonly offered package—you can explore two or more wrecks in one four-hour outing. For all necessary equipment—mask, fins, snorkel, scuba

CLOSE UP

Shocking Pink!

The sands of the world's beaches come in many hues, from basaltic black to gleaming quartz white, with a rainbow of red, green, yellow, and brown thrown in—and yes, even pink. Pink sand is considered choice by many beach connoisseurs, and Bermuda's south shore has plenty of it. You'll find the rosy tint of the island's sand most intense in the bright sun of midday, but in the gentler light of early morning and late afternoon the hue can appear darker, tending toward mauve.

In only a few regions where tropical coral reefs flourish offshore do pink-sand beaches form. What makes the sand pink is an amalgam of calcium-rich shells and fragments of invertebrate sea creatures, from minute, single-cell protozoa to spiny sea urchins. Chiefly responsible are foraminifera ("foram" for short), a type of protozoan that lives in great profusion in reef environments. The microscopic red *Homotrema rubrum* (red foram) variety is numerous both on the reefs and in the ocean sediments that surround Bermuda, and their persistent red pigment remains even in the microscopic "skeletons" these animals leave behind when they die. The red gets mixed in with other (predominantly white) reef debris—broken clam and snail shells, fragments of coral—and, when washed ashore, forms the island's signature pink sand.

The most visited pink-sand beaches are Warwick Long Bay Beach and Horseshoe Bay in Southampton. But just about any beach you visit on the south shore will have the famous sand in abundance.

---

apparatus, and wet suit (if needed)— it's $15 apiece. This operator is not to be confused with Dive Bermuda, despite the Web address. Kayaks are also on offer from $40 an hour, and snorkel gear is $20 an hour or $40 for 24 hours. ⊠ *Elbow Beach Hotel, 60 S. Shore Rd., Paget Parish* ☎ *441/232–2909* ⊕ *www.divebermuda.com* ⊠ *Robinson's Marina, Somerset Bridge, Sandys Parish* ☎ *441/234–1034.*

Dive Bermuda. This is an environmentally-friendly dive shop, as instructors go out of their way to protect Bermuda's reefs and fish. Dive Bermuda has been awarded National Geographic Dive Centre status and is the only center on the island to offer courses sanctioned by the world-renowned environmental organization. It has also received an environmental excellence award from PADI (Professional Association of Diving Instructors). For $200 you can opt for a Discover Scuba Diving course, which includes a lesson, dive, and equipment. For experienced divers, a single-tank dive costs $135 and a double-tank dive costs $195. Group rates and multiple dives cost less. ⊠ *Fairmont Southampton Resort, 101 S. Shore Rd., Southampton* ☎ *441/238–2332* ⊕ *www. bermudascuba.com.*

Fodor's Choice ★ **Triangle Diving.** For East End diving among wrecks and coral reefs, head for this outfitter at the Grotto Bay Beach Resort. A range of dive tours is offered, as well as PADI certification courses for $650. Friendly staff who really know their stuff and who never get tired of sharing their vast knowledge of Bermuda's wrecks make diving with this company all the more fun. The location also offers great access to one of Bermuda's most beautiful reefs at North Rock. Triangle is the only dive center on the island that offers enriched-air, or *nitrox*, diving. A Discover Scuba course for beginners, including lesson and dive, costs $160, while one-tank dives are $85 and two-tank dives are $120. ⊠ *Grotto Bay Beach Resort, 11 Blue Hole Hill, Bailey's Bay, Hamilton Parish* ☎ *441/293–7319* ⊕ *www.trianglediving.com.*

> ### SCUBA NEWBIES
>
> If you've never dived before but want to give it a try, Bermuda is a great place to start. All of the island's dive centers offer a Discover Scuba course, which allows first-time divers to take a brief lesson and follow an instructor on a shallow wreck or reef dive.

SNORKELING

The clarity of the water, the stunning array of coral reefs, and the shallow resting places of several wrecks make snorkeling in the waters around Bermuda—both inshore and offshore—particularly worthwhile. You can snorkel year-round, although a wet suit is advisable for anyone planning to spend a long time in the water in winter, when the water temperature can dip into the 60s. The water also tends to be rougher in winter, often restricting snorkeling to the protected areas of Harrington Sound and Castle Harbour. Underwater caves, grottoes, coral formations, and schools of small fish are the highlights of these areas.

Some of the best snorkeling sites are accessible only by boat. As the number of wrecks attests, navigating around Bermuda's reef-strewn waters is no simple task, especially for inexperienced boaters. If you rent a boat yourself, stick to the protected waters of the sounds, harbors, and bays, and be sure to ask for an ocean-navigation chart. These charts point out shallow waters, rocks, and hidden reefs.

For trips to the reefs, let someone else do the navigating—a charter-boat skipper or one of the snorkeling-cruise operators. Some of the best reefs for snorkeling, complete with shallow-water wrecks, are to the west, but where the tour guide or skipper goes often depends on the tide, weather, and water conditions. For snorkelers who demand privacy and freedom of movement, a boat charter (complete with captain) is the only answer, but the cost is considerable—$650 a day for a party of 18. By comparison, half a day of snorkeling on a regularly scheduled cruise generally costs $65 to $85, including equipment and instruction.

Fodor's Choice
★ **Church Bay.** When Bermudians are asked to name a favorite snorkeling spot, they invariably rank Church Bay in Southampton (at the western end of the south-shore beaches) at, or near, the top of the list. A small cove cut out of the coral cliffs, the bay is full of nooks and crannies, and the reefs are relatively close to shore. Snorkelers should exercise caution here (as you should everywhere along the south shore), as the water can be rough. ■TIP→ Bring your own snorkeling equipment, underwater camera, and fish food with you.

John Smith's Bay. This popular snorkeling spot off the south shore of Smith's Parish has several reefs close to the shore as well as the added safety of a lifeguard overseeing the beach. Beware, this site occasionally experiences rip currents.

Snorkel Park Beach. Off a rocky beach surrounded by the walls of the fort in the Dockyard, the Snorkel Park Beach is a cool place for kids. With a sunken cannon and other underwater features, it's worth a look if you're in the West End. You even get handed underwater fish cards so you can identify all the different species. There's a bar and restaurant, and you can rent umbrellas, shaded cabanas, and snorkel gear for a small fee. The beach is closed from November through April. ✉ *7 Maritime La., Dockyard, Sandys Parish* ⊕ *www.snorkelparkbeach. com* 🖃 *$5.*

Tobacco Bay. This beautiful bay is tucked in a cove near historic Fort St. Catherine's beach. Tobacco Bay offers wonderful snorkeling, public facilities, and equipment rentals, and there's a snack bar near the shore. This site is the most popular in St. George's and can get crowded.

Warwick Long Bay. On the south shore in Warwick, this ½-mi of beach is usually secluded and quiet. It's the perfect spot to check out Bermuda's underwater life without bumping into any other snorkelers. You'll have plenty of room to explore, and there's an inner reef very close to the shore.

West Whale Bay. Tiny West Whale Bay, off the western shore near the Port Royal Golf Course in Southampton, is quiet and usually uncrowded. The beach disappears during high tide, though, so check tide times first.

SNORKELING CRUISES

Snorkeling cruises, offered from April to November, are a less expensive albeit less personal way to experience the underwater world. Some boats carry up to 40 passengers to snorkeling sites but focus mostly on their music and bars (complimentary beverages are usually served on the trip back from the reefs). Smaller boats, which limit capacity to 10 to 16 passengers, offer more personal attention and focus more on the beautiful snorkeling areas themselves. Guides on such tours often relate interesting historical and ecological information about the island. To make sure you choose a boat that's right for you, ask for details before booking. Most companies can easily arrange private charters for groups.

Jessie James Cruises. Half-day trips aboard the 31-foot glass-bottomed boat *Pisces*, which holds up to 17 people, cost $65, $45 for children (ages 8–10). The boat takes you to three different sites, including at least two shipwrecks. ✉ *11 Clarence St., St. George's* ☎ *441/236–4804* ⊕ *www.jessiejames.bm.*

★ **Restless Native Tours.** Captain Kirk Ward has regularly scheduled sailing and snorkeling trips to the outer reefs on a 50-by-30-foot catamaran. With a crash course in Bermuda's marine life, plus fresh cookies on board, it's hard to resist this popular outfitter. The tours depart from wharfs all over the island. ☎ *441/531–8149* ⊕ *www.restlessnative.bm.*

SNORKELING EQUIPMENT RENTALS

Snorkeling equipment and sometimes underwater cameras are available for rent at most major hotels and at several marinas, as well as from the snorkeling concession stand at Warwick Long Bay. Grotto Bay Beach, Resort Rosewood Tucker's Point, Pompano Beach Club, and Fairmont Southampton Resort have dive operators on-site. A deposit or credit-card number is usually required when renting equipment.

Pompano Beach Club Watersports Centre. Equipment at Pompano rents for $6 per hour, for a mask, snorkel, and flippers. The water-sports center also rents low-powered vessels and kayaks, but it is only open from May through October. ⊠ *36 Pompano Beach Rd., Southampton Parish* ☎ *441/234–0222.*

H2O Sports. You can rent mask, snorkel, and flippers here for $20 per 24-hour period. Two of three pieces cost just $10. The staff will happily explain the best snorkeling spots to visit and what to look out for. ⊠ *Cambridge Beaches Resort, 30 Kings Point Rd., Somerset* ☎ *441/234–3082* ⊕ *www.h2osportsbermuda.com.*

SOCCER

6

Football (soccer) season runs from September through April in Bermuda. One of Bermuda's two national sports, football is massively popular among Bermudians, who often crowd matches in the evening and on weekends. You can watch local teams in various age divisions battle it out on fields around the island.

The Bermuda Hogges are the island's only professional football team. They play in the American United Soccer League Division Two against sides from places on the eastern coast of America like Richmond and Charlotte. They play their home games at the Bermuda National Sports Centre during the summer months. Tickets cost between $25 and $35.

TENNIS

Bermuda has one tennis court for every 600 residents, a ratio that even the most tennis-crazed countries would find difficult to match. Many are private, but the public has access to more than 70 courts in 20 locations. Courts are inexpensive and seldom full. Hourly rates for nonguests are about $15 to $20. You might want to consider bringing along a few fresh cans of balls, because balls in Bermuda cost $6 to $7 per can—two to three times the rate in the United States. Among the surfaces used in Bermuda are Har-Tru, clay, cork, and hard composites, of which the relatively slow Plexipave composite is the most prevalent. Despite Bermuda's British roots, the island has no grass court.

Wind, heat (in summer), and humidity are the most distinct characteristics of Bermudian tennis. From October through March, when daytime temperatures rarely exceed 80°F, play is comfortable throughout the day. But in summer the heat radiating from the court (especially hard courts) can make play uncomfortable between 11 am and 3 pm, so some clubs take a midday break. Most tennis facilities offer lessons, ranging

CLOSE UP

Aquatic Adventures

Whether it's renting a glass-bottomed kayak for a gentle paddle over the reefs, taking a motorboat for a spin, or spending an adrenaline-filled afternoon wakeboarding, getting out on the water is an essential part of the Bermuda experience.

As well as snorkeling tours and various other boat trips, you could try snuba, a kind of intermediary step between snorkeling and scuba diving. It involves a short training session and a shallow dive, usually at Daniel's Head Marine Park in Somerset. You don't need qualifications, experience, or too much cumbersome dive gear, so it is a popular option for people who have never dived before.

Bermuda Waterski and Wakeboard Centre. International competitor Kent Richardson represented Bermuda at nine World Championships and has also been in the Pan Am games. He took a trick skiing bronze medal at the Latin American games, but don't be intimidated—he's also a patient teacher. His business operates at the same location as Somerset Bridge Watersports at Robinson's Marina from mid-April to October. It's $190 for the hour, $100 per half hour. You can take your pick from waterskiing, wakeboarding, surfing, or tubing, or mix it up with a bit of everything. The price is for the time, which is split among however many people are on the boat. He can take up to six at a time, but three or four is usually a good number to allow a decent amount of time using the equipment. ✉ *Robinson's Marina, Somerset Bridge, Sandys Parish* ☎ *441/234–3354.*

Blue Hole Watersports. Based out of the Grotto Bay Resort, Blue Hole has you covered in the East End of

the island. Cruise the waters and soak up some rays in a Sun Cat, a low-powered floating deck chair, for $35 per half hour or $50 for an hour. You can rent kayaks; a single costs $20 for the first hour, and a double costs $30 for the first hour, then $15 per hour. Blue Hole also offers windsurfing and sunfish sailboat rentals for around $35 per hour, and motorboats starting at $90 for two hours. There's a gorgeous sheltered beach with a small wreck sunk just off-shore for snorkelers. A snorkeling set is $8 an hour or $24 for 24 hours. ✉ *Grotto Bay Beach Resort, 11 Blue Hole Hill, Bailey's Bay, Hamilton Parish* ☎ *441/293–2915, 441/293–8333* ⊕ *www.blueholewater.bm.*

Fantasea Bermuda. You're spoiled for choice with this one-stop recreational company. There are snorkeling tours, diving, sightseeing cruises, glass-bottom boat trips, and even banana boat rides. The whale-watching tours in March and April are immensely popular, when you can get close to the majestic humpbacks as they migrate north. Take your pick of a cruise-and-kayak or boat-and-bike ecotour for a closer look at some of the prettiest spots on the island. The three-hour Catamaran Coral Reef Snorkel aboard a luxury catamaran costs $65, while a 90-minute sunset sail with complimentary Dark 'n Stormy and live music costs $50. Inshore fishing trips are also offered at $95 per person. Most tours depart from Dockyard, near the cruise-ship terminal. Fantasea will even book golf tee times and spa treatments for you. ✉ *5 Point Pleasant Rd., Albuoy's Point, Hamilton* ☎ *441/236–1300* ⊕ *www.fantasea.bm.*

H2O Sports. Located at Mangrove Bay, Somerset, H2O offers just about everything there is to do on the water: sailing, boat rentals, kayaking, as well as instruction from experienced mariners. Formerly called Windjammer Watersports, it continues to rent 17-foot-long motorboats for $80 for the first hour, plus $30 for each additional hour. Mariners can take out a 17-foot sailboat at $80 for the first hour, and $10 for each additional. 90-minute sailing lessons are also available. See the island at speed with a guided Jet Ski tour for $135. Snorkeling gear costs $20 for 24 hours. ⊠ *Cambridge Beaches Resort, 30 Kings Point Rd., Sandys Parish* ☎ *441/234–3082* ✆ *h2osportsbermuda@yahoo.com* ⊕ *www. h2osportsbermuda.com.*

Pompano Beach Club. For a more relaxed aquatic experience, check out Pompano Beach Club. Several low-powered vessels are available, including a SunCat cruiser ($60 per hour), Hobie Cat sailboat ($60 per hour), two-person glass-bottom kayak ($40 per hour), and water tricycle ($30 per hour). Rates are cheaper for hotel guests. The water-sports center is open from May to October. Snorkeling equipment is also available to rent at $6 per hour. ⊠ *36 Pompano Beach Rd., Southampton Parish* ☎ *441/234– 0222* ⊕ *www.pompanobeachclub.com.*

Somerset Bridge Watersports. This West End outfitter rents 13- and 15-foot Boston Whalers and is right next to Somerset Bridge. Rates are $75 for two hours, $120 for four hours, $165 for six hours, or $200 for eight hours, plus the cost of gas. You can also take a speed tour of the western end of the island on a Jet Ski for $105 for a single and

$125 for a double. The tour takes you through Ely's Harbour, Mangrove Bay, above the Sea Gardens coral formations, and to the Vixen shipwreck site. Groups are kept small—no more than six Jet Skiers per guide. Single and double kayaks are also available starting at $15 an hour. ⊠ *Robinson's Marina, Somerset Bridge, Sandys Parish* ☎ *441/234–0914* ⊕ *www. bdawatersports.com.*

Snorkel Park Beach. This new family-friendly venue has all the water sports you could want in one location. It's tucked away through a limestone tunnel in the northwest corner of Dockyard, next to the National Museum of Bermuda, but it's just a stone's throw from the cruise-ship pier. Jet Ski tours are offered for $85 per half hour and $145 for an hour. Kayaks can be put to good use for $20 an hour, or you can rent a paddleboat for the same price. Snorkeling equipment is $10 an hour. The kids will love it, as they get free buckets and sand toys and there's a huge waterslide for them. Scuba dives can also be arranged. There's a bar and resaturant on-site, but there's also a $5 daytime admission. The beach is closed from November through April. ⊠ *7 Maritime La., Dockyard, undefined, Sandys Parish* ☎ *441/234–6989* ⊕ *www.snorkelparkbeach.com* ⊠ *$5.*

6

from $30 to $50 for 30 minutes of instruction, and racket rentals for $4 to $6 per hour or per play.

Coral Beach & Tennis Club. Introduction by a member is required to play at this exclusive club, which is the site of the XL Capital Bermuda Open tournament. Coral Beach has eight clay courts, three of which are floodlighted. It's open daily from 8:30 to 1 and from 2 to 6. Resident pro James Collieson is the man to talk to about scheduling lessons, which run $55 for a half hour and $100 for an hour. Tennis whites are required. ⊠ *34 S. Shore Rd., Paget Parish* ☎ *441/236–2233* ⊕ *www. coralbeachclub.com.*

Elbow Beach Tennis Facility. This facility is fortunate to have as its director of tennis David Lambert, who is also a former president of the Bermuda Lawn Tennis Association. There are five Plexipave courts on hand, three with lights, and hours of play are 8 am to 7 pm daily. Courts cost $10 per hour for guests of Elbow Beach Resort or $12 per hour for members of the public. Lessons and match play can be arranged for hotel guests or other visitors at $40 per half hour, $75 for the hour. This facility also rents rackets and repairs rackets. ⊠ *Elbow Beach Resort, 60 S. Shore Rd., Paget Parish* ☎ *441/236–8737* ⊕ *www.elbowtennisbda.com.*

Fairmont Southampton Tennis Club. Despite their position at the water's edge, the Plexipave hard courts here are reasonably shielded from the wind, although the breeze can be swirling and difficult. Six courts are at hand, costing $19 per hotel guest per day or $15 for a half-day. There's an added cost of $8 per hour to use the floodlights. Hours of service are daily from 8.30 to 6. Lessons from pro Mark Cordeiro are available at $45 per half hour or $90 per hour. ⊠ *Fairmont Southampton, 101 S. Shore Rd., Southampton Parish* ☎ *441/236–6950.*

P & R Tennis at Grotto Bay Beach Resort. A little more than a stone's throw from the L.F. Wade International Airport, Grotto Bay has four Plexipave cork-based courts, two lighted, with an hourly rate of $12, $15 under the lights. It's open daily, 8 to 7, with a midday break from 11–3 on weekdays. Tennis pros Paul Alves and Romar Douglas offer lessons from $35 per half hour and $55 per full hour. For juniors the cost is $25 per half hour and $40 per hour. Tennis attire is required. ⊠ *11 Blue Hole Hill, Bailey's Bay, Hamilton Parish* ☎ *441/293–8333, 441/293–3420.*

Pomander Gate Tennis Club. There are five hard courts available (four with lighting) at this scenic club located off Hamilton Harbour. Temporary membership is available for $35 per couple per week. Hours of play are 7 am to 11 pm on weekdays, until 10 pm on weekends. ⊠ *21 Pomander Rd., Paget Parish* ☎ *441/236–5400.*

Port Royal Tennis Courts. Port Royal Golf Course has four hard courts tucked away to the west of the clubhouse, two of which are floodlit. A host of pros, including head pro Steve Bean, are on hand to offer instruction. Lessons are $40 per half-hour and $75 per hour. Rates for court play are the cheapest on the island; $10 per hour in the day and $15 per hour at night—it's open until 10 pm. ⊠ *Port Royal Golf Course, 5 Middle Rd., Southampton Parish* ☎ *441/535–3695.*

W.E.R. Joell Tennis Stadium. This government-run facility is the busiest of Bermuda's tennis courts, the inland location ideal for combating strong winds. Of the eight all-weather courts available, five are Plexi-Cushion and three are Har-Tru. Three courts in the main stadium have floodlights. Hours are from 8 am to 10 pm weekdays and from 8 to 7 on weekends (closing time is 5 pm during winter months). Rates are $10 per hour during the day and $20 per hour at night. Tennis attire is required, and lessons are available starting at $35 per half hour and $75 per full hour. ✉ *2 Marsh Folly Rd., Pembroke Parish* ☎ *441/292–0105.*

TENNIS TOURNAMENTS

Bermuda Lawn Tennis Association. Established in 1964, the association is the governing body for tennis in Bermuda and hosts all the important tennis events on the island. Ask for an events calendar. ☎ *441/296–0834* ⊕ *www.blta.bm.*

International Beach Tennis Tournament. The pink sand of Horseshoe Bay hosts the island's beach tennis tournaments at the end of August. A cross between tennis and beach volleyball, the three-day tournament features "stars" of the game, plus an amateur division that anyone can enter. If you're not visiting in August, the Bermuda Beach Tennis Association runs regular pickup games at Horseshoe Bay every Sunday from 1 to 5 pm throughout the summer. ☎ *441/334–8669* ⊕ *www.bermudabeachtennis.com.*

XL Capital Bermuda Open. The clay courts at the Coral Beach & Tennis Club host this ATP Tour, a USTA-sanctioned event with the world's top professionals. Big names, such as Patrick Rafter and Todd Eldridge, have played in this event, as well as several of Bermuda's own tennis stars, such as James Collieson. Once held every April, it is no longer an annual event. In November there's back-to-back tournament activity at the club, too. The action begins with the Bermuda Lawn Tennis Club Invitational followed by the Coral Beach Club Invitational.

6

Golf

WORD OF MOUTH

"I'm impressed with the way the Bermuda courses have improved in recent years. The island really is a great golf destination now. Tucker's Point is a fine championship course, much better than the old Castle Harbour it replaced. Port Royal, my favorite, [has had] a complete makeover. And Mid Ocean is in great condition since it hosted the Grand Slam. Belmont Hills is sort of gimmicky, but fun, and Riddell's Bay is a super short course."

—7handicap

"Port Royal is a nice course, and the 16th hole is the whole enchilada. I had to hit my tee shot toward the ocean because of the wind."

—iamawfull

Updated by
Dale Leather-
man and
Simon Jones

Golf is an important facet of Bermuda sporting life, where golf courses make up nearly 17% of the island's 21.6 square mi. The scenery on the courses is quite often spectacular, with trees and shrubs decked out in multicolor blossoms against a backdrop of brilliant blue sea and sky. The layouts may be shorter than what you're accustomed to, but they're remarkably challenging, thanks to capricious ocean breezes, daunting natural terrain, and the clever work of world-class golf architects.

Of the seven 18-hole courses and one 9-hole layout on Bermuda, five are championship venues: Belmont Hills, the Mid Ocean Club, Port Royal, Riddell's Bay, and Tucker's Point. All are well maintained, but you should not expect the springy bent grass fairways and fast greens typical of U.S. golf courses. The rough is coarse Bermuda grass that will turn your club in your hands. Most clubs have TifEagle or Tifdwarf greens—finer-bladed grasses that are drought-resistant and putt faster and truer than Bermuda grass. Because the island's freshwater supply is limited, watering is usually devoted to the greens and tees, which means the fairways are likely to be firm and give you lots of roll. Expect plenty of sand hazards and wind—*especially* wind.

Many courses overseed with rye grass sometime between late September and early November to maintain color and texture through the cooler winter months. Some courses use temporary greens, whereas others keep their regular greens in play during the reseeding process. This makes for inaccurate putting situations; so if you're visiting in fall, call ahead to find out the condition of the greens. Though all courses now have carts, there's often a "cart path only" rule in force to protect the fairways, so expect to do some walking.

Many Bermudian tracks have holes on the ocean or atop seaside cliffs. They're wonderfully scenic, but the wind and that big natural water hazard can play havoc with your game.

All courses in Bermuda have dress codes: long pants or Bermuda (knee-length) shorts and collared shirts for both men and women. Denim is not allowed. ■TIP→ **Bermudian men always wear color-coordinated knee-high socks with their shorts on other occasions, but it's okay to go bare-legged on the golf course.**

Courses in Bermuda are rated by the United States Golf Association (USGA), just as they are in the States, so you can tell at a glance how difficult a course is. For example, a par-72 course with a rating of 68 means that a scratch golfer (one who usually shoots par) should be four under par for the round. High handicappers should score better than usual, too.

Reserve tee times before you leave home or ask your hotel concierge to do so as soon as you arrive. This is especially necessary to access the private courses. "Sunset" tee times, available at lower greens fees, generally start at 3 pm, but call ahead to be sure.

Lessons, available at all courses, cost $50 to $70 for a half hour, and $100 to $120 for an hour. Club rentals cost $25 to $45. Caddies are available only at the Mid Ocean Club, where you'll pay $65 per golf bag plus a tip of 10 to 15 percent.

GOLF COURSES

HAMILTON AND CENTRAL PARISHES

Belmont Hills Golf Club. Opened in June 2003, Belmont Hills was designed by California architect Algie Pulley Jr. and built on the site of the former Belmont Manor and Golf Club, a haven for celebrities in the early 1900s. "Hills" was added to the course name to reflect the dramatic design features that Pulley used to replace the previous, rather mundane layout. This is now a real shot-making test, heavily contoured and with more water than most other Bermuda courses. The sand in the bunkers is the same used at the famed Augusta National, site of the Masters. A waterfall connects two man-made lakes that can come into play on several holes. The final four holes are particularly challenging because of their tight landing areas bordered by out-of-bounds stakes. A bad hit or intervention by the ever-present wind can lead to lost balls and penalties. The pressure continues until the ball is in the hole, because the greens are heavily bunkered and multitiered. Putting surfaces are well-maintained TifEagle grass. Fairways are attractively defined by palm trees, and an automated irrigation system keeps everything lush. The course has the island's only double green, a 14,000-square-foot putting surface on holes 1 and 10.

Highlight Hole: The 7th hole, a 178-yard par 3, is bordered by a waterfall.

Clubhouse: The main clubhouse with a private members' lounge stands on the site of the former Belmont Hotel, overlooking the 9th hole. The building has lovely views of the Great Sound and Hamilton Harbour, plus an airy lounge, bar, and pro shop.

Blu. The clubhouse restaurant is an extraordinary dining experience.

7

TOP 5 GOLF

■ **Belmont Hills.** "Hills" is the operative word for this heavily contoured shot-maker's test.

■ **Mid Ocean.** Walk in famous footsteps with a caddy at your side.

■ **Port Royal.** After a year-long renovation completed in January 2009, the quintessential Robert Trent Jones Sr. course has never looked better.

■ **Riddell's Bay.** The island's oldest course has tight fairways to keep you on your toes.

■ **Tucker's Point.** A real class act, Tucker's Point is an entirely new layout on the old Castle Harbour track.

Secrets from a Golf Pro

Golf courses elsewhere are often designed with the wind in mind—long downwind holes and short upwind holes. Not so in Bermuda, where the wind is anything but consistent or predictable. **Quirky air currents** make play on a Bermudian course different every day. The wind puts a premium on being able to hit the ball straight, and grossly exaggerates any slice or hook.

The **hard ground** of most Bermudian courses means you must abandon the strategy you use on heavily watered tracks. Your ball will run a lot in the fairway, so don't overestimate the distance to hazards. Around the greens, it's wise to run the ball to the hole rather than chipping. Not only will you find it difficult to get under the ball

on the firm fairways, but your shot will be subject to the vagaries of the wind. If you're in the clinging Bermuda grass rough, your club face is likely to turn if you try to swing through it.

How should you prepare for a Bermuda trip? Practice **run-up shots** from close-cropped lies using a 5- or 6-iron—or a putter from just off the green. Use midirons to practice **punching shots** from the rough, angling back into the fairway rather than trying to advance the ball straight ahead and risk landing in the rough again. Putting surfaces are often undulating and grainier than bent grass, so putts will break less than you expect. They'll also die much more quickly unless you use a firm stroke.

Its eclectic menu includes fork-tender Angus steaks; innovative seafood dishes such as salmon, crab, shrimp, and avocado wrapped in a tortilla; and irresistible desserts. ☎ *441/232–2323.*

✉ *25 Belmont Hills Dr., Warwick Parish* ☎ *441/236–6400* ⊕ *www.newsteadbelmonthills.com* ✍ *Greens fees $120 daily, $60 sunset (walking only after 3:30 pm). Mandatory cart rentals $35 per person. Pull cart rentals (sunset only) $15. Shoe rentals $15. Tailor-made club rentals $60. Lessons $60 for 30 minutes, $100 per hour* 🏌 *18 holes. 6,017 yards. Par 70. Rating: blue tees, 68.8; white tees, 68.4; red tees, 69.4.*

Ocean View Golf Course. If you want to play with locals or just mingle to talk golf, Ocean View is the place to be after the workday ends. Only 10 minutes from Hamilton, it's very popular. Switch tees on your second loop of the 9 holes for an 18-hole round playing 5,658 yards to a par of 70. The first hole is a tough par 5 with a long, tight fairway flanked by a coral wall on one side and a drop-off to the shore on the other. The course is aptly named; there are panoramas from many holes as well as from the clubhouse and the restaurant patio. The club has a 260-yard driving range where the wind is often at your back, giving you a pleasant feeling that your drives are longer than they really are.

Highlight Hole: The green on the 192-yard, par-3 9th hole is cut into a coral hillside that's landscaped with colorful plants. It's a demanding shot when the wind is gusting from the north or west.

Clubhouse: Inside Ocean View's modest clubhouse is a small restaurant.

Golf Courses

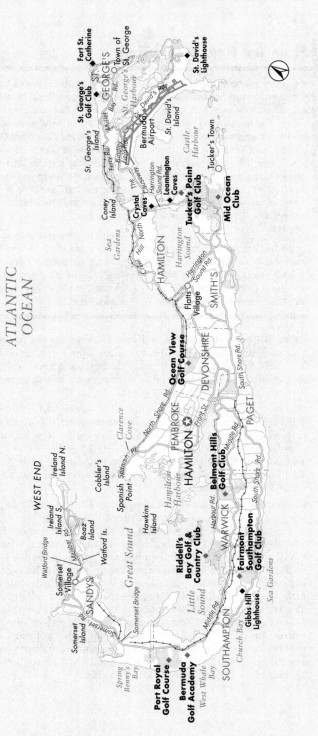

ATLANTIC OCEAN

WEST END

Fort St. Catherine
Town of St. George
St. George's
St. George's Golf Club
St. George's Island
St. David's Lighthouse
St. David's Island
Bermuda Airport
Mullet Bay Rd.
Ferry Rd.
Kindley Field Rd.
St. George's Harbour
St. David's Rd.

Coney Island
Crystal Caves
Leamington Caves
Harrington Sound Rd.
The Causeway
Tucker's Point Golf Club
Mid Ocean Club
Castle Harbour
Tucker's Town

Crawl Hill North
Sea Gardens
HAMILTON
Harrington Sound
Harrington Sound Rd.
Flatts Village
SMITH'S

Ocean View Golf Course
North Shore Rd.
PEMBROKE
DEVONSHIRE
South Shore Rd.
PAGET

Clarence Cove
Spanish Point
Spanish Pt.
HAMILTON
Front St.
Belmont Hills Golf Club
Hamilton Harbour
Harbour Rd.
Middle Rd.
WARWICK
Fairmont Southampton Golf Club
South Shore Rd.
Sea Gardens

Cobbler's Island
Hawkins Island
Riddell's Bay Golf & Country Club
Little Sound

Ireland Island N.
Ireland Island S.
Boaz Island
Watford Bridge
Malabar Rd.
Watford Is.
Somerset Village
Somerset Island
Somerset Rd.
Somerset Bridge
SANDYS
Great Sound

Spring Benny's Bay
West Whale Bay
Port Royal Golf Course
Bermuda Golf Academy
SOUTHAMPTON
Gibbs Hill Lighthouse
Middle Rd.
Church Bay

2 miles
3 km

KEY
+—+—+ Railway Trail

From Tee Time to Bed Time

If you stay in a hotel with its own golf course or one that has agreements with some of the golf clubs, it cuts out much of the planning you'll have to make on your own. For instance, the **Fairmont Southampton Resort** has its own 18-hole executive course and access agreement with **Riddell's Bay Golf & Country Club**. Tee times are blocked for hotel guests and a shuttle is provided to and from the hotel.

At the **Tucker's Point Club**, which opened its hotel and spa in the spring of 2009, you can contrast the old and the new in golf course designs without straying very far from the resort.

On-site is Roger Rulewich's fabulous design, laid down atop the old Castle Harbour Golf Club, designed by his mentor, Robert Trent Jones Sr. Literally next door is the classic **Mid Ocean Club**, a Charles Blair Macdonald track redesigned by Jones in 1953. You will have seen Mid Ocean on television during the 2007 and 2008 PGA Grand Slams, and you'll be anxious to try your luck.

When you make your lodging arrangements, check to see what golf packages and perks are available. Many hoteliers are also members at the clubs and are happy to facilitate arrangements.

Out of Bounds Restaurant and Bar. Overlooking the north shore, Out of Bounds Restaurant and Bar is open for breakfast and lunch. The small dining room has a menu with the usual burgers, sandwiches, and salads, as well as Bermudian favorites such as fish chowder and fish-cake sandwiches. ☎ *441/295–4916.*

✉ *2 Barker's Hill, off N. Shore Rd., Devonshire Parish* ☎ *441/295– 9092* ⊕ *www.oceanviewgolf.bm* ▤ *Greens fees (18 holes) $89 with cart, $75 walking before 3 pm; $65 sunset with cart or $55 walking. (9 holes) $74 with cart, $65 walking before 3 pm; $54 sunset with cart, $50 walking. Club rentals $40. Lessons $50 for half hour ⅃ 9 holes. 2,940 yards. Par 35. Rating: 68 playing white then blue tees, 68.7 playing yellow then red tees.*

Riddell's Bay Golf & Country Club. Opened in 1922, Riddell's Bay is Bermuda's oldest course and one of the island's "must plays" for its scenery and precise shot-placing demands. Designed by Devereaux Emmett, who went on to plot the Congressional Golf Club near Washington, D.C., it receives periodic fine-tuning and upgrading at the hands of Ed Beidel. Don't let the 5,800-yard length fool you; this tight layout is cleverly woven into a peninsula that is only 600 yards wide in some places. The first hole, a 424-yard par 4 (par 5 for women) doglegs to an elevated green, serving notice of difficulty to come. Positioned between Riddell's Bay and the Great Sound, and with Popplewell's Pond in the interior, the course has water views and a fair number of water encounters. For instance, the sea lies all along the right side of dogleg on hole 8, and the 9th demands a drive across an inlet. The 10th tee box perches above a beautiful inlet where boats are moored.

Highlight Hole: The 8th hole, a 360-yard par 4, doglegs along the water to a green near the brink. With a tailwind, big hitters often go for the green. The Gibbs Hill Lighthouse is a distant backdrop.

Clubhouse: The Riddell's Bay clubhouse, a refurbished 150-year-old farmhouse, has locker rooms, a well-stocked pro shop, a bar made of Bermuda cedar, a lounge overlooking the 18th green and 1st tee, and a dining room.

Riddell's Bay dining room. On the menu are salads (including a nice smoked salmon and goat cheese plate), sandwiches (the Riddell's Bay Fishcake is a signature dish), burgers and, of course, a fine fish chowder. The dining room is open 10 am to 3 pm weekdays and 8 am to 4 pm weekends.

✉ *Riddell's Bay Rd., Warwick Parish* ☎ *441/238–1060* ⊕ *www. riddellsbay.com* ✑ *Greens fees $155, including mandatory cart. Shoe rentals $15. Club rentals $40. Lessons $50 for half hour, $100 for hour* ⅃ *18 holes. 5,854 yards. Par 70 (72 for women). Rating: blue tees, 69; white tees, 67.*

ST. GEORGE'S AND EASTERN PARISHES

★ **Mid Ocean Club.** The elite Mid Ocean Club is a 1921 Charles Blair Macdonald design revamped in 1953 by Robert Trent Jones Sr. *Golf Digest* ranked it 45th in the top 50 courses outside the United States. Patrons include celebrities and politicians such as Michael Douglas and Catherine Zeta-Jones, New York City Mayor Michael Bloomberg, and Michael Jordan. Presidents Eisenhower, Bush Sr., and Clinton have also played here. The club has a genteel air, and a great sense of history. Even though it's expensive, you must play it at least once, walking it with a caddy to savor the traditional golf experience and the scenery.

There are many holes near ocean cliffs, but you'll want to linger on the back tee of the last hole, where the view up the coast is spectacular. You'll come away with memories of the course's many elevation changes and tight doglegs. One in particular is the 5th hole, Cape, where Babe Ruth is said to have splashed a dozen balls in Mangrove Lake as he tried to land too far down the fairway on the other side. Because Mid Ocean is the second-longest course on the island, the average woman player may have trouble reaching greens in regulation—and some men, too, especially when the wind is up.

If you haven't been here since 2006, you'll find the layout is now irrigated and the TifEagle greens are truer and faster than ever. Many trees were pruned or removed to increase airflow and encourage grass growth. This all happened in 2007 in preparation for the televised PGA Grand Slam, which the club hosted that year and again in October 2008. The tournament was held for years in Hawaii, so this was a coup for Mid Ocean and Bermuda.

Highlight Hole: The 433-yard 5th is a par-4 dogleg around Mangrove Lake. The elevated tees sit atop a hillside of flowering shrubbery, with the lake below. It's tempting to take a big shortcut over the water, but remember the Babe's experience. To the left of the green, a steep embankment funnels balls down into a bunker, setting up a delicate sand shot to the putting surface.

Clubhouse: Overlooking the 18th hole and the south shore, the Mid Ocean's pink clubhouse is classically Bermudian down to the interior cedar trim. The pro shop offers a range of golfing goodies. Several of the club's rooms commemorate famous American and British 20th-century politicians who played the course—there's the Churchill Bar, the Eisenhower Dining Room, and the MacMillan Television Room. The latter two are for members only, but you can have a drink in the bar.

Eden Room. Open to non-members for breakfast and lunch on Monday, Wednesday, and Friday, the Eden Room menu includes a wide selection of salads, soups, and sandwiches. 🕾 *441/293–0330.*

✉ *1 Mid Ocean Dr., off S. Shore Rd., Tucker's Town* 🕾 *441/293–1215* ⊕ *www.themidoceanclubbermuda.com* 🖳 *Greens fees $250 ($100 when playing with a member). Non-members must be sponsored by a club member (your hotelier can arrange this); non-member starting times available Mon., Wed., and Fri. except holidays. Caddies $55 for double or $65 for single per bag (tip not included). Cart rental $30 per person. Shoe rentals $6. Club rentals $45. Lessons $55 a half hour, $100 per hour.* ⛳ *18 holes. 6,548 yards. Par 71. Rating: blue tees, 73.0; white tees, 71.3; red tees, 75.0.*

St. George's Golf Club. Reopened in June 2011 after a three year closure, the St. George's Golf Club is one of Bermuda's prettiest golf courses, with panoramic sea views all the way around. The Robert Trent Jones, Sr. course dominates a secluded headland at the island's northeastern end. It might be a short course, but challenges still abound. Obstacles lurk at every corner, whether it is the steep bunker banks, the Atlantic Ocean, or the strong north wind that sweeps in from the sea. Play here while you can; the future of the course remains uncertain, as the lease is set to expire in June 2012. That lease could be extended, but there is also talk of a Nick Faldo- designed course as part of the Park Hyatt development.

Highlight Hole: On the par-4 thirteenth hole you can set your tee shot off straight across the Atlantic to cut off the dog-leg. Or play it safe and roll with the 294 yards by going down the fairway.

Clubhouse: The St. George's Club provides the perfect backdrop to this beautiful course. You can take advantage of the club's showers as well as a full bar and restaurant.

Griffin's Bistro and Bar. The cozy dining room–bar and patio, which are tended by a friendly and efficient staff, have a fine view of the north shore and the ramparts of Fort St. Catherine. Breakfast and lunch are served daily 8 am to 4 pm, and dinner after 6 pm on Friday. The menu includes sandwiches and salads as well as many local favorites such as fish-and-chips, grilled fresh fish, steaks, the award-winning Alfred's Fish Chowder, and St. David's fish cake (a codfish-and-mashed-potato concoction flavored with parsley and thyme).

✉ *6 Rose Hill, St. George's Parish* 🕾 *441/297–1200* ⊕ *www. stgeorgesgolf.bm* 🖳 *Greens fees $60. Club rentals $60. Golf hand cart $10.* ⛳ *18 holes. 4,043 yards. Par 62.*

Fodor's Choice
★

Tucker's Point Golf Club. If you remember the old Castle Harbour Golf Club, you'll recognize some of the views, but not the holes. Roger Rulewich, a former senior designer for the late Robert Trent Jones Sr., mapped out a stunning site layout in 2002, making the most of elevation changes and ocean views. It's longer than nearby Mid Ocean, and holds more surprises. On many

> **TAXI TO TEE**
>
> If you bring your own clubs, budget for taxis to get you to the various courses. It's dangerous to carry your golf bag on a scooter, and clubs are not allowed on public buses. Taxis are expensive, but most rides are relatively short.

holes you tee off toward the crest of a hill, not knowing what lies beyond. Topping the rise reveals the challenge, often involving a very elevated, sculpted green with a scenic vista. The course is fully irrigated and beautifully groomed. The final resort component—the 88-room Tucker's Point Hotel & Spa—opened in spring 2009. If you're not a guest at the hotel, you must have an introduction (your hotelier can do this) for playing and dining privileges.

Highlight Holes: There are many outstanding holes, but the par-4 17th is one of the most picturesque in Bermuda, with sweeping views of Tucker's Town and the Castle Islands. A rival is hole 13, where the perspective is the north coast and the Royal Navy Dockyard 20 mi away on the island's western tip.

Clubhouse: The 20,000-square-foot Tucker's Point Golf Clubhouse, a traditional Bermudian British–colonial design with covered verandas and tray ceilings, stands on a hilltop with a commanding view. Within are posh locker rooms, a large pro shop, and superb dining.

Grille. This elegant yet comfortable dining area has an extensive menu that includes sublime fish chowder, lamb, salmon, and tuna tartare, as well as catch-of-the-day and omelet specials. You can relax with a cocktail or dine alfresco on the second-floor veranda while enjoying a panorama of Castle Harbour and Tucker's Town. Lunch and dinner are served daily; in summer dinner is also served at the Beach Club. ☎ 441/298–6983.

✉ 9 Paynters Rd., St. George's Parish ☎ 441/298–6970 ⊕ www. tuckerspoint.com ⚑ Greens fees $250 with cart, $130 with cart for members' guests. Shoe rentals $15. Club rentals $75. Lessons $75 for half hour, $135 for hour ⚑ 18 holes. 6,500 yards. Par 70. Rating: blue tees, 71.2; white tees, 69.1; red tees, 69.7.

DOCKYARD AND WESTERN PARISHES

Bermuda Golf Academy. When you just want to practice or have some fun teaching the kids how to play golf in a relaxed environment, head for the Bermuda Golf Academy. The 320-yard driving range is floodlit at night until 10 and there are 40 practice bays. ■TIP→ **If you get a rainy day, fine-tune your game in one of the 25 covered bays.** You can also work on sand shots in the practice bunker or sharpen your putting on a practice green.

Especially attractive for families is the 18-hole miniature golf course, which features pagodas, a waterfall, waterways—even a drawbridge to hit over on the 16th hole. The minicourse is lighted at night and takes 45 to 60 minutes to complete. Adjacent are a new restaurant and small café.

East Meets West. As the name implies, the cuisine includes Japanese, Chinese, Balinese, English, Caribbean, Indian, and American. The café side has a wide range of hot sandwiches, wraps, salads, meins, noodles, and Indian dishes, plus full breakfasts. ☎ *441/238–8580*

✉ *10 Industrial Park Rd., off Middle Rd., Southampton Parish* ☎ *441/238–8800* 🖫 *Driving range $5, $6 after 5 pm and weekends. Miniature golf $12 adults, $8 children. Lessons $80 per hour.*

> ### DON'T REPLACE YOUR DIVOTS
>
> Bermuda grass is so called because it came to the U.S. from Bermuda, but it actually originated in Africa, where it's called Devil's Grass or Wire Grass. The grass is considered holy in India, where it's used to feed sacred cows. In ancient times, Romans boiled it and used the juice to stop bleeding. Bermuda grass is a creeping plant, putting down roots where nodes touch the earth. Once dislodged by your stroke, the mat of grass will not re-root, so don't bother to replace your divots. Instead, fill them with the sand and seed mixture on your cart.

Fairmont Southampton Golf Club. Spreading across the hillside below the high-rise Fairmont Southampton, this executive golf course is known for its steep terrain, giving players who opt to walk (for sunset tee times only) an excellent workout. The vertical drop on the first two holes alone is at least 200 feet, and the rise on the 4th hole makes 178 yards play like 220. The Ted Robinson design is a good warm-up for Bermuda's full-length courses, offering a legitimate test of wind and bunker play. The front nine has almost constant views of the ocean and is more difficult than the back nine, with tight holes calling for careful club selection.

Highlight Hole: The signature hole is the 214-yard 14th, but the most striking is the 174-yard 16th hole, which sits in a cup ringed by pink oleander bushes. The Gibbs Hill Lighthouse, less than a mile away, is the backdrop.

Clubhouse: Because the hotel and its restaurants are so close, there's no golf clubhouse per se, just a 10th-hole Golf Hut for snacks and drinks. The golf shop has a fine selection of quality golf wear and any essentials you might forget to bring. It has recently been completely renovated and is now twice as big.

Bacci. Above the Fairmont Southampton golf shop, this fine Italian restaurant overlooking the course is an excellent after golf option. ☎ *441/238–8000.*

Waterlot Inn. If you have a yearning for steak, catch the Fairmont Southampton hotel shuttle to the bottom of the hill, where the 320-year-old Waterlot Inn sits on the edge of the marina. It's unassuming from the outside, but inside it's all elegance, romance, and comfort, with beamed ceilings and windows overlooking the water and terrific sunsets. The Angus steaks here are among the best on the island, and the seafood is delectable, too. Waterlot Inn is open from 6–10 pm. ☎ 441/238–8000.

✉ *Fairmont Southampton Resort, 101 South Rd., Southampton Parish* ☎ *441/239–6952* ⊕ *www. fairmont.com/Southampton*

🎫 *Greens fees $84 before 2:30 pm with cart mandatory, $65 after 2:30 pm with cart or $45 walking. Pull-cart rental $7.50. Shoe rentals $10. Titleist club rentals $35. Lessons $50 a half hour, $100 per hour* 🏌 *18 holes. 2,684 yards. Par 54. Rating: 53.7.*

★ **Port Royal Golf Course.** One of three government-owned courses (Ocean View and St. George's are the others), Port Royal is a perennial local and visitor favorite. The course reopened in July 2009 after a year-long renovation that added irrigation, rebuilt tees and returfed them with Bermuda 419 grass, rebuilt and returfed greens with Tifeagle grass, and redesigned bunkers. Two holes, 12 and 13, have been rerouted and now play as a par 4 and par 3. The revamped course is 280 yards longer than before. It hosted the PGA Grand Slam in October 2009, 2010, and 2011, and is scheduled to host it in 2012.

One hole affected by the lengthening is the 16th, arguably Bermuda's best-known golf hole, which now plays 235 yards from the back tee. The green of this stunning par 3 occupies a treeless promontory with a backdrop of the blue waters and pink swands of Whale Bay. When the wind is blowing hard onshore, as it frequently does, this can be a tough green to reach. The holes leading up to the 16th are the icing on the cake, with ocean views on 7, 8, 9, and 15. The 1970 Robert Trent Jones Sr. layout has many elevated tees and greens and some clever doglegs. There are plenty of hills, on the back nine in particular.

Highlight Hole: Like the much-photographed 16th hole, the 412 yard, par-4 15th skirts the windswept cliffs along Whale Bay. The well-preserved remains of the Whale Bay Battery, a 19th-century fortification, stand next to the fairway.

Clubhouse: The Port Royal clubhouse also underwent renovation and reopened at the end of 2009. It is open daily at 10 am for lunch and dinner. Fresh Bermuda fish, burgers, peas and rice, and pasta are always on the menu. The bar has six flat-screen TVs, usually tuned to sports events.

✉ *Off Middle Rd., Southampton Parish* ☎ *441/234–0974, 441/234–4653 for automated tee-time reservations* ⊕ *www.portroyalgolf.bm* 🎫 *Greens fees: $180 including cart and practice balls. Sunset rates are $102 with cart, $95 walking. Shoe rentals $15. Club rentals $50. Lessons $60 for half hour* 🏌 *18 holes. 6,842 yards. Par 71. Rating: blue tees, 72.4; white tees, 70.2; red tees, 71.9; black tee 74.6.*

Shopping

WORD OF MOUTH

"My favorite inexpensive souvenirs are cedar Christmas ornaments from the Bermuda Craft Market in the Dockyard and linen tea towels with Bermudian flowers, cottages, or birds from The Irish Linen Shop. The Bermuda perfumery is great, too."
—cmcfong

"You won't find Versace, Tiffany, and Gucci here, but you will find some of the most exquisite inlaid coral, mother-of-pearl, and tanzanite jewelry for modest prices, as well as great shopping for Burberry, Mason Pearson, and other fine British goods."
—katalina_g

Updated By
Sirkka Huish

If you're accustomed to shopping in Neiman Marcus, Saks Fifth Avenue, and Bergdorf Goodman, the prices in Bermuda's elegant shops won't bother you. The island is a high-end shopping paradise; designer clothing and accessories, from MaxMara to Louis Vuitton, tend to be sold at prices comparable to those in the United States, but at least without the sales tax.

That doesn't mean bargain hunters are out of luck in Bermuda. Crystal, china, watches, and jewelry are often less expensive here and sometimes even on par with American outlet-store prices. Perfume and cosmetics are often sold at discount prices, and there are bargains to be had on woolens and cashmeres in early spring, when stores' winter stocks must go. The island's unforgiving humidity and lack of storage space mean sales are frequent and really meant to sweep stock off the shelves.

Art galleries in Bermuda attract serious shoppers and collectors. The island's thriving population of artists and artisans—many of whom are internationally recognized—produces well-reputed work, from paintings, photographs, and sculpture to miniature furniture, handblown glass, and dolls. During your gallery visits, look for Bruce Stuart's abstract paintings, Graeme Outerbridge's vivid photographs of Bermudian architecture and scenery, and Chelsey Trott's slim wood and bronze sculptures.

Bermuda-made specialty comestibles include rum and rum-based liqueurs and delicious local honey, which you can find in most grocery stores. Condiments from Outerbridge Peppers Ltd. add zip to soups, stews, drinks, and chowders. The original line has expanded to include Bloody Mary mix, pepper jellies, and barbecue sauce.

The duty-free shop at the airport sells liquor, perfume, cigarettes, rum cakes, and other items. You can also order duty-free spirits at some of the liquor stores in town, and the management will make arrangements to deliver your purchase to your hotel or cruise ship. If you choose to shop in town rather than at the airport, it's best to buy liquor at least 24 hours before your departure, or by 9:30 on the day of an afternoon departure, in order to allow enough time for delivery. With liquor, it pays to shop around, because prices vary. Grocery stores usually charge more than liquor stores. U.S. citizens age 21 and older who have been out of the country for 48 hours are allowed to bring home 1 liter of duty-free liquor.

SHOPPING DISTRICTS

Hamilton has the greatest concentration of shops in Bermuda, and Front Street is its pièce de résistance. Lined with small, pastel-color buildings, this most fashionable of Bermuda's streets houses sedate department stores and snazzy boutiques, with several small arcades and shopping alleys leading off it. A smart canopy shades the entrance to the 55

Front Street Group, which houses Crisson's. Modern Butterfield Place has galleries and boutiques selling, among other things, Louis Vuitton leather goods. The Emporium, a renovated building with an atrium, has a range of shops, from antiques to souvenirs.

St. George's Water Street, Duke of York Street, Hunters Wharf, Penno's Wharf, and Somers Wharf are the sites of numerous renovated buildings that house branches of Front Street stores, as well as artisans' studios. Historic King's Square offers little more than a couple of T-shirt and souvenir shops.

In the West End, Somerset Village has a few shops, but they hardly merit a special shopping trip. However, the Clocktower Mall, in a historic building at the Royal Naval Dockyard, has a few more shopping opportunities, including branches of Front Street shops and specialty boutiques. The Dockyard is also home to the Craft Market, the Bermuda Arts Centre, and Bermuda Clayworks.

> **TOP 5 SHOPPING**
>
> ■ Grab a fruit smoothie at Rock On for pre-shopping energy.
>
> ■ Check out Astwood Dickinson's collection of pins and charms replicating the island's flora and fauna.
>
> ■ Nab the Bermuda Blue fragrance, which combines the island's citrus and jasmine scents, available at A.S. Cooper and Gibbons Company.
>
> ■ Scour Dockyard Glassworks and the Bermuda Rum Company: their traditional black rum cakes are to die for.
>
> ■ Buy a beautiful coffee-table book from Trustworthy Gift Shop.

HAMILTON AND CENTRAL PARISHES

This is the place to head for all your shopping needs; Hamilton has Bermuda's largest concentration of stores. The main shopping streets are Front Street and Reid Street, but don't forget about all the side streets and alleyways, where some of the best stores are tucked away. Whether you want to buy a souvenir or gift for someone back home or splash out on a new outfit or a flashy piece of jewelry, Hamilton and the central parishes have something for you.

DEPARTMENT STORES

A.S. Cooper & Sons. Cooper's is best known for its extensive inventory of crystal and china, with pieces and sets by Waterford, Swarovski, Wedgwood, Royal Doulton, Lladro, Lalique, and Portmeirion, many sold at 15% to 20% less than U.S. prices. The store also carries tasteful Bermudian souvenirs, jewelry, fragrances, and cosmetics on the ground level. Brands on sale include Estée Lauder, Clinique, Clarins, Bobbi Brown, Lancome, YSL, and Elizabeth Arden. The main store also carries its private-label clothing collection for women and a ladies sportswear department, which carries Calvin Klein, Ralph Lauren, Lacoste, DKNY Jeans, Jones New York, Nick and Zoe, and other popular brands. There are several branches including one at the Fairmont Southampton resort,

KNOW-HOW

Clothing, china, and jewelry in Bermuda are sold at prices similar to those abroad, but since there's no sales tax, you can get good deals, especially on high-end goods. If you see something you like, go ahead and buy it—comparison shopping isn't fruitful on Bermuda, as prices are typically fixed island-wide. In all but a few stores, shoppers leaving the fitting rooms are expected to return unwanted items to the store floor. The island's bounty of craft markets and artists' studios offers a multitude of inexpensive souvenirs, from Bermuda honey to hand-painted pillows. Buyers and sellers don't really bargain, although a vendor may offer a discount if you buy something in bulk.

BUSINESS HOURS

Shops are generally open Monday to Saturday from 9 to 5 and closed on Sunday, although some supermarkets are open from 1 to 6 on Sunday. From April to October, some of the smaller Front Street shops stay open late and on Sunday. The shops in the Clocktower Mall at the Royal Naval Dockyard are usually open from Monday to Saturday 9:30 to 6 (11 to 5 in winter) and Sunday 11 to 5. Some extend their hours around Christmas. Almost all stores close for public holidays.

KEY DESTINATIONS

Department stores such as A.S. Cooper & Sons and Gibbons Co. are excellent one-stop shopping destinations, but you may have more fun exploring the boutiques on Front and Reid streets, and streets branching off them. For crafts, head to the Royal Naval Dockyard, where you can find artisans' studios and a permanent craft market. The town of St. George's has a bit of everything, including lots of small, unique boutiques, where you can find the perfect island outfit or a Bermuda-cedar model of a famous ship.

SMART SOUVENIRS

Small cakes from the Bermuda Rum Cake Company in the Dockyard make popular gifts and cost $14.95 duty-free. Men may want to pick up a pair of real Bermuda shorts, which come in an array of bright colors. They sell for about $45 in department stores. The Outerbridge line of sherry peppers and other sauces is available at grocery stores and souvenir shops. Locals use them to flavor fish chowder. A Bermudian cookbook makes a good accompaniment. An original photograph or painting is a meaningful, if expensive, souvenir. A coffee-table book of Bermudian art is another option. For something really offbeat, head to one of the music stores to take home the island's unique sound—yes, you really can buy a recording of Bermuda's tree frogs chirping through the night. The distinctive high-pitch sound is sure to remind you of your vacation.

WATCH OUT

A few stores in Bermuda sell Cuban cigars, but you may not bring them back to the United States.

It's illegal to export shipwreck artifacts or a Bermuda cedar carving or item of furniture that's more than 50 years old without a special permit from Bermuda Customs.

Bermuda Customs. ⊠ *Custom House, 40 Front St., Hamilton* ☎ *441/295–4816* ⊕ *www.customs. gov.bm.*

as well as the more specialized A.S. Cooper Man and A.S. Cooper Children's stores. Cooper's also owns Astwood Dickinson jewelry stores. ✉ *59 Front St., Hamilton* ☎ *441/295–3961* ⊕ *www.ascooper. bm* ✉ *Clocktower Mall, Dockyard* ✉ *22 Water St., St. George's.*

A.S. Cooper Children's. This kids' clothing shop has everything you'll need to dress your little one. From shorts and shirts in summer to long pants and jackets for Bermuda's rainy winter, it's all here. ✉ *27 Front St., Hamilton* ☎ *441/295–3961.*

A.S. Cooper Express. Flirty, bright clothes for junior girls in the know, from DKNY jeans and T-shirts to a great selection by Guess are stocked in this airy store. A full wall of accessories in a rainbow of colors is one of the many highlights here. ✉ *Washington Mall, 12 Reid St., Hamilton* ☎ *441/296–6525.*

A.S. Cooper Harbourside. A.S. Cooper's ready-to-wear shop stocks women's clothing, including plus sizes, accessories, and its own line of fragrances. Costume jewelery, homeware including candles, towels and bed linen, and other locally made gifts can also be found at this location. ✉ *Pier 6, 24 Front St., Hamilton* ☎ *441/295–3961.*

A.S. Cooper Man. This division of the classy department store is first-rate, with a staff who are reserved and courteous, but very helpful when needed. It is full of men's casual and dress clothes, plus accessories such as belts and wallets. The store is the exclusive Bermuda supplier of Polo Ralph Lauren. It also stocks brands such as Lacoste, Caribbean Joe, Perry Ellis, Chaps, and Helly Hansen. ✉ *29 Front St., Hamilton* ☎ *441/295–3961.*

Fodor's Choice **Gibbons Co.** One of Bermuda's oldest retailers (still run by the Gibbons ★ family) has transformed itself into a contemporary department store with a wide range of men's, women's, and children's clothing. Brands include Calvin Klein, Mango, and DKNY, and there's a substantial lingerie selection, as well as active and swim wear, accessories, and fashion jewelry. The perfume and cosmetics department stocks many French, Italian, English, and American lines at duty-free prices. The housewares department is the exclusive supplier of Denby tableware, which sells at a much lower price than in Canada or the United States. Gibbons also owns and operates a separate store, in the nearby Washington Mall, that sells bed, bath and home decor; Reid Street's Nine West, with shoes and accessories, and Twenty 5 Reid, with shoe brands such as Ann Klein and Marc Fisher; M.A.C. Cosmetics on Front Street; and the perfume stores in Dockyard and St. George's. ✉ *21 Reid St., Hamilton* ☎ *441/295–0022* ⊕ *www.gibbons.bm.*

Marks & Spencer. A franchise of the large British chain, Marks and Sparks (as it's called by everyone in Bermuda and England) is usually filled with locals attracted by its moderate prices for men's, women's, and children's clothing. Summer wear, including swimsuits, cotton jerseys, and polo shirts, is a good buy, as is underwear—but don't forget everything is in U.K. sizes rather than U.S. The chain's signature line of food and treats, plus wine from all over the world, is tucked away at the back of the store. ✉ *18 Reid St., Hamilton* ☎ *441/295–0031.*

8

ANTIQUES AND COLLECTIBLES

Bermuda Monetary Authority. This agency issues and redeems Bermuda currency, and also oversees financial institutions operating in and through Bermuda. At its offices in Hamilton, it sells collectors' coins, including replicas of the old Bermuda "hogge" money of the early 17th century. Cahow, Hawksville turtle, and gold shipwreck coins are among the many other pieces for sale. ⊠ *BMA House, 43 Victoria St., Hamilton* ☎ *441/295–5278* ⊕ *www.bma.bm.*

ART GALLERIES

Art House Gallery. Watercolors, oils, and limited-edition color lithographs by Bermudian artist Joan Forbes are displayed in this gallery. It's open Monday, Wednesday, and Friday from 10 to 4 or by appointment. ⊠ *80 S. Shore Rd., Paget Parish* ☎ *441/236–6746* ⊕ *www. arthousebermuda.com.*

★ **Bermuda Society of the Arts.** The island's oldest arts organization has four galleries, and many highly creative society members sell their work at the perennial members' shows and during special group exhibits. You can find watercolor, oil, and acrylic paintings; pastel and charcoal drawings; as some photographs, collages, and sculptures. Admission is free. ⊠ *17 Church St., 3rd fl. West Wing, City Hall, Hamilton* ☎ *441/292– 3824* ⊕ *www.bsoa.bm.*

Birdsey Studio. Renowned artist Alfred Birdsey, who painted Bermuda scenes for more than 60 years, died in 1996, but thanks to his daughter, Jo Birdsey Linberg, the studio remains open and the tradition continues. Watercolors cost from $100 and oils from $350 to $1,000. Prints of Birdsey's paintings are also available on note cards for $15. The studio is usually open weekdays 10:30 to 1, but call before you visit, as appointments are preferred. ⊠ *5 Stowe Hill, Paget Parish* ☎ *441/236–6658.*

Carole Holding Print & Craft Shops. Prices for artist Carole Holding watercolors of Bermuda's scenes and flowers range from $12 for small prints to more than $5,000 for framed originals. The artist's prints can also be found on linen, china, and clothing, including T-shirts and aprons, and she has her own line of jams, chutneys, and rum cakes. The shop also sells crafts by local artists, and there's a branch at the Clocktower Mall, Dockyard. ⊠ *81 Front St., Hamilton* ☎ *441/296–3431* ⊕ *www. caroleholding.bm* ⊠ *Fairmont Southampton Resort, Lower Level, South Shore Rd., Southampton* ☎ *441/238–7310.*

Desmond Fountain Gallery. From the moment you arrive in Bermuda, you will be surrounded by Fountain's sculptures, but his namesake gallery is the place to go to purchase his work. It features about 50 of his bronze statues, plus work by other local artists. Hours are 10–6 Monday through Saturday and 2–6 on Sunday. ⊠ *Elbow Beach Hotel, 60 S. Shore Rd., Paget* ☎ *441/232–3955* ⊕ *www.desmondfountaingallery.com.*

Kafu Hair Salon and Gallery. Proving that art can happen anywhere, artist and hairdresser Glen Wilks displays contemporary work, including paintings and sculpture, by local avant-garde artists at his salon. It's open until 8 pm Tuesday to Saturday. ⊠ *8 Parliament St., between Victoria and Dundonald, Hamilton* ☎ *441/295–5238* ⊕ *www.kafu.bm.*

Picturesque. Roland Skinner is one of the island's most-loved photographers. He captures the island's architecture, landscapes, and flora. The Front Street gallery showcases his portfolio, with photos selling from $100 to $800. ⊠ *129 Front St. E, Hamilton* ☎ *441/292–1452* ⊕ *www. picturesquebermuda.com.*

🐚 **X-Clue-Sive Creations Visual Arts Centre.** Pick up Doris Wade's hand-painted pottery here, or indulge your creative side and create your own souvenirs. Choose from about 100 bare shapes and paint to your heart's content. The studio will glaze and fire the piece in four to seven days. ⊠ *135 Front St, entrance is on King St, Hamilton* ☎ *441/296–1676.*

BOOKS

Bermuda Book Store. Owner Hannah Willmott doesn't believe in wasting space, so she crammed as many books as she could into her small bookstore. The shop is known for its cozy atmosphere and is well stocked with best sellers, children's books, and special Bermuda titles (including some out-of-print books), plus diaries and calendars. ⊠ *3 Queen St., Hamilton* ☎ *441/295–3698* ⊕ *www.bookstore.bm.*

★ **Bookmart.** The island's largest bookstore carries plenty of contemporary titles and classics, plus a complete selection of books on Bermuda. Paperbacks and children's books are in abundance, as well as every popular beauty, technology, and travel book you can think of. This is also the place to come for greeting cards, balloons, party supplies, and little gift items. Its café has a balcony overlooking Front Street, perfect for grabbing a sandwich or a drink after a hard day's shopping. ⊠ *Brown & Company, 4 Reid St., Hamilton* ☎ *441/279–5443* ⊕ *www. bookmart.bm.*

Metaphysical Bookshop. This incense-scented store sells books on meditation, alternative medicine, numerology, martial arts, philosophy, yoga, and self-help. Owner Kelvin Richardson also offers a bountiful supply of wind chimes, cards, candles, herbal health products, and other gift items. ⊠ *63 King St., Hamilton* ☎ *441/295–5683.*

CERAMICS AND GLASSWARE

Bluck's. A dignified establishment in business for more than 165 years, Bluck's is the island's only store devoted exclusively to crystal and china. Royal Doulton, Royal Copenhagen, and Herend china compete with Lalique, Waterford, Baccarat, and Kosta Boda crystal in glorious displays, and enamel boxes sit primly in their display cases. The courteous staff provides price lists upon request. New sellers include colorful linens, beautifully made napkin rings, and gold and silver photo frames encrusted with Swarovski crystals. ⊠ *4 Front St., Hamilton* ☎ *441/295–5367* ⊕ *www.blucksbermuda.com.*

8

CIGARS

House of Cigars: Chatham House. In business since 1895, this shop looks like an old-time country store. Thick, gray, lusty cigar smoke fills the air, and a life-size statue of a Native American princess greets you as you walk in. You can find top-quality cigars from the Dominican Republic, Jamaica, and Cuba (Romeo y Julieta, Bolivar, Partagas, Punch), Briar pipes, tobacco, and Swiss Army knives. Prices for handmade Cubans start at $5. ✉ *63 Front St., Hamilton* ☎ *441/292–8422.*

CLOTHING

CHILDREN'S CLOTHING

Daisy & Mac. This unmissable, pink-and-green boutique for little people is known locally as "the biggest little store in town." It sells children's shoes, toys, accessories, and fashionable clothes for newborns on up to 16 years. Brands include Diesel, Esprit Kids, and Ralph Lauren. There's also a small branch in the Clocktower Mall, Dockyard. ✉ *27 Queen St., Hamilton* ☎ *441/295–7477* 🌐 *www.daisyandmac.com.*

Phoenix Kidz. Head up the escalator at Phoenix Pharmacy, and you'll stumble upon a treasure trove for youngsters. The store sells a small range of clothes for children up to 24 months. Don't expect too much of a choice, but you can also take a look at its children's accessories and nursery furniture. ✉ *2nd fl., Phoenix Centre, 3 Reid St., Hamilton* ☎ *441/295–3838.*

Pirate's Port Boys. It's small and crowded, but it has bargains on casual clothing for girls and boys. It caters to boys from toddlers to teens and girls ages 7 to 14. There's also a Pirates Port women's wear store immediately opposite. ✉ *Lower Level, Washington Mall, 7 Reid St., Hamilton* ☎ *441/292–1080.*

MEN'S CLOTHING

David Winston. An upscale spot in the English Sports Shop, this handsome boutique carries international designer men's clothing and accessories. Hugo Boss, and Profuomo are well represented. The locals will tell you it's a great spot to pick up men's Italian shirts, ties, and belts. ✉ *The English Sports Shop, 49 Front St., Hamilton* ☎ *441/295–4866.*

The Edge. You can find trendy, casual clothing for men at this welcoming shop, including brand names such as Haight and Ashbury, Martin Gordon, and Report. There are also plenty of shoes, ties, belts, shades, and accessories to choose from. Although its main focus is on men's clothes, there's a small selection of women's clothes available, including the brand D.E.P.T. Also check out The Edge's end-of-line discount store, also on the lower level of Washington Mall. ✉ *Lower Level, Washington Mall, 7 Reid St., Hamilton* ☎ *441/295–4715.*

Sports Source. Popular with locals, Sports Source offers men's and youth urban wear and hip-hop gear. The labels are trendy, but the prices are reasonable. There's also a good selection of sneakers, football jerseys, and shorts. Visit Sports Source Youth at 49 Middle Road, Warwick, for a children's selection.

Sports Source Ladies. Sports Source Ladies sells women's casual and sports apparel as well as trendy athletic shoes ✉ *Washington Mall, Reid St., Hamilton* ✉ *Washington Mall, Reid St., Hamilton* ☎ *441/292–9442.*

MEN'S AND WOMEN'S CLOTHING

The Booth. Named after owner Darren Booth, this shop sells trendy men's and women's attire, including DC shoes, G-Shock watches, and jackets by Helly Hansen and North Face. It also stocks skateboards, backpacks, and a good selection of luggage. ⊠ *Lower level, Washington Mall, Church St., Hamilton* ☎ *441/295–5455.*

★ **English Sports Shop.** This shop specializes in knitwear, but walk through the front door and you can't miss the selection of colorful Bermuda shorts and knee-high socks. The store's own line of cotton sweaters is priced at $34.50,

> **TIME OF YOUR LIFE**
>
> While shopping on Reid Street, glance up and admire a famous city landmark hanging from the Phoenix Centre. The clock was imported from Boston in 1893 by watchmaker Duncan Doe. When you're at the Clocktower Mall in Dockyard, you'll notice the clocks on the two 100-foot towers tell different times. This isn't an error; one was installed to show the actual time and the other the time of the high tide.

and Italian Merino wool sweaters start at $76. Upstairs is a good supply of men's business and formal wear and children's clothes. Women's clothing and accessories are at the back of the store on the ground level. There are also branches at two hotels: Fairmont Southampton Resort and Fairmont Hamilton Princess. ⊠ *49 Front St., Hamilton* ☎ *441/295–2672* ⊠ *30 Water St., St. George's* ☎ *441/297–0142* ⊠ *Mangrove Bay, Somerset* ☎ *441/292–8946.*

French Connection. This chic urban-wear shop carries trendy skirts, pants, tops, and accessories for day and night. Women's clothing is on the ground level and men's is on the lower level. Follow the locals to the 50%–75% end-of-season sales. ⊠ *15 Reid St., Hamilton* ☎ *441/295–2112* ⊕ *www.calypsobermuda.com.*

★ **Makin' Waves.** Casual clothing and swimsuits by big-name brands Roxy, Billabong, O'Neill, Fox, and Quick Silver are sold at this beachy shop. There are plenty of shorts, T-shirts, and summer dresses to choose from, and surf gear is a speciality. You can also take your pick from Oakley sunglasses, incense, shell jewelry, beach bags, flip-flops, water shoes, and snorkeling and dive gear. ⊠ *Boyles Building, 31 Queen St., junction with Church St., Hamilton* ☎ *441/292–4609* ⊕ *www.makinwaves.bm* ⊠ *Former Club Malabar building, 1 Camber Rd., Dockyard* ☎ *441/234–5319.*

Mambo. Need a slice of Italian chic? Stop by this tiny shop that stocks funky Italian labels such as Dolce & Gabbana, Miss Sixty, Diesel, Just Cavalli, and True Religion jeans. ⊠ *Walker Arcade, 12 Reid St., Hamilton* ☎ *441/295–5698.*

Jeans Express. If denim is your favourite look, then this store is the place to go. It's crammed full of Levi's jeans in every style imaginable. All shapes and sizes are catered for and prices are reasonable compared to the U.S. Dockie's casual clothing is also sold. ⊠ *30 Queen St., Hamilton* ☎ *441/295–0084.*

Sasch. Part of the six-store Stefanel group, this boutique brings the very latest, hippest fashions in casual, business, and dress wear from

8

Bermuda Shorts in the Office

You may have heard of Bermuda's peculiar business fashion, and you may even have seen pictures of businessmen in shorts and long socks, but nothing can quite prepare you for the first sighting. First-time visitors have been spotted sniggering in shop doorways after discovering the bottom half of a blazer-and-tie-clad executive on his cell phone. After all, where else in the world could he walk into a boardroom wearing bright-pink shorts without anyone batting an eyelid? Only in Bermuda. These unique, all-purpose garments, however flamboyantly dyed, are worn with complete seriousness and pride. Bermudians would go so far as to say it's the rest of the world that is peculiar, and they have a point—particularly in the steaming humidity of the summer months.

What is surprising is how the original khaki cutoffs evolved into formal attire. They were introduced to Bermuda in the early 1900s by the British military, who adopted the belted, baggy, cotton-twill version to survive the sweltering outposts of the Empire. By the 1920s Bermudian pragmatism and innovation were at play as locals started chopping off their trousers at the knees to stay cool. Tailors seized on the trend and started manufacturing a smarter pair of shorts, and men were soon discovering the benefits of a breeze around the knees.

But for an island that has a love affair with rules there was always going to be a right and a wrong way to wear this new uniform. Bermudas had to be worn with knee-high socks, and a jacket and tie were the only acceptable way of dressing them up for business. But it didn't stop there. Obsession with detail prevailed, fueled by gentlemen who were disturbed at the unseemly shortness of other men's shorts. A law was passed to ensure propriety, and the bizarre result was patrolling policemen, armed with tape measures and warning tickets, scouring the capital for men showing too much leg. Officially, shorts could be no more than 6 inches above the knee, while 2 to 4 was preferable.

Other rigid but unwritten rules made it unheard of to wear them in hotel dining rooms after 6 pm or in churches on Sunday morning, and even to this day they are out of bounds in the Supreme Court, although in 2000, legislation was changed to allow them to be worn, even by ministers, in the House of Assembly. Viewed as conservative and respectable menswear for almost any occasion, they can be seen paired with tuxedo jackets and are even acceptable (provided they are black) at funerals.

But if Bermuda shorts are practical, smart dress for men, where does that leave the island's women during the sticky summer months? Wearing brightly colored cotton dresses and skirts, it would seem. Shorts are not considered ideal business wear for women and are only really acceptable on the beach and while shopping (but again, not if they're skimpy). In a country where pink is a man's color and men's bare legs are all but mandatory for six months of the year, perhaps the men feel the need to stamp their masculine pride on their pants.

—Vivienne Sheath

Florence to Bermuda. The clothes are high quality, made of primarily natural fibers in neutral colors. Large men may have trouble finding a good fit—most sizes are for smaller frames, and some styles are body hugging. There's also a small selection of trendy shoes and handbags at the back of the store. ⊠ *12 Reid St., Hamilton* ☎ *441/542–2226.*

27th Century Boutique. Khakis, polo shirts, and dress shirts predominate in this boutique's sizable men's section, and women can find sparkly tank tops and great-fitting black pants alongside office-appropriate blouses. Owner Sharon Bartram can help you assemble a perfect outfit—she has an excellent eye for style and detail. ⊠ *92 Reid St., Hamilton* ☎ *441/292–2628.*

WOMEN'S
CLOTHING

Benetton. This branch of the Italian brand has a wide variety of casual, chic women's and children's clothing in brash, bright colors and more subdued tones. ⊠ *24 Reid St., Hamilton* ☎ *441/295–2112* ⊕ *www.calypsobermuda.com.*

★ **Boutique C.C.** This English Sports Shop–owned store sells quality business wear for women of every age, but the highlight is the selection of evening wear. Look for reasonably priced cocktail dresses and classic suits along with stylish contemporary separates and trendy accessories. ⊠ *1 Front St., Hamilton* ☎ *441/295–3935.*

Fodor'sChoice
★

Calypso. Bermuda's fashionable set comes to this boutique to spend plenty of money on Italian leather shoes and sophisticated designer wear by Graham Kandiah. Calypso has the island's largest selection of swimwear, including Vilebrequin. Pick up a straw hat and sunglasses to make the perfect beach ensemble. Eclectic novelty items from Europe make great gifts. Calypso's shop in Butterfield Place, Voila!, carries Longchamp handbags and Johnston & Murphy men's shoes. There are branches at the Fairmont Southampton Resort, Fairmont Hamilton Princess Hotel, and Clocktower Mall at Dockyard. ⊠ *45 Front St., Hamilton* ☎ *441/295–2112* ⊕ *www.calypsobermuda.com.*

Cecile. Specializing in upscale European designer fashions, Cecile carries such labels as Valentino Red, Tibi, Emilio Pucci, Basler, and the perennial resort-wear favorite, Lilly Pulitzer. There's a good selection of evening wear and swimwear, including swimsuits by Gottex. Accessories such as scarves, jewelry, handbags, and belts can also be found. The boutique has great prices, often significantly lower than U.S. retail, on some of the world's foremost fashion names. To finish off that new outfit, Cecile's sister shoe store, Lusso, is just down the road. ⊠ *15 Front St., Hamilton* ☎ *441/295–1311.*

Eve's Garden Lingerie. Silk and satin panties, boxers, brassieres, and nightgowns, in sizes small to full-figure, are tucked away in this discreet shop at the back of the Emporium Building. You can also find massage oils and an adult section. Next door, owner Liz Adderley also runs the Bra Boutique selling a wide range of top-quality lingerie for all shapes and sizes. ⊠ *Emporium Building, 69 Front St., Hamilton* ☎ *441/296–2671.*

Luxury For Less. This shop overflows with a good selection of reasonably priced dresses, suits, shoes, handbags, fashion jewelry, and sunglasses. To make it easier to find what you want, clothes are in color-coordinated sections. There are smaller branches on Front Street and in the Clocktower Mall, Dockyard. ⊠ *19 Queen St., Hamilton* ☎ *441/295–9128.*

Jazzy Boutique. Lots of spandex and jeans are sold at this trendy juniors' clothing store. Plastic purses, faux-gem jewelry, and other colorful accessories tempt preteens of every ilk. There's also a good selection of shoes. Fortunately, the prices are quite affordable. ⊠ *Washington Mall, Reid St., Hamilton* ☎ *441/295–9258.*

MaxMara. Prices for this Italian designer's clothing average about 20% less in Bermuda than in the United States, although the accessories sell at much the same as U.S. prices. Although the boutique is much smaller than its counterpart on Madison Avenue, it still has a good selection of conservative casual wear and evening attire. You'll find the labels Maxmara, SportMax, and Studio. ⊠ *57 Front St., Hamilton* ☎ *441/295–2112* ⊕ *www.calypsobermuda.com.*

Revelation Boutique. Cool, contemporary linen and cotton clothing is the focus of Paulette Wedderburn's shop, which also has an impressive collection of formal wear. ⊠ *20 Ewing St., corner of Court, Hamilton* ☎ *441/296–4252.*

Secrets. Come to Secrets for sometimes understated, sometimes flashy, but always sexy lingerie. The shop also has massage oils, fun board games, and an adults section. ⊠ *Upper level of Washington Mall, Reid St., Hamilton* ☎ *441/295–0651.*

Sisley. Follow the trendsetters to this store to get your hands on the latest women's fashions, including suits, party dresses, and casual basics. This is a sister store to Benetton and is said to design its clothes with feminine flair. ⊠ *7 Front St., corner of Pa-La-Ville Rd., Hamilton* ☎ *441/295–2112* ⊕ *www.calypsobermuda.com.*

Stefanel. This popular Italian chain is good for simple, stylish, modern women's clothes, mostly made from cotton and other natural fabrics. Its own line of jackets, crocheted sweaters, and camisoles is particularly worth a look. The colors are neutral, sometimes with delicate small prints. Prices are commensurate with quality, but seasonal sales are rewarding. ⊠ *Walker Arcade, 12 Reid St., Hamilton* ☎ *441/295–5698.*

Vibe. Funky clothes, shoes, and accessories at reasonable prices make Vibe a choice shop for women who want to keep up with the latest styles. ⊠ *5 Burnaby St., Hamilton* ☎ *441/296–4883.*

Women's Secret. This Spanish brand offers a good range of fun and feminine underwear, lingerie, nightwear, loungewear, sportswear, and swimwear. ⊠ *14 Reid St., Hamilton* ☎ *441/295–2112* ⊕ *www. calypsobermuda.com.*

FOOD AND CANDY

Onion Jack's Trading Post. Onion Jack's own line of sweet and spicy sauces is sold here, along with various other food products. There are also plenty of T-shirts, caps, flip-flops, swimwear, sunglasses, and gifts. ⊠ *77 Front St., Hamilton* ☎ *441/295–1263* ⊕ *www.onionjacks.com.*

☺ **Treats.** You can find bulk candy in
★ just about every flavor here, but
the greatest draw to this tiny store
are the fun seasonal gifts and cute
baby toys. Look out for the educational and science toys. There's also
a selection of wooden toys, LEGOs,
board games, and a wide selection of Thomas the Tank Engine
toys. ✉ *Lower level of Washington Mall, 7 Reid St., Hamilton*
☏ *441/296–1123.*

SUPERSTAR GROCER
Dai James, a manager at Lindo's in Warwick, has become something of a cult hero as the star of a series of wacky TV adverts. Don't be surprised to hear locals asking Mr. Jones "Can you wrap?" In one advert he mistakenly starts to rap when a customer asks him to wrap her tomatoes.

GROCERY
STORES

A1 Paget. This grocery is near sev-
eral Paget accommodations and it's an easy enough walk to do with
bags of shopping. You could also stop here to grab a bite to eat before
hitting nearby Elbow Beach. ✉ *108 Middle Rd., Happy Valley Rd. Junction, Paget Parish* ☏ *441/236–0351* ⊕ *www.marketplace.bm.*

Down 2 Earth, Ltd. This natural-food and health shop sells everything
from tea and supplements to organic body products and home clean-
ers. Don't leave without grabbing a fruit smoothie or a vegetable juice
from the bar in the corner. There's seating on the porch. ✉ *56 Reid St.,
Hamilton* ☏ *441/292–5639.*

Esso City Tiger Market. Day or night, this gas station sells a good range of
fast food and sandwiches, as well as cigarettes, hot drinks, chips, soda
and aspirin. This is the only true 24-hour place on the island, as Esso
Warwick and Esso Collector's Hill are only open 24 hours on weekends.
✉ *37 Richmond Rd., Hamilton* ☏ *441/295–3776.*

Lindo's Family Foods, Ltd. Lindo's is a medium-size store with a good selection of groceries, plus organic foods, fresh seafood, and fine imported
French and Italian cheeses and pâtés. It's within walking distance of the
several Warwick accommodations. ✉ *128 Middle Rd., Warwick Parish*
☏ *441/236–1344* ✉ *4 Watlington Rd. E, Devonshire* ☏ *441/236–5623*
⊕ *www.lindos.bm.*

MarketPlace. The island's largest grocery store, and the chain's headquarters, MarketPlace offers homemade hot soups, stir-fries, salads,
dinners, and desserts for about $8 a pound. It's the place locals go for
lunch; many are drawn by the healthy-eating and organic sections. This
branch is open until 10 and also open Sunday 1–6. ✉ *Church St. near
Parliament St., Hamilton* ☏ *441/295–6006* ⊕ *www.marketplace.bm.*

★ **Miles Market.** Miles is Bermuda's Balducci's, with a large selection of
upscale or hard-to-get specialty food items and high-quality imported
and local meats and fish. There's also a mouth-watering range of Godiva
chocolate. Many items are on the expensive side, but the quality and
selection are unsurpassed in Bermuda. The supermarket delivers anywhere on the island. ✉ *96 Pitts Bay Rd., near Fairmont Hamilton Princess, Hamilton* ☏ *441/295–1234* ⊕ *www.miles.bm.*

Modern Mart. Part of the MarketPlace chain, but smaller than its flagship
Hamilton store, this location has all the essentials. It's easily accessible
from Sky Top Cottages, Paraquet Aaprtments, and other south-shore

8

hotels. It's also the nearest food stop to Elbow Beach. ⊠ *104 S. Shore Rd., Paget Parish* ☎ *441/236–6161.*

Rock On–The Health Store. Nutritional supplements, sports supplements, diet books, natural teas and remedies, and environmentally friendly toiletries are among the goods offered at one of Bermuda's

few health stores. But its biggest sellers are probably its protein shakes and bars. The staff is knowledgeable. ⊠ *Butterfield Pl., 67 Front St., Hamilton* ☎ *441/295–3468.*

The Supermart. English products, including the Waitrose brand, are the specialties of this grocery store. You can pick up a picnic lunch at the well-stocked salad-and-hot-food bar. ⊠ *125 Front St., between Court and King, Hamilton* ☎ *441/292–2064* ⊕ *www.supermart.com.*

JEWELRY AND ACCESSORIES

★ **Astwood Dickinson.** Established in 1904, this store has built a reputation for its exquisite unmounted stones, upscale jewelry, including designs by Baccarat and Tiffany and Co., and a wide range of Swiss watches. Cartier, Omega, Gucci, and Tag Heuer watches, among other famous names, are sold for up to 15% less than in the United States. The shop's Bermuda Collection, designed and created in the workshop, ranges from 18-karat gold charms to bejeweled pendants representing the island's flora and fauna. ⊠ *83–85 Front St., Hamilton* ☎ *441/292– 5805* ⊕ *www.astwooddickinson.com* ⊠ *Walker Arcade, 47 Front St., Hamilton* ☎ *441/292–4247* ⊠ *Clocktower Mall, Dockyard* ⊠ *Somers Wharf, St. George's.*

Crisson's. The only store in Bermuda carrying Rolex and Movado, Crisson's attracts well-heeled customers who come here to buy merchandise at prices 20% to 30% off those at home. Earrings are a specialty, and there's a large selection, as well as a handful of gold bangles and beads. There are smaller branches at Fairmont Hamilton Princess Hotel and Fairmont Southampton Resort. ⊠ *55 and 71 Front St., Hamilton* ☎ *441/295–2351* ⊕ *www.crisson.com* ⊠ *16 Queen St., Hamilton* ☎ *441/295–2351* ⊠ *Water St., St. George's* ☎ *441/297–0107* ⊠ *Clocktower Mall, Dockyard* ☎ *441/234–2233.*

E. R. Aubrey. Gold, sapphires, colored pearls, and tanzanite are the specialties of this Hamilton jeweler. The store also carries a large selection of certified diamonds and promises to match prices as long as they can be verified. ⊠ *19 Queen St., Hamilton* ☎ *441/295–9128* ⊠ *101 Front St., Hamilton* ☎ *441/296–3171* ⊠ *Clocktower Mall, Dockyard* ☎ *441/234–4577.*

Everrich Jewelry. This bargain jewelry store stocks countless styles of basic gold and silver chains, earrings, bangles, and rings. ⊠ *28 Queen St., Hamilton* ☎ *441/295–2110.*

Gem Cellar. Jewelers here make Bermuda-theme charms selling for $65 and up, including the Longtail national bird, the Hog Penny, and the Gombey dancer. They can also produce custom-designed gold and silver jewelry in two to three days. ⊠ *Walker Arcade, 47 Front St., Hamilton* 🕾 *441/292–3042.*

Kirk's Designs. Owner Kirk Stapff says he can design and produce any piece of jewelry you desire, "from A to Z." Just bring him an idea, and he'll work with you to create it. ⊠ *67 Front St., Hamilton* 🕾 *441/296–9428.*

Sovereign. Although this shop has fine gold and silver pieces and Casio and Citizen watches, head to the back of the store for one of the island's best selections of sunglasses—Prada, Dolce and Gabbana, Michael Kors, Ray Ban. This shop is also a good place for watch repairs and battery/strap replacements. ⊠ *13 Reid St., Hamilton* 🕾 *441/292–7933* ⊕ *www.sovereignjewellers.bm.*

Swiss Timing. Head here for watches, clocks, and jewelery from across Europe, including Germany, England, and Italy. The store has a great range of birthstone rings, earrings, necklaces, and bracelets, and you can have items custom designed. ⊠ *95 Front St., Hamilton* 🕾 *441/295–1376* ⊕ *www.swisstiming.bm.*

★ **Walker Christopher.** Here you can work with a jeweler to design your own exclusive piece or choose from classic diamond bands, strands of South Sea pearls, and the more contemporary hand-hammered chokers. The workshop also produces a line of Bermuda-inspired gold jewelry and sterling silver Christmas ornaments. ⊠ *9 Front St., Hamilton* 🕾 *441/295–1466* ⊕ *www.walkerchristopher.com.*

MUSIC

iStore. This large store is crammed full of the latest Mac gadgets and accessories. A full service center is also available with technicians on hand to help. A smaller store, specialising in iPods and accessories, is at 9 Reid Street in Hamilton. ⊠ *Upper level, Washington Mall, 7 Reid St., Hamilton* 🕾 *441/296–4622* ⊕ *www.istorebermuda.com.*

The Music Box. Stereos and other electronics are crammed into the window of this independent store. Inside is a small but diverse collection of new CDs (mostly R&B and hip-hop) and DVDs, as well as CD/DVD players and accessories. There's a handful of music books on sale and also the odd musical instrument. ⊠ *58 Reid St., Hamilton* 🕾 *441/295–4839.*

Sound Stage. Small but fairly comprehensive, Sound Stage stocks new-release, mainstream CDs and DVDs. All genres of music are covered. ⊠ *Upper Level, Washington Mall, 7 Reid St., Hamilton* 🕾 *441/292–0811.*

8

PHOTO EQUIPMENT

Kodak Express. This is a full-service photo lab that prints, adjusts, and restores your photos. There are also self-service booths so you can adjust and print your own photos without waiting. Photo frames, albums, and camera accessories are also sold. ✉ *Lower Level, Washington Mall, 7 Reid St., Hamilton* ☎ *441/295–2519* ⊕ *www.kodakexpress.bm.*

P-Tech. Point-and-shoot digital cameras, SLR cameras, digital photo frames, camcorders, and other small electronics such as iPod docking stations and home phones are all here. Brands to look for are Nikon, Canon, and Olympus. ✉ *5 Reid St., Hamilton* ☎ *441/295–5496* ⊕ *www.ptech.bm.*

NOVELTIES AND GIFTS

All Wrapped Up. Greeting cards, wrapping paper, and little gift items like aromatherapy oils, candles, photo frames, and ornaments are sold here. Head to the upper level in the Washington Mall to All Wrapped Up Home, which sells home decor, including vases and bathroom accessories. ✉ *Lower Level, Washington Mall, 7 Reid St., Hamilton* ☎ *441/295–1969* ⊕ *www.allwrappedup.bm.*

★ **Flying Colours.** This family-owned and -operated shop, established in 1937, has the island's largest selection of T-shirts, with creatively designed logos in hundreds of styles. The shop also carries everything for the beach—hats, towels, sarongs, flip-flops, sunglasses, toys for playing in the sand—plus high-quality souvenirs and gifts, like shell jewelry. It's smaller sister shop is Spinnakers at 99 Front Street. ✉ *5 Queen St., Hamilton* ☎ *441/295–0890* ⊕ *www.flyingcolours.bm.*

Foreign Cargo. Candles, oils, incense, and other gifts are among the offerings at this shop that also stocks larger wrought-iron home accessories and furniture. The store also has a catalog that you can consult and order from. ✉ *15 Burnaby St., Hamilton* ☎ *441/296–3054* ⊕ *www. foreigncargobda.com.*

Hodge Podge. This cluttered little shop, just around the corner from the Ferry Terminal and Visitors Service Bureau, offers pretty much what its name implies: postcards, sunblock, sunglasses, and T-shirts. It also sells imported shells and shell jewelry at low prices. ✉ *3 Point Pleasant Rd., Hamilton* ☎ *441/295–0647.*

The Irish Linen Shop. The stock is from all over the world and includes French table and bed linens from Le Jacquard Francais, Beauville, and Yves Delorme. Gifts from Michael Aram, Mariposa, and Cire Trudon are also available, as are European children's clothing from Papo d'Anjo and Chantal. This store is open until 9 pm on Wednesday in the summer to coincide with the Harbour Nights street festival. ✉ *31 Front St., Hamilton* ☎ *441/295–4089.*

Fodor'sChoice **The Island Shop.** Brightly colored island-theme artwork for ceramics,
★ linens, and pillows is designed by owner Barbara Finsness. A number of her original watercolors are available for purchase. She also stocks the store with cedar-handle handbags embroidered with Bermuda buildings, shell napkin rings, plates, monogrammed guest towels, rugs, chunky

jewelry, and elegant gifts, as well as candles and bath products. There are also branches at Somers Wharf, St. George's and at the Fairmont Southampton Resort. ⊠ *3 Queen St., Hamilton* ☎ *441/292–5292* ⊕ *www.islandexports.com* ✉ *Old Cellar La., 47 Front St, Hamilton* ☎ *441/292–6307.*

IN A FORMER LIFE
It may be hard to believe, but the shops at Old Cellar Lane used to be stables, sheltering horses and carriages for patrons of local businesses in a sort of municipal "parking lot."

★ **Otto Wurz.** It's hard to miss this Front Street store. Joke signs proclaiming such witticisms as "laugh and the world laughs with you, snore and you sleep alone" fill its windows. Inside, the theme continues with joke napkins, aprons, and quirky gift ideas that your friends and family will love. There's also a collection of silver and pewter jewelry, children's wood toys, and English silverware, and you can get your gifts engraved with personal messages. ⊠ *3 Front St., Hamilton* ☎ *441/295–1247.*

Pulp & Circumstance. If it's an original, quality gift you're after, look no further. What used to be two separate stores is now one bumper store crammed full of goodies. There are modern picture frames in all shapes and sizes, photo albums, ceramics, candles, bath products, and gifts for babies. There's also a great selection of greeting cards and other stationery items. Check out the Bermuda-theme notepaper with pictures of Gombey dancers or dinghies selling for $39 per box. ⊠ *7 Washington La., Hamilton* ☎ *441/292–9586* ✉ *Windsor Pl., 18 Queen St., Hamilton* ☎ *441/292–8886.*

★ **Sail On and Sunglass Alley.** This local favorite for more than two decade stocks a large selection of sunglasses, sandals, and wet weather gear, as well as sailing, swimwear, and name-brand fashions for adults and children. There's also a selection of wacky gifts, unusual books, and exclusive T-shirt designs. The store is tucked into a little alley off Front Street, and there's a traditional English red phone box outside. A unique collection of women's clothing, footwear, accessories, jewelry, swimwear, and eclectic gifts can be found at Sail On 2, the store's Washington Mall, Reid Street location. ⊠ *Old Cellar La., off Front St., Hamilton* ☎ *441/295–0808* ✉ *Washington Mall, 7 Reid St., Hamilton.*

★ **Trustworthy Gift Shop.** Proceeds from the sales of Bermuda-inspired coffee-table books, key chains, serving trays, spoons, ceramics, pens, and bags at this gift shop benefit the Bermuda National Trust. Look out for their specially designed bluebird boxes. ■ TIP→ **This is where you can find some of the most upscale gifts to take back home.** ⊠ *Old Cellar La., 47 Front St., Hamilton* ☎ *441/296–4164* ✉ *The Globe Hotel, 32 Duke of York St., St. George's* ☎ *441/297–1423.*

SHOES AND HANDBAGS

Boyle, W. J. & Son Ltd. Bermuda's leading footwear chain sells a wide range of men's, women's, and children's shoes. **Trends** on Reid Street has the most up-to-the-minute foot fashions, although the **Sports Locker** has a good stock of running shoes and flip-flops. The Church Street store specializes in children's shoes. ⊠ *Boyle's Building, 31 Queen St, Hamilton* ☎ *441/295–1887* ⊠ *Mangrove Bay, Somerset* ☎ *441/234–0530* ⊠ *Water St., St. George's* ☎ *441/297–1922* ⊠ *Trends, The Walkway, 22 Reid St., Hamilton* ☎ *441/295–6420* ⊠ *The Sports Locker, Windsor Place, 22 Queen St., Hamilton* ☎ *441/292–3300* ⊠ *Children's Shop, Church St., Hamilton* ☎ *441/292–6360.*

Calypso. Women looking for quirky, snazzy footwear should visit Calypso's main store first. The shoe and bag section is small but with choice, supertrendy, sometimes weird styles and colors. Items may cost a little more than you want to spend but you'll want them anyway. Serious bargains can be had during sales. Calypso has branches at Fairmont Hamilton Princess, Fairmont Southampton Resort, and Clocktower Mall in the Dockyard. ⊠ *45 Front St., Hamilton* ☎ *441/295–2112* ⊕ *www.calypsobermuda.com.*

The Harbourmaster. Tumi luggage and briefcases, among other brands, are sold at this store, which prides itself on having "everything pertaining to travel." Wallets, handbags, and gifts round out the stock. ⊠ *Lower level, Washington Mall, 7 Reid St., Hamilton* ☎ *441/295–5333.*

Locomotion Too. Italian, Spanish, and American shoes for women and children are sold in this small store. It has a wide selection of colored satin shoes, and staffers pride themselves on being able to find shoes to match any outfit. ⊠ *Upper Level, Washington Mall, 7 Reid St., Hamilton* ☎ *441/296–4030.*

★ **Louis Vuitton.** Come here to find the famous monogram on ladies' handbags, men's and women's briefcases, carry-on luggage, wallets, credit-card cases, and other leather goods. Prices here are the same as in the United States, except there's no tax. Small ladies' handbags start at about $765. Small, soft leather carry-ons cost up to $1,750, and briefcases start at $1,500 for soft-sided and $4,000 for hard-sided. ⊠ *Butterfield Pl., 67 Front St., Hamilton* ☎ *441/296–1940* ⊕ *www. louisvuitton.com.*

Fodor's Choice **Lusso.** This is the ultimate island boutique for designer footwear for
★ men and women, with shoes from Prada, Ferragamo, Jimmy Choo, and Fendi. If the shoes aren't enough to tempt you, the handbags, purses, wallets and belts definitely will. ⊠ *51 Front St., Hamilton* ☎ *441/295–6734.*

Perry Collection. This stylish store is worth a look, with an impressive collection of women's dress and casual shoes, including Coach, Kate Spade, Guess, and Juicy. It also sells handbags, wallets, jewelery and belts, and a small selection of children's shoes. Men shouldn't feel left out, as they are catered to at the Perry Footwear store at 44 Reid Street. They can choose from the brands Donald Pliner, Guess, and LaCoste. ⊠ *2 Reid St., corner of Church, Hamilton* ☎ *441/296–0014.*

The Shoe Centre. The Shoe Centre is a short distance from the shops of Front and Reid Street, but well worth the walk if you want a bargain. There's a good selection of men's, women's, and children's shoes starting from about $20. Don't miss the bargain basement on the lower level. ⊠ *42 Dundonald St., Hamilton* ☎ *441/292–5078.*

Trends. Pick up recognizable American and European handbag and shoe brands—from comfortable Aerosoles to the the likes of Enzo Angiolini and Joan & David—at this friendly, service-oriented shop. There are also colorful Cole Haan handbags, socks, and shoe accessories. ✉ *The Walkway, 22 Reid St., Hamilton* ☏ *441/295–6420.*

QUIK FIX

Heel Quik. Local shoes-in-distress swear by the friendly expert same-day service at Heel Quik. The store also cuts keys and carries shoe-care products and umbrellas. ✉ *Upper level, Washington Mall, 7 Reid St., Hamilton* ☏ *441/295–1559.*

SPA AND BEAUTY

The Body Shop. Pick up the fragrant skin, bath, and hair-care products you love so much at home at the Bermuda branch of this popular chain. A great selection of make-up is also offered. ✉ *Washington Mall, 7 Reid St., Hamilton* ☏ *441/292–5329.*

M.A.C. Cosmetics. This chic store has every beauty, make-up, and skin-care product you could ever want. Its trained make-up artists offer walk-in makeovers. ✉ *53 Front St., Hamilton* ☏ *441/295–8843* ⊕ *www.gibbons.bm.*

Peniston Brown Ltd.–The Perfume Shop. In addition to being the exclusive Bermuda agent for Guerlain's complete line of cosmetics and skin care products, Peniston Brown's boutique stocks perfume, soap, lotions, and bubble bath. It's also the island's exclusive seller of Chanel and Dior make-up. There's a branch in the Clocktower Mall, Dockyard. ✉ *Gibbons Co. Perfume Department, 21 Reid St., Hamilton* ☏ *441/295–5535* ⊕ *www.gibbons.bm* ✉ *6 Water St., St. George's* ☏ *441/405–0005.*

Sunshine Co. Although this beauty supplies shop caters mostly to professionals, it's open to the public on weekdays. The fantastic selection of OPI nail polish sells at $25 a bottle. Other nail-polish brands, a good selection of make-up, manicure tools, hair color, hair dryers, and curling irons is also available. ✉ *Dallas Bldg., 10 Park Rd., Hamilton* ☏ *441/295–6077.*

SPORTING GOODS

★ **CB Wholesale and Dive.** The best prices for dive gear are found, naturally, at Bermuda's most complete dive shop. The children's mask-and-snorkel set costs $30. You can find a large selection of wet suits, fishing gear, and wakeboards. ✉ *Unit 22, Washington Mall, Washington Lane, above La Trattoria, Hamilton* ☏ *441/292–3839.*

Flybridge Tackle. The only island store completely dedicated to fishing supplies, Flybridge Tackle offers everything except the fish. Plus, the avid fishermen on staff offer excellent advice about fishing in Bermuda. ✉ *26 Church St., across from City Hall, Hamilton* ☏ *441/295–1845.*

International Sports Shop. This store sells all your sporting needs including sneakers, football shirts, and exercise wear. Outdoor games, snorkel gear, and rackets are also available here. ✉ *16 Bermudiana Rd., Hamilton* ☏ *441/295–4183.*

The Pro Shop. Tucked away beneath the ground level, this shop sells men's and women's running and tennis clothes, football jerseys, and sneakers from all the main brands at reasonable prices. ⊠ *Kenwood Bldg., 17 Reid St., Hamilton* ☎ *441/292-7487.*

The Sports Locker. Here you can find athletic shoes, Teva sandals, and flip-flops. ⊠ *Windsor Pl., 22 Queen St., Hamilton* ☎ *441/292-3300.*

Sports 'R' Us. This store has Bermuda's largest selection of running shoes, plus gear and equipment for most sports. ⊠ *Shoppers Fair Bldg., 61 Church St., Hamilton* ☎ *441/292-1891.*

SportSeller. Big-name exercise gear, knapsacks, and running shoes are available at this shop, which also sells Speedo swimwear, sunglasses, and water bottles of every shape and size. ⊠ *Lower Level, Washington Mall, 7 Reid St., Hamilton* ☎ *441/295-2692.*

Upstairs Golf & Tennis Shop. Golf clubs, tennis rackets, and the accessories for those sports are the specialties of this store. You can find some of the best brands available, including Ping, Adams, Callaway, and Titleist for the golfer, and Yonex and Dunlop for the tennis player. Men's and women's sportswear is also sold. ⊠ *26 Church St., Hamilton* ☎ *441/295-5161.*

Winners Edge. This store sells everything to do with cycling including exercise wear, water bottles, and helmets, and it's the only store in Bermuda to sell Cannondale, Gary Fisher, and Trek equipment. The owners and staff include some of Bermuda's top cyclists; they'll be able to answer just about any biking question you throw at them. ⊠ *73 Front St., Hamilton* ☎ *441/295-6012* ⊕ *www.winnersedge.bm.*

STATIONERY AND ART SUPPLIES

Card Cove. This tiny cottage offers a good supply of cards, calendars, toys, and party supplies. ⊠ *19 Queen St., Hamilton* ☎ *441/295-0727.*

The Complete Office. This one-stop office shop is where you can find everything from toners and computer paper to pens and staples. ⊠ *17 Reid St., Hamilton* ☎ *441/292-4333.*

The Royal Gazette Stationery Store. Pens, pencils, envelopes, writing paper, copy paper, file boxes, and notepads are plentiful at this well-stocked stationery store. It's also home to Artcetera, where you can buy paint, charcoal, pastels, sketching pads, canvases, and almost anything else an aspiring artist might need to capture Bermuda in color or black and white. ⊠ *32 Reid St., corner of Burnaby St., Hamilton* ☎ *441/295-4008.*

TOYS

The Annex Toys. Upstairs at the Phoenix Pharmacy, this large toy department has an up-to-date selection of toys and games for all ages. There's a good supply of kites and beach toys, as well as shelves full of board games and puzzles. ⊠ *Phoenix Centre, 3 Reid St., Hamilton* ☎ *441/279-5450* ⊕ *www.phoenixstores.bm.*

Magic Moments. Party planners will find gift-bag loot, balloons, banners, feather boas, costumes, wigs, and almost anything else you might need for a theme party. ✉ *Corner of Reid and Queen Sts., Hamilton* ☎ *441/296–8848.*

People's Pharmacy. Head to the back room of this large pharmacy for one of the island's biggest selections of toys and games—from cuddly toys and rattles for babies to computer games and board games for teens. There's also a corner play area with coloring and reading books and a TV showing the Disney channel. ✉ *62 Victoria St., Hamilton* ☎ *441/292–7527* ⊕ *www.peoplespharmacy.bm.*

WINES AND SPIRITS

Burrows Lightbourn. This wine and spirits merchant has a great selection in stores all over the island. Visitors who want to take duty-free alcohol back home make significant savings on the retail price. ✉ *127 Front St., Hamilton* ☎ *441/295–1554* ✉ *Harbour Rd., Paget* ☎ *441/236–0355* ✉ *Water St., St. George's* ☎ *441/297–0409.*

Front Street Wine & Spirits. Here's your one-stop shop for candy, wines, beer, souvenirs, and assorted snacks. ✉ *57 Front St., Hamilton* ☎ *441/292–6620.*

Gosling's Ltd. The maker of Bermuda's Black Seal Rum also stocks wines and other liquors at its stores. The helpful and knowledgeable staff provides excellent advice. You can only buy one bottle of Black Seal rum to consume on the island and then another to export—and the latter will cost you less than the one you plan to drink in Bermuda. The store also sells T-shirts, ties, and hats with Gosling's logo, a black seal. There's another branch on Dundonald Street in North Hamilton. ✉ *Front and Queen Sts., Hamilton* ☎ *441/298–7337* ⊕ *www.goslingsrum.com.*

8

ST. GEORGE'S AND EASTERN PARISHES

If you want to combine shopping with a leisurely stroll, this is the direction to head in. Water Street and Duke of York Street in St. George's are great for taking everything in at your own speed. There's a varied selection of stores, and no one will hurry you along. St. George's is the perfect day-trip, as you can pick up some bargains, stop for lunch, and go sightseeing in the same location. There's also a handful of stores in Flatts Village, which you may want to visit on your way to the Bermuda Aquarium and Zoo.

ART GALLERIES

Bermuda Memories. Local artists display their work depicting Bermuda's houses, scenery, and wharfs in this specialty shop on the town square. The store, which prides itself on being 100% Bermudian, also stocks ceramics, textiles, gifts, and jewelry. ✉ *1 King's Sq., St. George's* ☎ *441/297–8104.*

Otto Trott Art Studio. Trott is known for his beautiful oil paintings of landscapes and local characters. His work can be found at other galleries, but often his best pieces are here. Small watercolors are priced at $500, oils from about $1,000 to $5,000. A lot of the artist's work

Yo, Ho, Ho and a Bottle of Rum

One of the distinct pleasures of a visit to Bermuda is getting to sample a bit of island rum and rum-based products. Gosling's Black Seal Rum is perhaps the best loved by locals. It's darker and thicker than the usual stuff, with a hint of a caramel flavor—especially when mixed with carbonated ginger beer to make a Dark 'n Stormy, a famous Bermuda drink (treat it with respect and caution).

Gosling's is one of Bermuda's oldest companies, and its Hamilton liquor shop was established in 1806. Gosling's Black Seal Rum was sold in barrels until just after World War I, and inherited its name from the black sealing wax that sealed the barrel corks. In its 151-proof variety, Black Seal will test the strongest drinker.

Many prefer to buy it in the standard 80 proof.

Bermuda's Rum Swizzle, another popular drink, also uses the ubiquitous Black Seal Rum, along with a splash of club soda, lime juice, and sugar. Gosling also produces three liqueurs that are big favorites—Bermuda Gold, Bermuda Banana Liqueur, and Bermuda Coconut Rum. These liqueurs can be ordered everywhere, from poolside bars to late-night jazz clubs. They're even found in cakes, as you soon discover in gift shops and on restaurant menus. Classic Bermuda rum cakes are a delicious, nontoxic way to taste the island's famous export. Fear not if rum's not your thing: Guinness and Heineken are among the widely available imported beers.

is on display at the Landfall Restaurant next door. The gallery is open by appointment. ⊠ *151 N. Shore Rd., Crawl Hill, Hamilton Parish* ☎ *441/293–1050* ⊕ *www.ottotrott.com.*

BOOKS

The Book Cellar. In a small space underneath the Tucker House, this shop crams in a surprisingly large selection of books about Bermuda and an interesting assortment of novels in addition to contemporary best sellers. Coffee-table books and children's books are plentiful. ⊠ *5 Water St., St. George's* ☎ *441/297–0448.*

CERAMICS AND GLASSWARE

Vera P. Card. Lladro and Swarovski crystal figurines are available at almost identical prices elsewhere, but this store has the largest selection, including open-edition and limited-edition gallery pieces. The shop's collection of more than 250 Hummel figurines is one of the world's largest. Limited-edition porcelain plates and vases depicting Bermuda scenes cost $69 to $300. There are also brightly painted chiming cuckoo clocks. Fine and costume jewelry is also sold. ⊠ *Above the Carriage House restaurant, 22 Water St., St. George's* ☎ *441/295–1729* ⊠ *7 Water St., St. George's* ☎ *441/297–1718.*

CLOTHING

Davidson's of Bermuda. Davidson's offers exactly what you would expect of an island clothing store—light, comfortable cotton shirts, pants, and shorts for adults. There's also a large selection of children's clothes from baby to about 9 years. The store includes plenty of gift ideas including aprons, teddy bears, bags, tobacco, and accessories. There are branches in the Fairmont Southampton Resort and the Fairmont Hamilton Princess, too. ✉ *Water St., St. George's* ☎ *441/297–8363* ✉ *Clocktower Mall, Dockyard* ☎ *441/234–0959.*

Flatts Men's Wear. Owner Mick Adderley runs this popular out-of-town shop selling men's clothing, shoes, and accessories, including Dickies work clothes. It also has a small selection of specially made clothes in big-and-tall sizes. ✉ *13 N. Shore Rd., Flatts Village* ☎ *441/292–0360.*

Frangipani. This little store sells colorful women's fashions with a South-east Asian island–resort look. Cotton, silk, and rayon leisure wear are the backbone of the stock. Don't miss the hand-strung, brightly colored, beaded necklaces, bracelets, and earrings, as well as eye-catching ethnic bags. ✉ *13 Water St., St. George's* ☎ *441/297–1357.*

CRAFTS

★ **The Bounty.** The spicy smell of cedar is the first thing to greet you in this tiny shop, where owner Kersley Nanette and his staff handcraft teak and cedar model ships. The focus is on tall ships of the 17th and 18th centuries. Prices range from $150 to $5,000. Models of the *Sea Venture* and *Deliverance* are especially popular. Call for an appointment weekdays 9 to 5. ✉ *2A Old Maid's La., St. George's* ☎ *441/297–2143.*

FOOD AND CANDY

GROCERY STORES **Arnold's Family Market.** Close to Robin's Nest and Mazarine by the Sea, this grocery store is always open, even on public holidays. The extended hours might be one reason why prices aren't cheap, but if you come on the first Tuesday of the month, you'll get 10% off cash purchases. The two Arnold's Express stores in Hamilton—on Queen Street and Front Street—are open until midnight. ✉ *113 St John's Rd., Pembroke Parish* ☎ *441/292–3310.*

The Gourmet Boutique. If you appreciate the finer things in life, this store is the place for you with its range of luxury food products. The family-run business brings some European flair to Bermuda with the sale of caviar, foie gras, and smoked salmon. There's also Galler chocolate, preserves, and Whittard tea and coffee. ✉ *10 Queen St., corner of Reid St., Hamilton* ☎ *441/296–9425* ⊕ *www.the-gourmet-boutique.com.*

Harrington Hundreds Grocery & Liquor Store. Harrington is a must for those observing special diets or seeking unusual ingredients. As well as all your usual groceries, it has the island's best selection of wheat-free foods, including gluten-free pastas, breads, and cookies. It's close to but not within walking distance of Spittal Pond and Pink Beach Club. ✉ *99 S. Shore Rd., Smith's Parish* ☎ *441/293–1635.*

8

Robertson's Drug Store. This is so much more than a pharmacy, as it's crammed full of goodies. It stocks great greetings cards, many toiletries, and unusual toys. ⊠ *24 York St., St. George's* ☎ *441/297–1736.*

Shelly Bay MarketPlace. This branch of the MarketPlace chain is the only large grocery store on North Shore Road. It stocks everything you could need. There's also a huge parking lot and a handful of other stores nearby. ⊠ *110 N. Shore Rd., Hamilton Parish* ☎ *441/293–0966.*

Somers Supermarket. Despite its small size, Somers has a large selection, with hot food, salads, and sandwiches made fresh daily. It offers free delivery service within St. George's, and it's open Monday to Saturday from 7 am to 9 pm, and Sunday from 8 to 7. ⊠ *41 York St., St. George's* ☎ *441/297–1177.*

NOVELTIES AND GIFTS

Another World Gift Shop. You can find every permutation of gift in this shop—from "Bermuda" T-shirts to plates to funky knickknacks. ⊠ *7 King's Sq., St. George's* ☎ *441/297–0670.*

Bermuda Linens and Gifts. Specialty items include hand-embroidered table, bed, and bath linens; christening gowns; and infant wear. There's also a selection of home decor and gifts. ⊠ *16 Somers Wharf, St. George's* ☎ *441/734–2954* ⊕ *www.bermudalinens.com.*

Crackerbox. Shells, shells, and more shells are what you can find in this adorable souvenir shop. Big bins of them invite rummaging, and you can buy just one or a whole handful. Also for sale are charms and jewelry made from shells and sea glass (bits of colored glass worn smooth from tumbling in the ocean or machine-tumbled to look that way). ⊠ *15 York St., St. George's* ☎ *441/297–1205.*

SPA AND BEAUTY

Fodor's Choice ★ **Bermuda Perfumery.** This historic perfumery, which opened in 1928, creates and manufactures all its own perfumes, using the scents of Bermuda's flowers and citrus trees as inspiration. New perfumes are constantly being created, but try out Coral and Lili for women and Navy, 32 North, and Somers for men. You can also tour the facilities to learn how modern and traditional techniques of perfumery are combined. There's also a small museum dedicated to the history of perfumery. ⊠ *Stewart Hall, 5 Queen St., St. George's* ☎ *441/293–0627* ⊕ *www.lilibermuda.com.*

WINES AND SPIRITS

Bermuda Duty Free Shop. Before you head home, this airport store invites you to put together your own package of Bermuda liquors at duty-free prices. Gosling's Black Seal Rum and rum cakes are among the native products. ⊠ *L.F. Wade International Airport, 3 Cahow Way, St. George's* ☎ *441/293–2870.*

DOCKYARD AND WESTERN PARISHES

New stores continue to spring up as the West End begins to threaten Hamilton as a shopping hot spot. Dockyard is the place to go for those quirky gift ideas that you won't be able to find anywhere else. You will find a vast selection of goodies on offer at Bermuda Craft Market and Bermuda Glassworks and Bermuda Rum Cake Company, and just round the corner you have the ClockTower Mall. Don't picture a mall with floor-to-roof stores, but rather more of a quaint indoor selection of little stores and boutiques. It offers many of the same stores as Hamilton, but with the added bonus of avoiding the crowds. Just a few miles along the road you will find the village of Somerset, which has a few stores to browse.

ART GALLERIES

★ **Bermuda Arts Centre at Dockyard.** Sleek and modern, with well-designed displays of local art, this gallery is in one of the stone buildings of the former Royal Naval Dockyard. The walls are adorned with paintings and photographs, and glass display cases contain exquisitely crafted ceramics, jewelry, and wood sculpture. Exhibits change every month. Several artists' studios inside the gallery are open to the public. Much of the work on show is for sale; there's also a small shop selling prints and a variety of art-related gifts. ⊠ *4 Maritime La., Dockyard* ☏ *441/234–2809* ⊕ *www.artbermuda.bm.*

CRAFTS

Bermuda Clayworks. Customized house number and name plaques and tableware are among the brightly painted pottery pieces created in this little shop. The salt-fire pottery and porcelain is also worth a look. Head to the back of the store to see Bermudian artists at work in the open studio. ⊠ *7 Camber Rd., Dockyard* ☏ *441/234–5116* ⊕ *www.bermudaclayworks.com.*

Bermuda Craft Market. The island's largest permanent craft outlet is the Dockyard's old Cooperage building, which dates from 1831. Dozens of artists show their work here, and this is the place to go to find that unusual gift, from Bermuda-cedar hair clips to Bermuda chutney and jam. Hand-painted glassware, sterling-silver jewelry, and sand sculptures are also among the pretty offerings. ⊠ *The Cooperage, 4 Maritime La., Dockyard* ☏ *441/234–3208.*

FOOD AND CANDY

GROCERY STORES **Heron Bay MarketPlace.** Part of the island-wide MarketPlace chain, this one has a large selection of fresh vegetables, as well as meats and seafood. It's convenient to Longtail Cliffs and Marley Beach, but not on foot. ⊠ *227 Middle Rd., Southampton Parish* ☏ *441/238–1993.*

Somerset MarketPlace. The largest grocery store on the island's western end, it's convenient to Whale Bay Inn, but take a moped or taxi. ⊠ *48 Somerset Rd., Sandys Parish* ☏ *441/234–0626.*

NOVELTIES AND GIFTS

Fodor's Choice
★

Dockyard Glassworks and Bermuda Rum Cake Company. Pull up an armchair and watch as artists turn molten glass into vases, plates, miniature tree frogs, and other collectibles. Afterward, help yourself to the rum-cake samples. Flavors include traditional black rum, chocolate, coconut, rum swizzle (with tropical fruit juices), coffee, banana, and ginger. You can buy the cakes duty-free for $14.95, $28, and $38 or pickup a specially presented cake in a tin for $42. Black-rum fruitcake and loquat cakes are also sold for $17.50. If you buy glassware, the company will pack the purchase and deliver it to your hotel or cruise ship for a $5 fee. A small outlet in St. George's sells a collection of glasswork in addition to the cakes. ⊠ *Building No. 9, 1 Maritime La., Dockyard* ☎ *441/234–4216* ⊕ *www.bermudarumcakes.com* ⊠ *3 Bridge St., St. George's* ☎ *441/297–3908.*

Littlest Drawbridge Gift Shop. Bermuda-cedar treasures, such as bowls, candle holders, and letter openers, are the highlight of this closet-size shop. Resort wear, handcrafted pottery, pens, and incense cones are also on sale. ⊠ *Clocktower Mall, Dockyard* ☎ *441/234–6214.*

Cruising to Bermuda

WORD OF MOUTH

"Dockyard = King's Wharf. This is where the majority of the water sports/tour activity is based. The brand-new cruise terminal is there, and the shopping and browsing availability is more than what you'll find in St George's. There's also a fast ferry service directly to Hamilton, plus buses that leave Dockyard straight for the gorgeous South Shore beaches."

—txgirlinbda

9

Updated by
Linda Coffman

Wouldn't you like to arrive in Bermuda relaxed, unpacked, and already in vacation mode? While Bermuda is only a two-hour flight from most East Coast cities, a cruise is more than simply transportation. There's nothing quite as traditional, or gracious, as a Bermuda arrival by sea.

In today's bigger-and-newer-is-better marketplace, major cruise lines are divesting their fleets of smaller and older ships. Unfortunately, those were the only cruise ships able to squeeze through the entrances into Hamilton and St. George's harbors. That narrows your selection to the few smaller ships remaining, and larger vessels that dock only at King's Wharf. In any case, you'll have access to the entire island by taxi, moped, public bus, high-speed ferry, or shore excursion.

Departure points for Bermuda cruises run the length of the Eastern seaboard, including Baltimore, Boston, New York, Norfolk, and Philadelphia. Departures are sometimes scheduled from other mid-Atlantic ports, such as Charleston, as well as those in Florida, so check with the cruise line or your travel agent. The Bermuda cruise season runs from mid-April through mid-November. However, a few ships make occasional port calls during off-season months.

Increasingly popular are round-trip itineraries originating in northeastern embarkation ports that include a single day or overnight port call in Bermuda before continuing south to the Bahamas or Caribbean. In addition to these Bermuda/Bahamas and Bermuda/Caribbean itineraries, "special" voyages or one-way ship-repositioning cruises are often available at the beginning or end of the usual Bermuda season, when cruise lines move their ships to the Caribbean for winter months.

CHOOSING A CRUISE

Your choice of cruise line to Bermuda is narrowed by the government's firm control over the annual number of cruise ships and visitors to the island. That figure has increased in recent years, allowing more passengers to experience all Bermuda has to offer while still receiving the best service and hospitality. Although most ships to Bermuda are big, floating-resort type vessels, each has its own personality, which is determined by its amenities, theme, and, of course, passengers.

Your cruise experience will be shaped by several factors. To decide whether a particular ship's style will suit you, you need to consider your lifestyle and vacation expectations and then do a bit of research: Is there a full program of organized activities each day? What happens in the evening? What kind of entertainment is offered after dark? How often will you need to dress up for dinner? Are there facilities for kids and teens?

Space and passenger-to-crew ratios are equally important. The latter indicates the number of passengers served by each crew member—the lower the ratio, the better the level of service. The space ratio (the gross tonnage of a ship divided by its passenger capacity) allows you to compare ships' roominess. The higher the ratio, the more spacious the vessel feels: at 40:1 or higher a ship will feel quite roomy. Less than 25:1 will cramp anyone's style.

ACCOMMODATIONS

CABIN SIZE

The term "stateroom," used on some ships, is usually interchangeable with "cabin." Price is directly proportional to size and location of your chosen accommodations, and most cabins are more compact than you would expect. The higher you go in the ship, the more expensive the quarters tend to be.

Suites are the roomiest and best-equipped accommodations, but they may differ in size, facilities, and price even on the same ship. Steward service may be more attentive to passengers staying in suites; top suites on some ships are even assigned private butlers. Most suites have a sitting area with sofa and chairs, but sleeping areas aren't necessarily separated from it with more than a curtain. However, some top suites have entirely private bedrooms, walk-in closets, and a guest bathroom. Occasionally the main bathroom has a separate shower and a whirlpool bath.

LOCATION

Today's cruise ships have stabilizers that make seasickness mostly a problem of the past. However, if you're susceptible to motion sickness, try to book a cabin amidships (close to the middle of the ship) as the bow (front) and stern (back) pitch up and down far more when the waves are uncooperative. Ships also experience a side-to-side motion known as roll. The closer your deck is to the true center of the ship—which is halfway between the bottom of the hull and the highest deck and midway between the bow and the stern—the less you will feel the ship's movement. Some cruise lines charge more for cabins amidships; most charge more for higher decks.

Outside cabins have portholes or windows (which cannot be opened). Upper-deck views from outside cabins may be partially obstructed by lifeboats or overlook a public promenade. Because outside cabins are more desirable, most newer ships are configured with only or mostly outside cabins; outside cabins on upper decks are increasingly being built with private verandas. Cabins that overlook a

9

TOP 5 CRUISING

■ Climb up Gibbs Hill Lighthouse for an expansive view of the inlets and harbors.

■ Absorb Bermuda's nautical and military history at the National Museum of Bermuda.

■ Ride on the ferries to rub shoulders with Bermudians.

■ Watch gossips and nagging wives get drenched in a dunking stool during the town crier's St. George's reenactment.

■ Marvel as ships gingerly inch through the cuts at Hamilton harbor with *very* little room to spare.

public promenade have mirrored windows, so that passersby can't see in by day; after dark, you'll need to draw your curtains.

Inside cabins on older vessels are often smaller, and some are oddly shaped. On newer ships, inside cabin floor plans are virtually identical to those of outside cabins. As long as you don't feel claustrophobic without a window—and most cruise lines hang curtains or place mirrors on the wall to create the illusion—inside cabins are generally an excellent value.

Cruise brochures in print and online show a ship's layout deck by deck, and include the approximate location and shape of every cabin and suite. Use the deck plan to make sure the cabin you choose is not directly above or below public rooms or near the ship's engine, both of which can be noisy; and make sure that you're close to stairs or an elevator if you want to avoid walking down a long passageway every time you return to your cabin. If you can access detailed layouts of typical cabins, you can determine what kind of beds each cabin has, whether it has a window or a porthole, and what furnishings are provided.

SHARING

Most cabins are designed to accommodate two people. When more than two share a cabin, the third and fourth passengers are usually offered a substantial discount, thereby lowering the per-person price for the entire group. An additional discount is sometimes offered when children share a cabin with their parents.

COSTS

The average daily price of a Bermuda cruise varies dramatically depending on several circumstances. The cost of a cruise on a luxury line such as Regent Seven Seas Cruises or Crystal Cruises may be three to five or more times the cost of a cruise on a mainstream line such as Royal Caribbean or Norwegian Cruise Line. Although Bermuda has a relatively short cruising season, you can often save money by cruising in April, before the island experiences ideal beach weather or late in the season, but that is the time when hurricanes are most likely.

Solo travelers should be aware that single cabins have virtually disappeared from cruise ships. Taking a double cabin can cost twice the advertised per-person rates (which are based on double occupancy); passengers traveling on their own must pay a single supplement, which usually ranges from 125% to 200% of the double-occupancy per-person rate. Some cruise lines will find same-sex roommates for singles; each then pays the per-person, double-occupancy rate.

EXTRAS

Aside from the cost of your cruise there are additional expenses to consider, such as airfare to the embarkation port city. These days, virtually all cruise lines offer air add-ons, which are sometimes less expensive than the lowest available airline fare. Shore excursions can also be a substantial expense; the best shore excursions are not cheap. But if you skimp too much on your excursion budget you can deprive yourself of an important part of the Bermuda cruising experience. Finally, there will be many extras added onto your shipboard account during the cruise, including drinks (both alcoholic and nonalcoholic), activity fees (you pay to play bingo), dining in specialty restaurants, spa services, and even cappuccino and espresso on most ships.

TIPPING

Tipping is another add-on. At the end of the cruise, it's customary to tip your room steward, dining-room waiter, and the person who buses your table. You should expect to pay an average of $11 to $14 per day in tips. Most major cruise lines do not use the traditional method of tipping the service staff in cash at the end of the cruise, opting instead to add the recommended amount per day to your onboard account, which you may adjust upward or downward according to the level of service you receive. Bar bills generally include an automatic 15%–18% gratuity, so the one person you don't need to tip is your bartender. Some high-end cruise lines have no-tipping-required policies, though most passengers tip anyway. Each cruise line offers guidelines.

THE BERMUDA CRUISE FLEET

To avoid overcrowding, the Bermudian government limits the number of regular cruise-ship visits to the island. Cruise lines with weekly sailings are Holland America Line, Norwegian Cruise Line, and Royal Caribbean International. In addition, cruise lines such as Carnival Cruise Lines, Seabourn Cruises, Silversea Cruises, MSC Cruises, Regent Seven Seas Cruises, Princess Cruises, and Oceania Cruises each have at least one Bermuda cruise or a Bermuda port call on their 2012 schedules.

MAINSTREAM CRUISE LINES

9

Generally speaking, the mainstream lines have two basic ship sizes—large cruise ship and megaship—in their fleets. These vessels have plentiful outdoor deck space, and many have a wraparound outdoor promenade deck that allows you to stroll or jog the ship's perimeter. In the newest cruise ships, traditional meets trendy. You can find atrium lobbies and expansive sun and sports decks, picture windows instead of portholes, and cabins that open onto private verandas. For all these resort-style innovations, the newest ships still feature onboard classics—afternoon tea, complimentary room service, and lavish pampering. The smallest cruise ships carry 1,000 passengers at most, whereas the largest accommodate more than 3,000 passengers and are filled with diversions.

If you're into big, bold, brassy, and nonstop activity, these huge ships offer it all. The centerpiece of most megaships is a three-, five-, or even eleven-story central atrium. However, these giant vessels are most readily distinguished by their profile: the boxy hull and superstructure rise as many as 14 stories out of the water and are capped by a huge sun or sports deck with a jogging track and one or more swimming pools. From their casinos and discos to their fitness centers, everything is bigger and more extravagant than on other ships. You may want to rethink a cruise aboard one of these ships if you like a bit more intimacy, since you'll be joined by up to 3,000 fellow passengers. Keep in mind that megaships are limited to docking at the Royal Navy Dockyard—they are simply too big to slip into the harbors at Hamilton and St. George's.

HOLLAND AMERICA LINE

Holland America was founded in 1873 as the Netherlands-America Steamship Company (NASM), a shipping and passenger line. It was headquartered in Rotterdam and provided service to the Americas, so became known as Holland America Line (HAL). Within 25 years, HAL owned a fleet of six cargo and passenger ships, and was known as one of the first lines to offer passage to the Dutch West Indies in the late 19th century, via the newly opened Suez Canal. The line was a principal carrier of immigrants from Europe to the United States until well after the turn of the century, carrying 850,000 to new lives in the New World.

Though transportation and shipping were the primary sources of revenue, in 1895 the company offered its first vacation cruise. Moving forward to 1989, HAL became a wholly owned subsidiary of Carnival Corp., the largest cruise company in the world. Today, the premium cruise liner has a fleet of 15 ships offering nearly 500 cruises to 350 ports of call in more than 100 countries. More than 720,000 cruise passengers a year embark on two-day to six-month itineraries visiting all seven continents. The line is best known for its Caribbean, Alaska, Europe, and Mexico cruises, as well as its extensive round-the-world trips. The line's ships range from the smaller and older S-Class vessels; the midrange R-Class; the Vista class, and the newest and largest Signature class. HAL's newest ship is the 2,106-passenger MS Nieuw Amsterdam, which entered service in 2010.

HAL's ships are a lot smaller than many of its competitors and lack many of the modern activities such as rock climbing and ice-skating, however the line has always prided itself on its quality of service. As far back as the 1920s, the ships became known as "the spotless fleet" for their cleanliness, and in the 1950s and 1960s the company's advertising slogan was "It's good to be on a well-run ship." Winner of numerous awards and accolades, HAL was named the best overall cruise value in the industry for 17 years running by the members of the World Ocean & Cruise Liner Society.

A top-notch dining experience is a top priority for the fleet, which teamed up with *Food and Wine* magazine to offer gourmet demonstrations and seminars by top chefs and wine experts. An onboard children's culinary program was also introduced in 2007. Self-guided iPod art tours are available on all ships; the fleet's highlighted pieces include Andy Warhol's famed Queen Beatrix series and Susanna Holt's life-size bronze sculptures of wildlife. The 2012 Bermuda season will see Veendam sailing from New York once again, with port calls at Hamilton.

HAL applies an automatic gratuity to passengers' shipboard accounts: $11 per passenger per day. A 15% gratuity is added to bar charges and dining room wine charges. ☎ *877/932–4259 ⊕ www. hollandamerica.com.*

Veendam. This elegant S-class ship, which came into service in 1996, has undergone extensive renovation to bring its features into line with the newest ships in the Holland America Line fleet. It boasts the two-tiered Rotterdam Dining Room with five-course menus, the upscale Pinnacle Grill alternative restaurant, Canaletto Restaurant where Italian fare is served at dinner in the Lido buffet, a larger swimming pool and restyled pool area, multiple lounges, a $2-million art and antiques collection, and a wide teak promenade deck. It's specially designed to carry fewer passengers while providing them with more space for maximum comfort. Most accommodations received an upgrade in 2009, when two decks of balcony cabins were added to the rear of the ship and new Lanai cabins with mirrored-glass doors opening onto the Promenade deck and a spa category that includes spa amenities were introduced. All accommodations are designated no-smoking; however, smoking is allowed on private balconies with the exception of those in the spa category. On board you have a good choice of dining facilities, a spa and salon, a coffeehouse with an extensive library and Internet access, Wi-Fi throughout the ship, and activities for children and teens. Digital workshops are also offered to passengers on topics such as blogging, social networking, and digital photography. ⇆ *675 cabins, 1,350 passengers, 10 passenger decks ☞ Safe, refrigerator, Wi-Fi, 3 restaurants, bars, pools, gym, spa, children's programs (ages 3–17), laundry facilities, laundry service.*

NORWEGIAN CRUISE LINE

Fodor's Choice ★

Norwegian Cruise Line (NCL) was established in 1966, when one of Norway's oldest and most respected shipping companies, Oslo-based Klosters Rederi A/S, acquired the *Sunward* and repositioned the ship from Europe to the then-obscure Port of Miami. With the formation of a company called Norwegian Caribbean Lines, the cruise industry was changed forever. NCL launched an entirely new concept with its regularly scheduled cruises to the Caribbean on a single-class ship, with an informal kind of luxury. No longer simply a means of transportation, the ship became a destination unto itself, offering guests an affordable alternative to land-based resorts. The *Sunward*'s popularity prompted other cruise lines to build ships to accommodate the burgeoning market, eventually turning Miami into the world's number-one cruise-ship embarkation port. NCL led the way with its fleet of sleek, new ships. In another bold move, NCL purchased the former *France* in 1979 and rebuilt the grand ocean liner for Caribbean cruising. Rechristened *Norway,* she assumed the honored position as flagship of the fleet until she was retired from service in 2003. The late 1980s brought new ships and a new corporate name when Norwegian Caribbean Lines became Norwegian Cruise Line in 1987. Freestyle Cruising created a sensation in the industry when Asian shipping giant Star Cruises acquired NCL early in 2000—the new owners were confounded that Americans meekly conformed to rigid dining schedules and dress codes. All that changed with NCL's introduction of a host of flexible dining options that allow passengers to choose open seating in the main dining rooms or dine

9

in any of a number of à la carte and specialty restaurants at any time and with whomever they please. With the retirement of its older and smaller ships, the Freestyle Cruising concept now applies to the entire NCL fleet. The line has even loosened the dress code to resort casual at all times and relaxed the disembarkation process by inviting passengers to remain in their cabins until it's time to leave the ship (instead of gathering in a lounge to wait for their numbers to be called). NCL's passenger list usually includes a wide range of ages, including families and couples, mostly from the United States and Canada.

A long-term agreement between NCL and the Bermuda government assures that the cruise line will sail at least two of its newest and largest ships to Bermuda through 2019. The 2012 season will see *Norwegian Gem* and *Norwegian Star* sailing from New York and *Norwegian Dawn* sailing from Boston. All will dock at King's Wharf, Dockyard.

NCL applies a service charge to passengers' shipboard accounts of $12 per passenger per day for those three and older. Passengers in suites who have access to concierge and butler services are asked to offer a cash gratuity at their own discretion. A 15% gratuity is added to bar tabs and 18% is added to spa bills. ☎ *305/436–4000 or 800/327–7030* ⊕ *www.ncl.com.*

Ⓒ **Norwegian Gem.** This 2007 Jewel-class ship offers the best of everything: numerous dining alternatives, a variety of entertainment options, an impressive spa and fitness center, and a pool deck complete with waterslides and hot tubs. For quieter pursuits, escape the crowds in the ship's tranquil library, which is also a good spot to gaze at the sea if your book proves to be less than compelling. Cabins are reasonably large and stylish, with plenty of storage. Standard features include a small sitting area with sofa, chair, and table, a mini-refrigerator, personal safe, broadband Internet connection, duvets on beds, and a wall-mounted hair dryer. Interconnecting staterooms in a variety of categories are perfect for families. For even more space and upgraded amenities, move up to the luxury Courtyard Villas Complex, where guests have exclusive access to a private pool deck, plus butler service and concierge. Kids love the four-lane bowling alley, a daily kids' club, and a two-story Nintendo Wii screen in the lobby atrium. ↘ *1,197 cabins, 2,394 passengers, 15 passenger decks � Safe, refrigerator, DVD (some), Wi-Fi, 10 restaurants, bars, pools, gym, spa, children's programs (ages 2–17), laundry service.*

Ⓒ **Norwegian Star and Norwegian Dawn.** Purpose-built for NCL's Freestyle cruising concept Dawn-class ships, *Norwegian Star* (launched in 2001) and *Norwegian Dawn* (introduced in 2002) *have* numerous dining options, a variety of entertainment selections, and enormous spas. These ships unveiled NCL's super deluxe Garden Villa accommodations, English pubs, and 24-hour dining. Their cabins are reasonably large, with stylish decor and nice-looking cherry-veneer cabinetry; minisuites with private verandas are especially nice. Most accommodations have compartmentalized bathrooms with toilet, sink, and shower separated by sliding-glass doors, and many are family-friendly with interior connecting doors. Extensive children's facilities (including a children's pool) and separate teen disco are definite pluses, as is Wi-Fi access throughout the ship. Major refurbishments on both vessels have refreshed the interiors to bring them in line with newer ships in the fleet. *1,174/1,184 cabins, 2,348/2,368 passengers, 11 passenger decks & Safe, refrigerator (some), DVD (some), Wi-Fi, 10 restaurants, bars, pools, gym, spa, children's programs (ages 2–17), laundry service.*

ROYAL CARIBBEAN INTERNATIONAL

Royal Caribbean International. Big, bigger, biggest! More than two decades ago, Royal Caribbean International (RCI) launched the first of the modern mega–cruise ships for passengers who enjoy traditional cruising with a touch of daring and whimsy tossed in. These large-to-giant vessels are indoor-outdoor wonders, with every conceivable activity in a resortlike atmosphere, including atrium lobbies, shopping arcades, large spas, expansive sundecks, and rock-climbing walls. Several ships have such elaborate facilities as 18-hole miniature-golf courses, ice-skating rinks, and in-line skating tracks. These mammoth ships quickly overshadowed the smaller vessels in Royal Caribbean's fleet, which have all retired from service over the years. Passengers now have six generations of megaships to choose from and, happily, RCI regularly rejuvenates its older vessels, adding new facilities to mirror the latest trends.

The centerpiece of Royal Caribbean megaships is the multideck atrium, a hallmark that has been duplicated by many other cruise lines. The brilliance of this design is that all the major public rooms radiate from this central point, so you can learn your way around these huge ships within minutes of boarding. Ships in the Vision series are especially bright and airy, with sea views almost anywhere you happen to be. The main problem with Royal Caribbean's otherwise well-conceived vessels is that, when booked to over 100% capacity, there are too many people on board, making for an exasperating experience at embarkation and disembarkation. However, small annoyances aside, Royal Caribbean is one of the best-run and most popular cruise lines. Coming to Bermuda for the 2012 season will be *Enchantment of the Seas*, sailing from Baltimore, Maryland, and *Explorer of the Seas*, sailing from Cape Liberty, New Jersey.

Although the line competes directly with Carnival and Norwegian Cruise Line for passengers—active couples and singles in their 30s to 50s, as well as a large family contingent—there are distinct differences in ambience and energy. Royal Caribbean is a bit more sophisticated and subdued, even while delivering a good time on a grand scale.

Tips can be prepaid when the cruise is booked, added onto shipboard accounts, or given in cash on the last night of the cruise. Suggested gratuities per passenger per day are $5 for the cabin steward ($7.25 for suites), $3.75 for the waiter, $2.15 for the assistant waiter, and $0.75 for the headwaiter. A 15% gratuity is automatically added to alcoholic-beverage and bar bills. ☎ *305/539–6000 or 800/327–6700* ⊕ *www.royalcaribbean.com.*

☾ **Enchantment of the Seas.** Having undergone an "extreme makeover" in 2005, the lengthened and fully refurbished *Enchantment of the Seas* is on par with her sister ships.

GOOD TO KNOW

Duty-free prices at Bermuda liquor stores only apply when purchases are delivered directly to your ship. Carry-outs carry a premium price tag.

This ship is serious fun for thrill seekers, with bungee trampolines, massive suspension bridges spanning the pool deck, and a rock-climbing wall. The Centrum is an open atrium packed with shops and bars, and there's a pool deck, plus a splash deck for children. There are plenty of dining options like the two-tier dining room with two dinner seatings or an open seating ("My Timing Dining") option, the more casual buffet-style Windjammer Café, and a coffee and ice cream bar. For a more upscale dinner, there is the line's specialty steak house, Chops Grille, which charges a supplement and requires reservations. Room service is available 24 hours; however there is a charge after midnight. Light woods, pastel colors, a vanity-desk, a TV, a safe, a hair dryer, and a sitting area with sofa, chair, and table are typical features in all accommodations categories. Cabins are light and comfortable, although the smallest can be a tight squeeze for more than two adults. For larger families, family suites have private balconies, a small refrigerator, and sleep up to eight, while family ocean-view staterooms sleep six. ⇗ *1,126 cabins, 2,252 passengers (2,446 at full occupancy), 11 passenger decks* ☞ *Safe, Wi-Fi, 3 restaurants, bars, pools, gym, spa, children's programs (ages 3–17), laundry service.*

☾ **Explorer of the Seas.** Royal Caribbean's enormous Voyager-class vessels are among the world's largest cruise ships and represent the highest space-per-guest ratio in the RCI fleet. Innovative and eye-popping features include ice-skating rinks, basketball courts, shopping promenades, in-line skating tracks, 18-hole miniature-golf courses, and rock-climbing walls. Spectacular three-story dining rooms have two dinner seatings or an open seating ("My Timing Dining") option. There are also other dining choices, both casual (the buffet-style Windjammer Café and an actual Johnny Rockets diner) and reservation-only (Portofino, serving Italian fare for an extra fee). Room service is available 24 hours; however, there is a charge after midnight. As on all Royal Caribbean ships, accommodations are cheery; however, while cabins are larger than on earlier ships, the least expensive can be a tight squeeze for more than two occupants. Suites have the advantage of more floor space and larger closets; other cabins have twin beds convertible to a queen and bathrooms with hair dryers and sizable vanity areas; some inside staterooms have a view overlooking the gigantic atrium. RCI boasts that staterooms designed for families can sleep up to eight. ⇗ *1,557 cabins, 3,114 passengers (3,835 to 3,844 at full occupancy), 14 passenger decks* ☞ *Safe, refrigerator, DVD (some), Wi-Fi, 3 restaurants, bars, pools, gym, spa, children's programs (ages 3–17), laundry service.*

BEFORE YOU GO

To expedite your preboarding paperwork, most cruise lines have convenient forms on their Web sites. As long as you have your reservation number, you can provide the required immigration information, reserve shore excursions, and even indicate special requests from the comfort of your home. Less "wired" cruise lines might mail preboarding paperwork to you or your travel agent for completion after you make your final payment and request that you return the forms by mail or fax. No matter how you submit them, be sure to make copies of any forms you fill out and to bring them with you to the pier to shorten the check-in process.

TRAVEL DOCUMENTS

After you make the final payment to your travel agent, the cruise line will issue your cruise tickets and vouchers for airport-to-ship transfers, or you may be able to print them yourselves from the line's Web site. Depending on the airline, and whether you have purchased an air-sea package, you may receive your flight reservations or e-ticket vouchers at the same time; you may also receive vouchers for shore excursions, although cruise lines generally issue these aboard ship. Should your travel documents not arrive when promised, contact your travel agent or call the cruise line.

Children under the age of 18 who are not traveling with both parents almost always require a letter of permission from the absent parent(s). Airlines, cruise lines, and immigration agents can deny minor children initial boarding or entry to foreign countries without proper proof of identification and citizenship *and* a permission letter from absent or noncustodial parents. Your travel agent or cruise line can help with the wording of such a letter.

A WORD ABOUT PASSPORTS

It is every passenger's responsibility to have proper identification. If you arrive at the embarkation port without it, you will not be allowed to board, and the cruise line will issue no fare refund. Most travel agents know the requirements and can guide you to the proper agency to obtain what you need if you don't have it.

Everyone must have proof of citizenship and identity to travel abroad. Effective June 1, 2009, travelers were required to present a passport or other approved document denoting citizenship and identity for all land *and* sea travel into the United States. Like most rules, there is a confusing exception—U.S. citizens traveling within the so-called "Caribbean Region" (which includes Bermuda) on closed-loop cruises (cruises that begin and end in the same port) are still permitted to depart from or enter the U.S. with proof of identity, which includes a government-issued photo ID, such as a driver's license, along with proof of citizenship, such as a certified birth certificate with seal issued by the state where you were born. However, you may still be required to present a passport when you dock at a foreign port, depending on the islands or countries that your cruise ship is visiting. And if your cruise begins in one U.S. port and ends in a different port, you will be required to have a passport. Check with your cruise line to ensure you have the appropriate documents for the stops you'll be making on your cruise.

WHAT TO PACK

Cruise wear falls into three categories: casual, informal, and formal. Cruise documents should include information indicating how many evenings fall into each category. You will know when to wear what by reading your ship's daily newsletter—each evening's dress code will be prominently announced.

> **FRUGAL FUN**
>
> Riding the ferry is an outstanding—and inexpensive—way to see Bermuda from the water. Bus and ferry passes, while sold on board some cruise ships, are usually less expensive when purchased at the ferry landing.

For the day, you'll need casual wear, including swimwear, a cover-up, and sandals for pool and beach. Time spent ashore touring and shopping calls for shorts topped with T-shirts or polo shirts and comfy walking shoes. Conservative is a rule to live by in Bermuda, and mix-and-match will save room in your suitcase. Forget denim, which is too hot, and concentrate on lighter fabrics that will breathe in the heat. At night, casual means khaki-type slacks and polo or sport shirts for men and sundresses, skirts, or casual pants outfits for women. By sticking to a few colors and adding accessories, you can mix and match for a different look every night.

Informal dress—sometimes called "resort casual" or "country club casual"—is a little trickier. It applies only to evening wear and can mean different things depending on the cruise line. Informal for women is a dressier dress or pants outfit; for men it almost always includes a sport coat, and a tie is optional. Check your documents carefully.

Formal night means dressing up, but these days even that is a relative notion. You'll see women in everything from simple cocktail dresses to elaborate, glittering gowns. A tuxedo (either all black or with white dinner jacket) or dark suit is required for gentlemen. For children, Sunday best is entirely appropriate.

Men can usually rent their formal attire from the cruise line, and if they do so, it will be waiting when they board. Be sure to make these arrangements in advance; your travel agent can get the details from the cruise line. But if you're renting a tux, buy your own studs: a surefire way to spot a rented tuxedo is by the inexpensive studs that come with it. Also, many men with a little girth consider a vest more comfortable than a cummerbund.

An absolute essential for women is a shawl or light sweater. Aggressive air-conditioning can make public rooms uncomfortable, particularly if you're sunburned from a day at the beach.

Put things you can't do without—such as prescription medication, spare eyeglasses, toiletries, a swimsuit, and change of clothes for the first day—in your carry-on. Most cruise ships provide soap, shampoo, and conditioner.

CRIME ON BOARD

Crime aboard cruise ships has occasionally become headline news, thanks in large part to a few well-publicized cases. Most people never have any type of problem, but you should exercise the same precautions aboard ship that you would at home. Keep your valuables out of sight—on big ships virtually every cabin has a small safe in the cabin. Don't carry too much cash ashore, use your credit card whenever possible, and keep your money in a secure place, such as a front pocket that's harder to pick. Single women traveling with friends should stick together, especially when returning to their cabins late at night. When assaults occur, it often comes to light that alcohol, particularly over-indulgence in alcohol, is a factor. Be careful about whom you befriend, as you would anywhere, whether it's a fellow passenger or a member of the crew. Don't be paranoid, but do be prudent.

Your cruise is a wonderful opportunity to leave everyday responsibilities behind, but don't neglect to pack your common sense. After a few drinks it might seem like a good idea to sit on a railing or lean over to get a better view of the ship's wake. Passengers have been known to fall. "Man overboard" is more likely to be the result of carelessness than criminal intent.

ACCESSIBILITY ISSUES

As recently as the early 1990s, "accessibility" on a cruise ship meant little more than a few inside staterooms set aside for passengers with mobility issues. Most public restrooms and nearly all en suite bathrooms had a "step-over" threshold. Newer ships are more sensitive to the needs of passengers with disabilities, but many older ships still have physical barriers in both cabins and public rooms. And once you get off the ship your problems will be compounded.

All cruise lines offer a limited number of staterooms designed to be wheelchair- and scooter-accessible. Booking a newer vessel will generally assure more choices and better accessibility. Auxiliary aids, such as flashers for the hearing impaired and buzzers for visually impaired passengers, as well as lifts for swimming pools and hot tubs, are available upon request. However, more than the usual amount of preplanning is necessary for smooth sailing if you have special needs.

Some people with limited mobility may find it difficult to embark or disembark the ship when docked due to the steep angle of gangways during high or low tide at certain times of day. In some situations, crew members may offer assistance that involves carrying guests, but if the sea is choppy, that might not be an option.

Passengers who require continuous oxygen or have service animals have further hurdles to overcome. You can bring both aboard a cruise ship, but your service animal will not be allowed to go ashore with you in Bermuda without an import permit, which must be requested in advance.

ARRIVING AND DEPARTING

Most cruise-ship passengers fly to the port of embarkation. If you book your cruise far enough in advance, you'll be given the opportunity to purchase an air & sea package, which sometimes saves you money on your flight. By making your own airline arrangements, though, you may find airfare low enough to cover a pre-cruise night in a hotel if you have the time to fly in a day early. With frequent flight delays and cancellations these days, it's always a good idea to arrive in your port city the day before sailing—you will be more refreshed at boarding time and you don't want to "miss the boat"!

If you buy an air & sea package from your cruise line, a uniformed cruise-line agent will meet you to smooth your way from airport to pier. You'll need to claim your own bags and give them to the transfer driver so they can be loaded on the bus. Upon arrival at the pier, luggage is automatically transferred to the ship for delivery to your cabin. The cruise-line ground-transfer system can also be available to independent fliers. However, be sure to ask your travel agent how much it costs; you may find that a taxi or shuttle service is less expensive and more convenient.

Many people prefer to drive to embarkation ports if they are close enough to home; secure parking is always available, either within the port or nearby. Additionally, some nearby hotels might offer free parking while you sail if you spend one pre-cruise night there.

BOARDING

Once the planning, packing, and anticipation are behind them, veteran cruise passengers sometimes view embarkation day as anticlimactic. However, for first-time cruise travelers, embarking on their first ship can be more than exhilarating—it can be downright intimidating. What exactly can you expect?

CHECK-IN

Once inside the cruise terminal, you'll see a check-in line. Actual boarding time is often scheduled to begin at noon, but some cruise lines will process early arrivals and then direct them to a "holding" area. During check-in, you'll be asked to produce your documents and any forms you were asked to complete ahead of time, plus proof of citizenship, and a credit card (to cover onboard charges). You're issued a boarding card that usually doubles as your stateroom key and shipboard charge card. At some point—usually before you enter the check-in area—you and your hand luggage will pass through a security procedure similar to those at airports.

The lines for check-in can be long, particularly at peak times. If check-in starts at noon but continues to 4 pm, you can expect lines to trail off as the boarding deadline approaches. While the gangway is generally not removed until 30 minutes before sailing, U.S. government security regulations require cruise lines to submit certain passenger information to law enforcement authorities at least 60 minutes prior to departure. To meet that requirement, they must have the necessary information in their computers at least 90 minutes before departure. If you arrive too late and your information is not in the system before the deadline, you run the risk being denied boarding even though the ship won't be sailing for over an hour (i.e., if your cruise departs at 5 pm, you must be on the ship no later than 3:30).

Everyone is anxious to get on board and begin their vacation, so if you arrive at one of the busy periods, keep in mind that this is not the time to get cranky if you have to wait.

BOARDING THE SHIP

Once boarding begins, you'll inevitably have your first experience with the ship's photographer and be asked to pose for an embarkation picture. It only takes a second, so smile. You are under no obligation to purchase any photos taken of you during the cruise, but they're a nice souvenir.

Procedures vary somewhat once you're greeted by staff members lined up just inside the ship's hull; however, you'll have to produce your boarding card for the security officer. At some point, either at the check-in desk or when boarding the ship for the first time, you'll be photographed for security purposes—your image will display on a monitor when your boarding card is "swiped" into a computer as you leave and reboard the ship throughout the cruise. Depending on the cruise line, once aboard you'll be directed to your cabin, or a steward will relieve you of your carry-on luggage and accompany you. Stewards on high-end cruise lines not only show you the way, but hand you a glass of champagne as a welcome-aboard gesture. However, if you board at noon or shortly thereafter, you might be directed to the dining room or buffet restaurant where you can have lunch while your cabin is being readied for your arrival.

ON BOARD

As you settle in, check out your cabin to make sure that everything is in order. Try the plumbing and set the air-conditioning to the temperature you prefer. Your cabin may feel warm while docked but will cool off when the ship is underway. You should find a copy of the ship's daily schedule in the cabin. Take a few moments to look it over—you'll want to know what time the muster drill takes place (a placard on the back of your cabin door will indicate directions to your emergency station), as well as meal hours and the schedule for various activities and entertainments.

Rented tuxedoes are either hanging in the closet or will be delivered sometime during the afternoon; bon-voyage gifts sent by your friends or travel agent usually appear as well. Be patient if you're expecting deliveries, particularly on megaships. Cabin stewards participate in the ship's turnaround and are extremely busy, although yours will no doubt introduce himself at the first available opportunity. It will also be a while before your checked luggage arrives, so your initial order of business is usually the buffet if you haven't already had lunch. Bring along the daily schedule to examine in detail while you eat.

While making your way around the ship, no doubt you'll notice bar waiters offering trays of colorful and exotic drinks, often in souvenir glasses that you can keep. Beware—they are not complimentary! If you choose one, you will be asked to sign for it. Again, like the photos, you're under no obligation to purchase; however, the glasses are fun souvenirs.

Do your plans for the cruise include booking shore excursions and indulging in spa treatments? The most popular tours sometimes sell out, and spas can be very busy during sea days, so your next stops should be the shore-excursion desk to book tours and the spa to make appointments if you haven't already done so online. You may even want to take care of those tasks on the way to the buffet.

Dining-room seating arrangements are another matter for consideration. Some people like to check the main dining room to determine where their table is located. If it's not to your liking, or if you requested a large table and find yourself assigned to a small one, you'll want to see the headwaiter. He'll be stationed in a lounge with his charts handy to make changes. The daily schedule will indicate where and when to meet with him. If you plan to dine in the ship's specialty restaurant, make those reservations as soon as possible to avoid disappointment.

PAYING FOR THINGS ON BOARD

Let's step back a moment and take a look at what happened when you checked in at the pier. Because a cashless society prevails on cruise ships, an imprint was made of your credit card or you had to place a cash deposit for use against your onboard charges. Then you were issued a charge card that usually doubles as your stateroom key. Most onboard expenditures are charged to your shipboard account with your signature as verification, with the possible exception of casino gaming—even so, you can often get cash advances against your account from the casino cashier.

An itemized bill is provided at the end of the voyage listing your purchases. In order to avoid surprises, it's a good idea to set aside your charge slips and request an interim printout of your bill from the purser to insure accuracy. On some ships you can even access your account on your stateroom TV. Should you change your mind about charging onboard purchases, you can always inform the purser and pay in cash or traveler's checks instead. If your cash deposit was more than you spent, you'll receive a refund.

TIPPING

One of the most delicate—yet frequently debated—topics of conversation among cruise passengers involves the matter of tipping. Who do you tip? How much? What's "customary" and "recommended?" Should parents tip the full amount for children or is just half adequate? Why do you have to tip at all?

When transfers to and from your ship are a part of your air & sea program, gratuities are generally included for luggage handling. In that case, do not worry about the interim tipping. However, if you take a taxi to the pier and hand over your bags to a stevedore, be sure to tip him. Treat him with respect and pass along at least $5.

During your cruise, room-service waiters generally receive a cash tip of $1 to $3 per delivery. A 15% gratuity will automatically be added to each bar bill during the cruise. If you use salon and spa services, a similar percentage might be added to the bills there as well. If you dine in a specialty restaurant, it may be suggested that you extend a one-time gratuity for the service staff.

There will be a "disembarkation talk" on the last day of the cruise that explains tipping procedures. If you're expected to tip in cash, which is increasingly rare these days, small white tip envelopes will appear in your stateroom that day. If you tip in cash, you usually give the tip envelope directly to each person on the last night of the cruise. Tips generally add up to about $11 to $12 per person (including children) per day.

Most lines now either automatically add gratuities to passengers' onboard charge accounts or offer the option. If that suits you, then do nothing further. However, you're certainly free to adjust the amounts up or down to more appropriate levels or ask that the charge be removed altogether if you prefer distributing cash gratuities.

9

DINING

All food, all the time? Not quite, but it's possible to literally eat away the day and most of the night on a cruise. A popular cruise directors' joke is, "You came on as passengers, and you will be leaving as cargo." Although it's meant in fun, it does contain an element of truth. Food—tasty and plentiful—is available 24 hours a day on most cruise ships, and the dining experience at sea has reached almost mythical proportions. Perhaps it has something to do with legendary midnight buffets, the absence of menu prices, or maybe it's the vast selection and availability.

RESTAURANTS

Every ship has at least one main restaurant and a Lido, or casual, buffet alternative. Increasingly important are specialty restaurants. Meals in the primary and buffet restaurants are included in the cruise fare, as is round-the-clock room service on most lines, with Royal Caribbean being the exception—while room service is available 24 hours, there is an automatic per-order charge after midnight. Midday tea and snacks, and late-night buffets are also complimentary on ships that offer them. Most mainstream cruise lines levy a surcharge for dining in alternative restaurants that may, or may not, also include a gratuity, although there generally is no additional charge on luxury cruise lines.

> ### GOOD TO KNOW
>
> It isn't stinginess on the part of the cruise line that forbids bringing snacks ashore. Fruits, vegetables, seeds, plants, and meat are not allowed to be removed from the ship by regulation of the Bermuda government.

You may also find a pizzeria or a specialty coffee bar on your ship—popular favorites cropping up on ships old and new. Pizza is complimentary, but expect an additional charge for specialty coffees at the coffee bar and, quite likely, in the dining room as well. You'll also be charged for alcoholic beverages and soft drinks during meals; iced tea, regular coffee, tap water, and fruit juice are the most common complimentary beverages.

There's often a direct relationship between the cost of a cruise and the quality of its cuisine. The food is sophisticated on some (mostly expensive) lines, among them Crystal Cruises, Silversea Cruises, and Regent Seven Seas Cruises. In the more moderate price range, Oceania Cruises and Azamara Club Cruises have gained renown for their culinary stylings. The trend toward featuring signature dishes and even entire menus designed by acclaimed chefs has spread throughout the cruise industry; however, on most mainstream cruise lines, the food is of the quality that you would find at any good hotel banquet—perfectly acceptable but certainly not gourmet.

SEATINGS

If your cruise ship has traditional seatings for dinner, the one decision that may set the tone for your entire cruise is your dinner seating. Which is best? Early dinner seating is generally scheduled between 6 and 6:30 pm, and late seating can begin from 8:15 to 8:45 pm. So the "best" seating depends on you, your lifestyle, and your personal preference.

Families with young children and older passengers often choose an early seating. Early seating diners are encouraged not to linger too long over dessert and coffee because the dining room has to be readied for late seating. Late seating is viewed by some passengers as more romantic and less rushed.

Cruise lines understand that strict schedules no longer satisfy the desires of all cruise passengers. Most cruise lines now include alternatives to the set schedules in the dining room, including an open seating option, and casual dinner menus in their buffet facilities, where more flexibility is allowed in dress and meal times. À la carte restaurants are showing up on more ships and offer yet another choice, though usually for an additional charge.

Open seating is primarily associated with more upscale lines; it allows passengers the flexibility to dine any time during restaurant hours and be seated with whomever they please.

CHANGING TABLES

Most cruise lines advise that, although dining preferences may be requested by your travel agent, no requests are guaranteed. Table assignments are generally not confirmed until embarkation; however, every effort is made to satisfy all guests. If there's a problem, see the headwaiter for assistance. Changes after the first evening are generally discouraged; however, there will be a designated place to meet with dining-room staff and iron out seating problems during embarkation day. Check the daily program or ask at the reception desk for the time and location.

SPECIAL DIETS

Cruise lines make every possible attempt to ensure dining satisfaction. If you have special dietary considerations—such as low-salt, kosher, or food allergies—be sure to indicate them well ahead of time and check to be certain your needs are known by your waiter once you're on board. In addition to the usual menu items, spa, low-calorie, low-carbohydrate, or low-fat selections, as well as children's menus, are usually available. Requests for dishes not featured on the menu can often be granted if you ask in advance.

WINE

Wine typically costs about what you would expect to pay at a nice lounge or restaurant in a resort or in your local liquor store (depending on where you live). Wine by the bottle is a more economical choice at dinner than ordering it by the glass. Any wine you don't finish will be kept for you and served the next night. Gifts of wine or champagne ordered from the cruise line (either by you, a friend, or your travel agent) can be taken to the dining room. Wine from any other source will incur a corkage fee of approximately $15 to $25 per bottle.

THE CAPTAIN'S TABLE

Legend has it that a nouveau-riche passenger's response to an invitation to dine with the captain during a round-the-world cruise was, "I didn't shell out all those bucks to eat with the help!" Although there are some cruise passengers who decline invitations to dine at the captain's table, there are far more who relish such an experience. You will know you have been included in that exclusive coterie when an embossed invitation arrives in your stateroom on the day of a formal dinner. RSVP as soon as possible—if you are unable to attend, someone else will be invited in your place.

Who is invited? If you're a frequent cruiser, occupy an owner's suite, or if you hail from the captain's hometown and speak his native language, you may be considered. Honeymoon couples are sometimes selected at random, as are couples celebrating a golden wedding anniversary. Unattached female passengers often round out an uneven number of guests. Requests made by travel agents on behalf of their clients sometimes do the trick.

DRINKING ON BOARD

It's difficult to avoid the ship's bars since they are social centers, but alcoholic drinks are not usually included in your cruise fare, and bar bills can add up quickly. Drinks at the captain's welcome-aboard cocktail party and at cocktail parties held specifically for repeat cruisers are usually free. But if you pick up that boldly colored welcome-aboard cocktail as your ship pulls away from the dock, you may well be asked to sign for it, and the cost will then be added to your shipboard account. You should expect to pay about the same for a drink on board a cruise ship as you would pay in a bar at home: $5 to $6 for a domestic beer, $5.75 to $9 for a cocktail, $6 to $9 for a glass of wine, $1.50 to $2 for a soft drink. On virtually all ships an automatic 15% gratuity will be added to your tab. Also note that specialty coffees like cappuccino—even in the dining room after dinner—will add a $3 to $4 charge to your onboard account. To save money on your bar bill, you can follow a few simple strategies. In lounges, request the less expensive bar brands or the reduced-price drink of the day. On some ships, discounted "beverage cards" for unlimited fountain soft drinks and/or a set number of mixed drinks are available.

In international waters there are, technically, no laws against teenage drinking, but almost all ships require passengers to be over 21 to purchase alcoholic beverages.

ENTERTAINMENT

It's hard to imagine, but in the early years of cruise travel shipboard entertainment consisted of little more than poetry readings and recitals that exhibited the talents of fellow passengers. Those bygone days of sedate amusements in an intimate setting have been replaced by lavish showrooms where sequined and feathered showgirls strut their stuff on stage amid previously unimagined special effects.

Seven-night Bermuda cruises usually include two original production shows. One of these might be a Las Vegas–style extravaganza and the other a best-of-Broadway show featuring old and new favorites from the Great White Way. Other shows highlight the talents of individual singers, dancers, magicians, comedians, and even acrobats. Don't be surprised if you're plucked from the audience to take the brunt of a comedian's jokes or act as the magician's temporary assistant. Sit in the front row if appearing onstage appeals to you.

Whether it's relegated to a late-afternoon interlude between bingo and dinner or a featured evening highlight, the passenger talent show is often a "don't miss" production. From pure camp to stylishly slick, what passes for talent is sometimes surprising but seldom boring. Stand-up comedy is generally discouraged; however, passengers who want their performance skills to be considered should answer the call for auditions and plan to rehearse the show at least once.

Enrichment programs have become a popular pastime at sea. It may come as a surprise that port lecturers on many large contemporary cruise ships offer more information on shore tours and shopping than insight into the ports of call. If more cerebral presentations are important to you, consider a cruise on a line that features stimulating enrichment programs and seminars. Speakers may include destination-oriented historians, popular authors, business leaders, radio or television personalities, and even movie stars.

LOUNGES AND NIGHTCLUBS

If you find the show-lounge stage a bit intimidating and want to perform in a more intimate venue, look for karaoke. Singing along in a piano bar is another shipboard favorite for would-be crooners.

Other lounges might feature easy-listening music, jazz, or combos for pre- and post-dinner social dancing. Later in the evening, lounges pick up the pace with music from the 1950s and '60s; clubs aimed at a younger crowd usually have more contemporary dance music during the late-night hours.

CASINOS

A sure sign that your ship is in international waters is the opening of the casino. All ships currently offering Bermuda itineraries feature casinos.

The rationale for locating casinos where most passengers must pass either through or alongside them is obvious—the unspoken allure of winning. In addition to slot machines in a variety of denominations, cruise-ship casinos might feature roulette, craps, and a variety of poker games—Caribbean stud poker, Let It Ride, Texas Hold 'Em, and blackjack, to name a few. Cruise lines strive to provide fair and professional gambling entertainment and supply gaming guides that set out the rules of play and betting limits for each game.

Casino hours vary based on the itinerary or location of the ship; most are required to close while in port, whereas others may offer 24-hour slot machines. Every casino has a cashier for convenience, and you may be able to charge a cash advance to your onboard account.

OTHER ENTERTAINMENT

Most vessels have a room for screening movies. On older ships and some newer ones, this is often a genuine movie theater; on other ships it may be a multipurpose room or even a giant screen on the Lido deck. Over the course of a weeklong voyage a dozen films may be screened, each repeated several times. Traditional theaters are also used for lectures, religious services, and private meetings.

With a few exceptions, cruise ships equip their cabins with closed-circuit TVs showing movies (continuously on some newer ships), shipboard lectures, and regular programs (thanks to satellite reception). Ships with in-cabin VCRs or DVDs usually provide a selection of movies at no charge (a deposit is sometimes required).

Most medium- and large-size ships have video arcades, and nearly all ships now have computer centers and feature Wi-Fi—either bow-to-stern or in hotspots.

SPAS

With all the usual pampering and service in luxurious surroundings, simply being on a cruise can be a stress-reducing experience. Add to that the menu of spa and salon services at your fingertips and you have a recipe for total sensory pleasure. The spas have become among the most popular of shipboard ser-

> ### GOOD TO KNOW
>
> Your ship's spa treatments are often available at a significantly reduced price during port days. Pamper yourself—and your wallet.

vices, so book your blisstime as soon as possible. Some cruise lines allow you to book services in advance.

Some of the more exotic spa offerings sound good enough to eat. A Milk and Honey Hydrotherapy Bath; Coconut Rub & Milk Ritual Wrap or Float; and a Javanese Steam Wrap incorporating cinnamon, ginger, coffee, sea salt, and honey are just a few of the tempting items found on spa menus. Not quite as exotic sounding, other treatments and services are nonetheless therapeutic for the body and soul. Steiner Leisure is the largest spa and salon operator at sea (the company even operates the Mandara and the Greenhouse spas), with facilities on more than 100 cruise ships worldwide.

In addition to facials, manicures, pedicures, massages, and sensual body treatments, other hallmarks of Steiner Leisure are salon services and products for hair and skin. Founded in 1901 by Henry Steiner of London, a single salon prospered when Steiner's son joined the business in 1926 and was granted a royal warrant as hairdresser to Queen Mary in 1937. In 1956 Steiner won its first cruise-ship contract, to operate salons on Cunard Line ships. By the mid-1990s, Steiner Leisure began taking an active role in creating shipboard spas offering a wide variety of wellness therapies and beauty programs for both women and men.

SPORTS AND FITNESS

Onboard sports facilities might include a court for basketball, volleyball, tennis—or all three—a jogging track, or even an in-line skating track. Some Royal Caribbean ships offer such innovative and unexpected features as rock-climbing walls and ice-skating rinks. For the less adventurous, there's always table tennis and shuffleboard.

Naturally, you can find at least one swimming pool, and possibly several. Cruise-ship pools are generally on the small side—more appropriate for cooling off than doing laps—and the majority contain filtered saltwater. But some are elaborate affairs, with waterslides. Princess Grand–class ships have challenging, freshwater "swim against the current" pools for swimming enthusiasts who want to get their low-impact exercise while on board.

Golf is a perennial seagoing favorite of players who want to take their games to the next level and add Bermuda's most beautiful and challenging courses to their scorecards. Shipboard programs can include clinics, use of full-motion golf cages, and even individual instruction from resident pros using state-of-the-art computer analysis. Once ashore, escorted excursions include everything needed for a satisfying round of play, including equipment and tips from the pro, and pre-scheduled tee times at exclusive courses. Unless you find avid golfers with firsthand insight into Bermuda courses who are anxious to make up a group from the ship themselves, you may find it more expedient to book golf outings through the cruise line rather than take your chances at locating a course with a convenient tee time, arranging costly transportation, and being paired with strangers. You may not save time or money by letting the cruise line arrange a golf outing; however, when they do it, they handle the details and make sure you return to the ship on time.

FITNESS CENTERS

Cruise vacations can be hazardous to your waistline if you're not careful. Eating "out" for all meals and sampling different cuisines tends to pile on unaccustomed calories. But shipboard fitness centers have become ever more elaborate, offering state-of-the-art exercise machines, treadmills, and stair steppers, not to mention weights and weight machines. As a bonus, many fitness centers with floor-to-ceiling windows have the world's most inspiring sea views.

If you prefer a more social atmosphere as you burn off sinful chocolate desserts, there are specialized fitness classes for all levels of ability. High-impact, energetic aerobics are not for everyone, but any class that raises the heart rate can be toned down and tailored to individual capabilities. Stretching classes help you warm up for a light jog or brisk walk on deck, and sit-for-fitness classes are offered for mature passengers or those with delicate joints. Fees are sometimes charged for specialty classes, such as Pilates, spinning, and yoga. Most ships have personal trainers on board to get you off on the right foot, also for a fee.

SHIPBOARD SERVICES

9

COMMUNICATIONS

Just because you're out to sea does not mean you have to be out of touch. Ship-to-shore telephone calls can cost $5 to $15 a minute, so it makes economic sense to use email to remain in contact with your home or office. Most ships have basic computer systems, whereas some newer vessels offer more high-tech connectivity—even in-cabin hook-ups or wireless connections for your own laptop computer or one you can rent on board. Expect charges in the 75¢ to $1 per minute range for usage. Ships usually offer some kind of package so that you get a reduced per-minute price if you pay a fee up front; the more minutes in the package, the lower the per-minute cost.

The ability to use your own cell phone from the high seas is a relatively new alternative that is gaining popularity. It can also be cheaper than using a cabin phone. It's a rather ingenious concept: the ship acts as a cell "tower" in international waters—you use your own cell phone and number when roaming at sea. Before leaving home, ask your cell-phone service provider to activate international roaming on your account. When in port, depending on the agreements your

mobile-service provider has established, you may be able to connect
to local networks. Rates for using
the maritime service, as well as any
roaming charges from Bermuda,
are established by your mobile-service carrier and are worth checking
into before you leave home.

LAUNDRY AND DRY CLEANING

Most cruise ships offer valet laundry and pressing (and some also have
dry-cleaning) service. Expenses can add up fast, especially for laundry, as charges are per item and the rates are similar to those charged
in hotels. If doing laundry is important to you and you do not want
to send it out to be done, some cruise ships have a low-cost or free
self-service laundry room (they usually feature an iron and ironing
board in addition to washer and dryer). If you book one of the top-
dollar suites, laundry service may be included for no additional cost.
Upscale ships, such as those in the Regent Seven Seas Cruises and
Crystal Cruises fleets, have complimentary self-service launderettes.
On other lines, such as Princess Cruises, Carnival Cruise Lines, and
Holland America Line's *Veendam*, you can do your own laundry for
about $3 or less per load. Ships in the Royal Caribbean fleet and
Norwegian Cruise Line vessels sailing to Bermuda do not have self-
service laundry facilities.

LIBRARY

Cruise-ship libraries run the gamut from a few shelves of relatively
uninspiring titles to huge rooms crammed with volumes of travel
guides, classics, and the latest best sellers. As a rule, the smaller the
ship, the more likely you are to find a well-stocked library. The space
allotted to the library falls in proportion to the emphasis on glitzy
stage shows—on small ships the passengers are more likely to lean
toward quiet diversions. On ships with sophisticated entertainment
centers in staterooms, you may find videotape or DVD movies as well
as books in the library.

PHOTO SHOP

A Bermuda cruise is a series of photo opportunities, and ships' photographers are on hand to capture boarding, sail-away, port arrivals, and
other highlights, such as the captain's reception. Photographers seem
to pop up everywhere and take far more pictures than you could ever
want; however, they're a unique remembrance, and there's no obligation to purchase them. Prices for the prints, which are put on display,
range from $15 to $29, depending on size.

Film, batteries, single-use cameras, digital storage cards, and related
merchandise may also be available in the ship's photo shop. Some ships'
photography staffers are capable of processing your film or your digital
prints right on board.

SHORE-EXCURSION DESK

Manned by a knowledgeable staff, the shore-excursion desk can offer not only the sale of ship-sponsored tours, but may also be the place to learn more about ports of call and garner information you'll need to tour independently. Although staff members and the focus of their positions vary widely, the least you

can expect is basic information and port maps. Happily, some shore-excursion staff members possess a wealth of information and share it without reservation. On some ships the port lecturer may emphasize shopping and "recommended" merchants, with little to impart regarding sightseeing or the history and culture of ports.

SHORE EXCURSIONS

Shore excursions are optional tours organized by the cruise line and sold aboard the ship. Most tours last two to four hours and all are meant to optimize your time on the island—the cruise line does the research about what to see and do, and you just go along for the ride. You'll sometimes pay more for these ship-packaged tours than if you booked them independently, either before you leave home or after arriving in port. However, with only two or three days at your disposal, the convenience, and assurance that a spot on the tour you're looking forward to is available, may be worth the price. Popular tours often sell out and may not be obtainable at any price once you are ashore. Fees are generally $20–$30 per person for walking tours, $45–$75 per person for island tours, $50–$80 for snorkeling trips, and $150–$175 for diving trips. Prices for children are usually less. For exact durations and pricing, consult your cruise line. Also keep in mind that tour fees and time estimates can vary.

Naturally, you're always free to explore on your own. With its excellent taxi service, Bermuda is a good, although pricey, island for hiring a car and driver. A taxi tour of the island, including such historic and photogenic sights as Gibbs Hill Lighthouse and Somerset Bridge, costs about $37 per hour for up to four passengers or $50 for up to six passengers. Public transportation, including buses and ferries, is convenient to all cruise terminals and the sale of all-day passes might even be offered by the shore-excursion desk on your ship.

GOING ASHORE

Ships calling in Hamilton dock alongside the pier, so you can walk right off the ship to the center of town and major attractions. From the Royal Navy Dockyard, pubs, shopping, and transportation are a short walk from the pier. Before anyone is allowed to proceed down the gangway, however, the ship must be cleared for landing. Immigration and customs officials board the vessel to examine paperwork and sort through red tape. It may be more than an hour before you're allowed ashore. Your ship ID acts as your boarding pass, which you'll need to get back

9

on board. You may also be advised to take a photo ID ashore, such as your passport or driver's license.

One advantage of a Bermuda itinerary is that cruise ships remain docked at night, which affords the opportunity to dine ashore and sample the nightlife. There's a downside to onboard life, though. Although most shipboard services—dining, lounges, and the fitness center and spa—continue to hum along as usual, duty-free shops and casinos are required by Bermuda government regulations to remain closed when in port. In addition, professional entertainment in the show lounge is curtailed, although a movie might be screened there instead. Some ships offer a "Bermuda Night" tropical-theme deck party.

> ## A WHOLE NEW WORLD
>
> Experience a whole different type of Bermuda nightlife—reserve a night snorkel tour from your ship's shore excursion desk. The island's coral reef comes alive when the sun goes down as nocturnal creatures of the deep emerge from the safety of their caves and crevices. Participants are provided with a dive light as well as snorkel gear, but the real treat is when the lights are turned off to reveal the extraordinary effects of bioluminescence—microscopic creatures that create light as you swim through them.

RETURNING TO THE SHIP

Cruise lines are strict about sailing times, which are posted at the gangway and elsewhere and announced in the daily schedule of activities. Be sure to be back on board at least a half hour before the announced sailing time or you may be stranded. If you're on a shore excursion that was sold by the cruise line, however, the captain will wait for your group before casting off. That's one reason why many passengers prefer ship-packaged tours.

If you're not on one of the ship's tours and the ship sails without you, immediately contact the cruise line's port representative, whose phone number is usually listed on the daily schedule of activities. You may be able to hitch a ride on a pilot boat, although that is unlikely. Passengers who miss the boat must pay their own way to the next port, and for a Bermuda cruise that means the U.S. disembarkation port (where you will not be allowed to fly unless you have brought a valid passport).

DISEMBARKATION

All cruises come to an end eventually, and it hardly seems fair that you have to leave when it feels like your vacation has just begun, but leave you must. The disembarkation process actually begins the day before you arrive at your ship's home port. During that day your cabin steward delivers special luggage tags to your stateroom, along with customs forms and instructions.

The night before you disembark, you'll need to set aside clothing to wear the next morning when you leave the ship. Many people dress in whatever casual outfits they wear for the final dinner on board, or change into travel clothes after dinner. Also, do not forget to put your passport or other proof of citizenship, airline tickets, and medications in your hand luggage.

After you finish packing, attach your new luggage tags (they are color- or number-coded according to post-cruise transportation plans and flight schedules). Follow the instructions provided and place the locked luggage outside your stateroom door for pickup during the hours indicated.

A statement itemizing your onboard charges is delivered before you arise on disembarkation morning. Plan to get up early enough to check it over for accuracy, finish packing your belongings, and vacate your stateroom by the appointed hour. Any discrepancies in your onboard account should be taken care of before leaving the ship, usually at the purser's desk.

> **WORD OF MOUTH**
>
> "My husband and I are taking my 90-year-old parents on a cruise to Bermuda in October. We're looking for something to do with them when we dock at King's Wharf."
>
> —ovingtonl
>
> "King's Wharf is mostly shops—if that's what they're into, great! My parents weren't, so we took the ferry to St. George's and then one to Hamilton. Both have carriage rides through town—very nice. The ferry was easy for my mom to negotiate. She loved St. George's because the town is small and everything is close by."
>
> —CDonahue

Room service is not available on most ships on the last morning; however, breakfast is served in the main dining room and the buffet restaurant. After breakfast, there's not much to do but wait comfortably in a lounge or on deck for your tag color or number to be called. Disembarkation procedures can sometimes be drawn out by passengers who are unprepared. This is no time to abandon your patience or sense of humor.

Remember that all passengers must meet with customs and immigration officials before disembarkation, either on the ship or in the terminal. Procedures vary and are outlined in your instructions. In some ports, passengers must meet with officials at a specified hour (usually very early) in an onboard lounge; in other ports, customs forms are collected in the terminal, and passports or other identification papers are examined there as well.

Once in the terminal, locate your luggage and proceed to your motor coach or taxi, or retrieve your vehicle from the parking lot.

CUSTOMS AND DUTIES

U.S. CUSTOMS

Before a ship lands, each individual or family must fill out a customs declaration, regardless of whether anything was purchased abroad. If you have less than $800 worth of goods, you will not need to itemize purchases. Be prepared to pay whatever duties are owed directly to the customs inspector, with cash or check.

U.S. Customs might preclear your ship when you sail in and out of certain ports. It's done on board before you disembark. In most ports you must collect your luggage from the dock and then stand in line to pass through the inspection point. This can take up to an hour.

U.S. CITIZENS Duties are the same for returning cruise passengers as for all other travelers, with a few exceptions. On certain Caribbean itineraries that include a visit to Bermuda, you're entitled to bring back $800 worth of goods duty-free. ⇨ *For general customs and duty information, see Customs and Duties in Travel Smart Bermuda.*

> **ON THE SEASHORE**
>
> For a "free" souvenir, sea glass (broken bits of glass and china that have been tumbled by the sea to make them nice and smooth) is deposited in fairly large quantities by the surf at Alexandra Battery Beach Park. The beach park is easy to find on any local map and only about a mile walk from St. George's.

NON-U.S. CITIZENS If you hold a foreign passport and will be returning to your home country within hours of docking, you may be exempt from all U.S. Customs duties. Everything you bring into the United States must leave with you when you return home. When you reach your own country, you will have to pay appropriate duties there.

SENDING PACKAGES HOME

You may also send packages home duty-free, with a limit of one parcel per addressee per day (except alcohol or tobacco products or perfume worth more than $5). You can mail up to $200 worth of goods for personal use and $100 worth of goods as a gift. Mailed items do not affect your duty-free allowance on your return.

Travel Smart Bermuda

WORD OF MOUTH

"Rain, when it does come, is usually in the form of fast moving, very brief, and widely scattered showers. Not unusual for it to sprinkle in one area and there be bright sun 1/4 mile away. Often you can see rain miles out at sea and that rain never comes close to shore."

—RoamsAround

"The ferries are now high-speed and it is only about a 25 minute ride. It cost $4.00/person one way. If you are in Bermuda for more than a couple of days and want to get around by ferry or bus, buy a pass. A sheath of 15 tickets was only $30."

—Tanya

GETTING HERE AND AROUND

It's easy to get to Bermuda by air from the United States, and the price is cheaper than it once was, as more discount airlines have added flights from major East Coast hubs. For those who would rather cruise than fly, there are options as well, with the Bermuda cruise season starting in late spring and going through early fall.

▌ AIR TRAVEL

Flying time to Bermuda from most East Coast cities is about 2 hours; from Toronto, 3 hours; and 7 hours from London Gatwick.

Most flights arrive around noon, making for particularly long waits to get through immigration; however, British Airways flights and a couple of American Airlines flights from New York arrive in the evening.

At many airports outside Bermuda travelers with only carry-on luggage can bypass the airline's front desk and check in at the gate. But in Bermuda everyone checks in at the airline's front desk. U.S. customs has a desk here, too, so you won't have to clear customs at home when you land. Passengers returning to Britain or Canada will need to clear customs and immigration on arrival.

Airlines and Airports Airline and Airport Links.com. Links to many of the world's airlines and airports. ⊕ *www. airlineandairportlinks.com.*

Airline Security Issues Transportation Security Administration. Answers for almost every flight question that might come up. ⊕ *www.tsa.gov.*

AIRPORTS

Bermuda's gateway is L.F. Wade International Airport (BDA), formerly Bermuda International Airport, on the East End of the island. It's approximately 9 mi from Hamilton (30-minute cab ride), 13 mi from Southampton (40-minute cab ride), and 17 mi from Somerset (50 minutes by cab). The town of St. George's is about a 15-minute cab ride from the airport.

Airport Information L.F. Wade International Airport (BDA) ☎ *441/293–2470* ⊕ *www. bermudaairport.com.*

▌TIP→ **Ask the local tourist board about hotel and local transportation packages that include tickets to major museum exhibits or other special events.**

GROUND TRANSPORTATION

Taxis, available outside the arrivals gate, are the usual and most convenient way to leave the airport. The approximate fare (not including tip) to Hamilton is $25; to St. George's, $15; to south-shore hotels, $35; and to Sandys (Somerset), $50. A surcharge of $1 is added for each piece of luggage stored in the trunk or on the roof. Fares are 25% higher between midnight and 6 am and all day on Sunday and public holidays. Fifteen percent is an acceptable tip.

Bermuda Triangle Tours provides transportation to hotels and guesthouses aboard air-conditioned six- to 25-seat vans and buses. Reservations are recommended. Prices are $35 per person to Hamilton or $40 per person to Southampton, so for most people a taxi is the cheaper option.

Contacts Bermuda Triangle Tours ☎ *441/293–5806, 888/308–4687* ⊕ *www. bermudatriangletours.bm.* **The Bermuda Industrial Union Taxi Co-op** ☎ *441/292– 4476.* **BTA Dispatching Ltd.** ☎ *441/296–2121* ⊕ *www.taxibermuda.com.* **First Step Taxi Service.** First Step Taxi Service (wheelchair accessible) ☎ *441/293–0301, 441/735–7151, 441/516–9876.* **Island Taxi Services** ☎ *441/295–4141* ⊕ *www. islandtaxiservices.com.*

FLIGHTS

Nonstop service to Bermuda is available year-round on major airlines from Atlanta, Boston, Newark (NJ), New York City, Washington, D.C., Baltimore, Philadelphia, Toronto, Miami, and London, and seasonally from Charlotte.

Fares from New York City may be found for under $300 on some of the budget airlines, but the average price is closer to $500 and can be as high as $800 in peak season, whereas fares from Toronto are typically about $400. Fares from Gatwick vary from $900 in low season to $1,300 in high season on British Airways. Flight regularity and price are subject to rapid change, and airlines recommend that travelers check their Web sites for up-to-the-minute information.

Airline Contacts Air Canada ☎ *888/247–2262.* **American Airlines** ☎ *800/433–7300.* **Continental Airlines** ☎ *800/523–3273 for U.S. and Mexico reservations, 800/231–0856 for international reservations.* **Delta Airlines** ☎ *800/221–1212 for U.S. reservations, 800/241–4141 for international reservations.* **jetBlue** ☎ *800/538–2583.* **USAirways** ☎ *800/428–4322 for U.S. and Canada reservations, 800/622–1015 for international reservations.* **WestJet** ☎ *888/937–8538* ⊕ *www.westjet.com.*

▌BOAT TRAVEL

The Bermuda Ministry of Transport maintains excellent, frequent, and on-time ferry service from Hamilton to Paget and Warwick (the pink line), Somerset and the Dockyard in the West End (the blue line), Rockaway in Southampton (the green line), and, weekdays in summer only, the Dockyard and St. George's (the orange line).

A one-way adult fare to Paget or Warwick is $2.50; to Somerset, the Dockyard, or St. George's, $4. The last departures are from Hamilton at 8:30 pm from mid-April through mid-November, 7 pm from mid-November through mid-April. Sunday ferry service is limited and ends

around 6 pm. You can bring a bicycle on board free of charge, but you'll pay $4 extra to take a motor scooter to Somerset or the Dockyard. Discounted one-, two-, three-, four-, and seven-day passes are available for use on both ferries and buses. They cost $12, $20, $28, $35, and $45 respectively. Monthly passes are also offered at $55. The helpful ferry operators can answer questions about routes and schedules and can even help get your bike on board. Schedules are published in the phone book, posted at each landing, and also available at the Ferry Terminal, Central Bus Terminal, Visitors Service Bureaus, and most hotels.

Information Ministry of Transport, Department of Marine and Ports Services ☎ *441/295–4506 Hamilton Ferry Terminal* ⊕ *www.seaexpress.bm.*

▌BUS TRAVEL

Bermuda's pink and blue buses travel the island from east to west. To find a bus stop outside Hamilton, look for either a stone shelter or a pink or blue pole. For buses heading to Hamilton, the pole is pink; for those traveling away from Hamilton, the pole is blue. Remember to wait on the proper side of the road. Driving in Bermuda is on the left. Bus drivers will not make change, so purchase tickets or discounted tokens or carry plenty of coins.

In addition to public buses, private minibuses serve St. George's. The minibus fare depends upon the destination, but you won't pay more than $5. Minibuses, which you can flag down, drop you wherever you want to go in this parish. They operate daily from about 7:30 am to

11 pm. Smoking is not permitted on buses.

Bermuda is divided into 14 bus zones, each about 2 mi long. Within the first three zones, the rate is $3 (coins only). For longer distances, the fare is $4.50. If you plan to travel by public transportation often, buy a booklet of tickets (15 14-zone tickets for $30, or 15 three-zone tickets for $20). You can also buy a few tokens, which, unlike tickets, are sold individually. In addition to tickets and tokens, there are one-, two-, three-, four-, and seven-day adult passes ($12, $20, $28, $35, and $45 respectively). Monthly passes are also available for $55 each. All bus passes are good for ferry service and are available at the central bus terminal. Tickets and passes are also sold at many hotels and guesthouses. Passes are accepted on both buses and ferries.

Hamilton buses arrive and depart from the Central Bus Terminal. An office here is open weekdays from 7:15 am to 7 pm, Saturday from 8 am to 6:30 pm, and Sunday and holidays from 8:30 am to 5:30 pm; it's the only place to buy money-saving tokens.

Buses run about every 15 minutes, except on Sunday, when they usually come every half hour or hour, depending on the route. Bus schedules, which also contain ferry timetables, are available at the bus terminal in Hamilton and at many hotels. The timetable also offers an itinerary for a do-it-yourself, one-day sightseeing tour by bus and ferry. Upon request, the driver will be happy to tell you when you've reached your stop. Be sure to greet the bus driver when boarding—it's considered rude in Bermuda to ask a bus driver a question, such as the fare or details on your destination, without first greeting him or her.

Bus Information Public Transport Bermuda ☎ *441/292–3851* ⊕ *www.gov.bm.* **St. George's Minibus Service** ☎ *441/297–8199, 441/297–8492.*

▌ CAR TRAVEL

You cannot rent a car in Bermuda. The island has strict laws governing overcrowded roads, so even Bermudians are only allowed one car per household. A popular, albeit possibly somewhat dangerous, alternative is to rent mopeds or scooters (⇨ *below*), which are better for negotiating the island's narrow roads.

▌ CRUISE SHIP TRAVEL

⇨ For information about cruising to Bermuda, see Chapter 9.

▌ MOPED AND SCOOTER TRAVEL

Because car rentals are not allowed in Bermuda, you might decide to get around by moped or scooter. Bermudians routinely use the words "moped" and "scooter" interchangeably, even though they're different. You must pedal to start a moped, and it carries only one person. A scooter, on the other hand, which starts when you put the key in the ignition, is more powerful and holds one or two passengers.

Think twice before renting a moped, as accidents occur frequently and are occasionally fatal. The best ways to avoid mishaps are to drive defensively, obey the speed limit, remember to stay on the left-hand side of the road—especially at traffic circles—and avoid riding in the rain and at night.

Helmets are required by law. Mopeds and scooters can be rented from cycle liveries by the hour, the day, or the week. Liveries will show first-time riders how to operate the vehicles. Rates vary, so it's worth calling several liveries to see what they charge. Single-seat scooter rentals cost from $55–$75 per day or from about $200–$250 per week. All liveries tack a mandatory $30 insurance-and-repair charge on top of the bill, whereas others include the cost of insurance, breakdown service, pickup and delivery, and a tank of gas in the quoted price. A $20 deposit may also be charged for the lock, key, and helmet. You must be at least 16 and have a valid driver's license to rent. Major hotels have their own cycle liveries, and all hotels and most guesthouses will make rental arrangements.

GASOLINE

Gas for cycles runs from $3 to $4 per liter, but you can cover a great deal of ground on the full tank that comes with the wheels. Gas stations will accept major credit cards. It's customary to tip attendants—a couple of dollars is adequate.

PARKING

On-street parking bays for scooters are plentiful and easy to spot. What's even better is they're free!

ROAD CONDITIONS

Roads are narrow, winding, and full of blind curves. Whether driving cars or scooters, Bermudians tend to be quite cautious around less-experienced visiting riders, but crowded city streets make accidents all the more common. Local rush hours are weekdays from 7:30 am to 9 am and from 4 pm to 6 pm. Roads are often bumpy, and they may be slippery under a morning mist or rainfall. Street lamps are few and far between outside of the cities, so be especially careful driving at night.

ROADSIDE EMERGENCIES

The number for Bermuda's emergency services is 911. Scooters are often stolen, so to be safe you should always carry the number of your hire company with you. Also, don't ride with valuables in your bike basket, as you are putting yourself at risk of theft. Passing motorists can grab your belongings and ride off without your even knowing it.

RULES OF THE ROAD

The speed limit is 35 kph (22 mph), except in the World Heritage Site of St. George's, where it is a mere 25 kph (about 15 mph). The limits, however, are not very well enforced, and the actual driving speed in Bermuda hovers around 50 kph (30 mph). Police seldom target tourists for parking offenses or other driving infractions.

Drunk driving is a serious problem in Bermuda, despite stiff penalties. The blood-alcohol limit is 0.08. The courts will impose a $1,000 fine for a driving-while-intoxicated infraction, and also take the driver off the road for at least one year. Despite much discussion, there's currently no law against using a mobile phone even while driving a scooter.

Rental Companies Eve Cycles ⊠ *10 Dockyard Terr., Dockyard* ☎ *441/236-6748* ⊕ *www.evecycles.com.* **Oleander Cycles** ⊠ *6 Valley Rd., off Middle Rd., Paget* ☎ *441/236-5235* ⊠ *26 York St., St. George's* ☎ *441/297-0478* ⊠ *26 Middle Rd., Southampton* ☎ *441/234-0629* ⊠ *Maritime Lane, Dockyard, Sandys* ☎ *441/234-2764.* **Smatt's Cycle Livery Ltd.** ☎ *441/295-1180.* **Wheels Cycles** ⊠ *74 Front St., Hamilton* ☎ *441/292-2245.*

▌TAXI TRAVEL

Taxis are the fastest and easiest way to get around the island; unfortunately, they are also the most costly and can take a long time to arrive. Four-seater taxis charge $6.40 for the first mile and $2 for each subsequent mile. Between midnight and 6 am, and on Sunday and holidays, a 25% surcharge is added to the fare. There's a $1 charge for each piece of luggage stored in the trunk or on the roof. Taxi drivers accept only American or Bermudian cash, but not bills larger than $50, and they expect a 15% tip. You can phone for taxi pickup, but you may wait while the cab navigates Bermuda's heavy traffic. Don't hesitate to hail a taxi on the street.

For a personalized taxi tour of the island, the minimum duration is three hours, at $40 per hour for one to four people and $55 an hour for five or six, excluding tip.

Taxi Companies The Bermuda Industrial Union Taxi Co-op ☎ *441/292-4476.* **Island Taxi Services** ☎ *441/295-4141* ⊕ *www.islandtaxiservices.com.* **BTA Dispatching Ltd.** ☎ *441/296-2121.* **First Step Taxi Service.** (wheelchair accessible) ☎ *441/293-0301, 441/735-7151, 441/516-9876.*

ESSENTIALS

■ ACCOMMODATIONS

Accommodation standards in Bermuda—whether you prefer a guesthouse or a five-star hotel—are generally high, and strongly regulated by the Bermuda Department of Tourism. However, prices tend to reflect this quality, and you should be warned that there are no true budget options. (Camping is not allowed and there are no hostels on the island.) Staying in a hotel can mean anything from a luxury resort setting to something more similar to a three-star hotel in the U.S. Another option is to stay in more home-like accommodations—either by renting a room in a guesthouse (a commercial establishment roughly similar to a room in a bed-and-breakfast, though some can be very upmarket) or a cottage.

Most hotels and other lodgings require you to give your credit-card details before they will confirm your reservation. If you don't feel comfortable emailing this information, ask if you can fax it (some places even prefer faxes). However you book, get confirmation in writing and have a copy of it handy when you check in.

Be sure you understand the hotel's cancellation policy. Some places allow you to cancel without any kind of penalty—even if you prepaid to secure a discounted rate—if you cancel at least 24 hours in advance. Others require you to cancel a week in advance or penalize you the cost of one night. Small inns and bed-and-breakfasts are most likely to require you to cancel far in advance. Most hotels allow children under a certain age to stay in their parents' room at no extra charge, but others charge for them as extra adults; find out the cutoff age for discounts.

⇨ *For price categories, consult the price chart found at the beginning of the "Where to Stay" chapter.*

APARTMENT AND HOUSE RENTALS

Rental houses, apartments, and villas are all over Bermuda and may be owned by individuals, consortiums, and developers, so booking might be anything from calling the owner in person to booking on a Web site. ⊕ *www.bermuda.com* has a fairly extensive list of the better-known properties.

Contacts Villas International ☎ *415/499–9490, 800/221–2260* ⊕ *www.villasintl.com.*

BED-AND-BREAKFASTS

If you're part of the "no-frills" crowd, guesthouses in Bermuda offer bed-and-breakfast–style accommodation. Some have their own Internet sites; most are listed on ⊕ *www.bermuda.com.*

Reservation Services Bed & Breakfast.com. ☎ *512/322–2710, 800/462–2632* ⊕ *www.bedandbreakfast.com.*

HOME EXCHANGES

With a direct home exchange, you stay in someone else's home while they stay in yours. Some outfits also deal with vacation homes, so you're not actually staying in someone's full-time residence, just their vacant weekend place.

▌ COMMUNICATIONS

INTERNET

You should have no trouble bringing a laptop through customs into Bermuda, though you may have to open and turn it on for inspection by security officers. It's a good idea to bring proof of purchase with you so you will not run into any difficulty bringing the computer back to the States, especially if it's a new machine.

Most hotels charge connection fees each time a laptop is hooked up to the Internet ($3 to $10), with additional charges (10¢ to 30¢ per minute) during the connection. The Fairmont Southampton Resort, Fairmont Hamilton Princess, and Rosewood Tucker's Point have fully-equipped business centers where guests can use hotel computers for Internet access (connection charges still apply).

If you do not have an Internet connection at your hotel, there is only one place in Hamilton where you can log on. But it will cost you—$10 an hour is an average rate.

Contacts Cybercafes. Cybercafes lists more than 4,000 Internet cafés worldwide. ⊕ *www. cybercafes.com.* **Logic Internet Cafe** ✉ *10–12 Burnaby St., next to The Spot, Hamilton* ☏ *441/296–9600* ◷ *8–6 Mon.–Fri. Closes at 8 on Wed. in summer.*

PHONES

The good news is you can now make a direct-dial telephone call from virtually any point on earth. The bad news? You can't always do so cheaply. Calling from a hotel is almost always the most expensive option; hotels usually add huge surcharges to all calls, particularly international ones. In some countries you can phone from call centers or even the post office. And then there are mobile phones (⇨ *see Mobile Phones below)*, which are sometimes more prevalent—particularly in the developing world—than landlines; as expensive as mobile phone calls can be, they are still usually a much cheaper option than calling from your hotel.

Destination-specific international calling cards from North Rock Communications in Hamilton offer the cheapest way of calling. You can use them on any phones, including public pay phones and mobile phones. You can also get standard international cards from pharmacies, some supermarkets, and many gas stations, which will also get you a better rate than calling directly from the hotel.

The country code for Bermuda is 441. When dialing a Bermuda number from the United States or Canada, simply dial 1 + 441 + local number. You do not need to dial the international access code (011).

CALLING WITHIN BERMUDA

Telephone service in Bermuda is organized and efficient, though service may be interrupted during storms.

When in Bermuda, call 411 for local phone numbers. To reach directory assistance from outside the country, call 441/555–1212.

To make a local call, simply dial the seven-digit number.

You can find pay phones similar to those in the United States on the streets of Hamilton, St. George's, and Somerset as well as at ferry landings, some bus stops, and public beaches. Deposit 50¢ (U.S. or Bermudian) before you dial. Most hotels charge from 30¢ to $1 for local calls.

CALLING OUTSIDE BERMUDA

The country code for the United States is 1.

Most hotels impose a surcharge for long-distance calls, even those made collect or with a phone card or credit card. Many toll-free 800 or 888 numbers in the United States aren't honored in Bermuda. Consider buying a prepaid local phone card rather than using your own calling card. In many small guesthouses and apartments the phone in your room is a private line from which you can make only collect, credit-card, or local calls. Some small hotels have a telephone room or kiosk where you can make long-distance calls.

You can find specially marked AT&T USADirect phones at the airport, the cruise-ship dock in Hamilton, and King's Square and Ordnance Island in St. George's. You can also make international calls with a calling card from the main post office. You can make prepaid international calls from the Cable & Wireless Office, which also has international telex, cable, and fax services, Monday through Friday from 9 to 4:45.

To call the United States, Canada, and most Caribbean countries, simply dial 1 (or 0 if you need an operator's assistance), then the area code and the number. For all other countries, dial 011 (or 0 for an operator), the country code, the area code, and the number. Using an operator for an overseas call is more expensive than dialing direct. For calls to the United States, rates are highest from 8 am to 6 pm and discounted from 6 pm to 8 am and on weekends.

Access Codes AT&T USADirect ☎ 800/872–2881. **MCI Call USA** ☎ 800/888–8000, 800/888–8888. **Sprint Express** ☎ 800/623–0877.

International Calls Bermuda General Post Office ☎ 441/297–7893. **Cable & Wireless Office** ☎ 441/297–7000.

CALLING CARDS

Buy a prepaid phone card for long-distance calls. They can be used with any touch-tone phone in Bermuda, although they can only be used for calls outside Bermuda. Rates are often significantly lower than dialing direct, but the down side is that some hotels will charge you for making the call to your card's 800 number. Phone cards are available at pharmacies, shops, gas stations, and restaurants. The phone companies Cable & Wireless, Tele-Bermuda, and Logic Communications sell prepaid calling cards in denominations of $5 to $50. The cards can be used around the world as well as in Bermuda.

Phone-Card Companies Cable & Wireless ☎ 441/297–7022. **Logic Communications** ☎ 441/296–9600. **North Rock**

Communications ☎ 441/540–2700. **TeleBermuda International** ☎ 441/296–9000.

MOBILE PHONES

If you have a multiband phone (some countries use different frequencies than what's used in the United States) and your service provider uses the world-standard GSM network (as do T-Mobile, AT&T, and Verizon), you can probably use your phone abroad. Roaming fees can be steep, however: 99¢ a minute is considered reasonable. And overseas you normally pay the toll charges for incoming calls. It's almost always cheaper to send a text message than to make a call, since text messages have a very low set fee (often less than 25¢).

If you just want to make local calls, consider buying a new SIM card (note that your provider may have to unlock your phone for you to use a different SIM card) and a prepaid service plan in the destination. You'll then have a local number and can make local calls at local rates. If your trip is extensive, you could also simply buy a new cell phone in your destination, as the initial cost will be offset over time.

■TIP➔ **If you travel internationally frequently, save one of your old mobile phones or buy a cheap one on the Internet; ask your cell phone company to unlock it for you, and take it with you as a travel phone, buying a new SIM card with pay-as-you-go service in each destination.**

Most travelers can use their own cell phones in Bermuda, though you should check with your provider to be sure. Cell-phone rentals are available from stores in Hamilton, some of which will even deliver the phone to you. A typical charge is $2 a day for the rental while local calls will cost 60¢ a minute. Incoming international calls will also cost 60¢ a minute, but outgoing international calls will cost $1.10 a minute.

Contacts Cellular Abroad. Cellular Abroad rents and sells GMS phones and sells SIM cards that work in many countries. ☎ 800/287–5072 ⊕ www.cellularabroad.com. **Mobal.** Mobal

LOCAL DO'S AND TABOOS

CUSTOMS OF THE COUNTRY

Bermudians tend to be quite formal in attire as well as in personal interactions. Casual dress, including bathing suits, is acceptable at hotels and resorts, but locals seldom venture into Hamilton in anything less than long shorts and sports shirts for men, and slacks-and-blouse combinations or dresses for women. Some restaurants and clubs, particularly those connected to hotels, request that men wear jackets, and more formal establishments require ties during dinner, but there are plenty of places in Hamilton and beyond where you can dress casually and dine well. If you have dinner reservations you should arrive promptly, but be aware that in other situations the phenomenon known as "Bermuda time" prevails. If you make plans to meet a local, don't be surprised if they're 20 minutes late.

In downtown Hamilton the classic Bermuda shorts are often worn by banking and insurance executives, but the outfit always includes knee-high socks, dress shoes, and jacket and tie. When it comes to dress, err on the formal side. It's an offense in Bermuda to appear in public without a shirt, even for joggers. This rule may seem arcane, but most Bermudians appreciate this decorum. Decorum is also expected at the beach.

GREETINGS

Courtesy is the rule when locals interact among each other. In business and social gatherings use the more formal Mr. and Ms. instead of first names, at least until a friendship has been established, which sometimes takes just a few minutes. Always greet bus drivers with a friendly "Good morning" or "Good afternoon" when you board public buses. This is an island custom, and it's nice to see each passenger offer a smile and sincere greeting when boarding and exiting the bus. In fact, saying "Good morning" to people on the street is also a custom. Obviously if you're walking down a crowded street you needn't say it to everyone you pass, but in less crowded situations, especially when eye contact is made, some recognition should be given. You'll be surprised at the friendly response you receive.

In general, respect and appreciation are shown quite liberally to public servants in Bermuda. Although one underlying reason may be the fact that the residents of this small island seem to know everyone, and personal greetings on the streets are commonplace, it also seems that a genuinely upbeat and friendly attitude is part of the national character.

OUT ON THE TOWN

The key to interaction with any Bermudian is to be polite and formal, and that goes for your waiter or any other person serving you. Rudeness will get you nowhere. Public displays of affection are quite okay, but you might want to keep it in moderation; generally people are fairly reserved. Gay and lesbian travelers in particular may experience some negative reactions when showing affection in public, such as holding hands.

SIGHTSEEING

Bathing suits are best kept for the beach only, and overly skimpy attire is traditionally frowned upon, though attitudes are more tolerant of tourists. While the problem is far less prevalent than in most places of the world, there are a few street beggars and it's best not to give them anything—for one, due to Hamilton's small size you're likely to see the same beggar again and again, and if you give them something once they'll repeatedly approach you. A firm, but polite, refusal is best. You shouldn't eat or drink on the buses, and you'll gain approval by giving up your seat for elderly or pregnant women.

rents mobiles and sells GSM phones (starting at $29) that will operate in 140 countries. Per-call rates vary throughout the world. ☎ 888/888–9162 ⊕ www.mobalrental.com.
Planet Fone. Planet Fone rents cell phones, but the per-minute rates are expensive. ☎ 888/988–4777 ⊕ www.planetfone.com.

Rentals BermudaCellRental.com ☎ 441/232–2355 ⊕ www.BermudaCellRental. com. **FKB Transact** ☎ 441/272–2001.

CUSTOMS AND DUTIES

On entering Bermuda, you can bring in duty-free up to 50 cigars, 200 cigarettes, and 1 pound of tobacco; 1 liter of wine and 1 liter of spirits; and other goods with a total maximum value of $30. To import plants, fruits, vegetables, or pets, you must get an import permit in advance from the Department of Environmental Protection. Merchandise and sales materials for use at conventions must be cleared with the hotel concerned before you arrive. Be prepared for a bit of a wait, as the Customs Office has a reputation for being very thorough. If there are a lot of passengers this process can add an hour or so if you're unlucky. It goes without saying, but you should definitely not bring in any drugs such as marijuana, as drug checks are very thorough and the penalties are harsh.

Information in Bermuda Bermuda Customs ☎ 441/295–4816 ⊕ www.customs.gov.bm. **Department of Environmental Protection** ☎ 441/236–4201 ⊕ www.animals.gov.bm.

U.S. Information U.S. Customs and Border Protection ⊕ www.cbp.gov.

EATING OUT

Bermuda has a surprising number of restaurants serving just about any type of foreign cuisine imaginable: Indian, Thai, Japanese, Chinese, British, French—you name it. Truly Bermudian cuisine is, however, harder to come by. Codfish and potatoes, the national dish, tends to appear

on some pub-food menus and also in a number of diner-style restaurants. Vegetarians are generally well catered to, and most places have no problem with young children, but check ahead at some of the higher-class establishments just to make sure.

⇨ *For information on food-related health issues, see Health, below.*

MEALS AND MEALTIMES

Unless otherwise noted, the restaurants listed in this guide are open daily for lunch and dinner.

A word of warning to those who are used to eating out late: it can be difficult to find a place that serves food after 10 pm. Your last option is a burger van called Jorjays, which is usually open late into the night on Front Street.

PAYING

It's customary to ask for your check when you're finished, instead of waiting for the server to bring it. All major credit cards are accepted island-wide.

⇨ *For price categories, consult the price chart found at the beginning of the "Where to Eat" chapter.*

⇨ *For guidelines on tipping see Tipping below.*

RESERVATIONS AND DRESS

Regardless of where you are, it's a good idea to make a reservation if you can. We only mention them specifically when reservations are essential (there's no other way you'll ever get a table) or when they are not accepted. For popular restaurants, book as far ahead as you can (often 30 days), and reconfirm as soon as you arrive. (Large parties should always call ahead to check the reservations policy.) We mention dress only when men are required to wear a jacket or a jacket and tie.

WINES, BEER, AND SPIRITS

Bermuda's two national drinks, the Dark 'n Stormy (dark rum and ginger beer) and the Rum Swizzle (a mixed fruit cocktail with dark and light rum), both rely on the locally produced Gosling's Rum. These drinks are everywhere—so watch out! The only locally produced beers are available at North Rock Pub in Smith's Parish or at the Frog and Onion Pub in Dockyard. Otherwise available beers are fairly standard North American and European brands, and wines are plentiful. Liquor can't be bought from a liquor store on a Sunday or after 9 pm any day of the week.

▌ ELECTRICITY

The local electrical current is the same as in the United States and Canada: 110 volt, 60 cycle AC. All appliances that can be used in North America can be used in Bermuda without adapters. Winter storms bring occasional power outages.

▌ EMERGENCIES

Police, ambulance, and fire services are all at 911. Pharmacies usually open around 8 am, some stay open until 9 pm. People's Pharmacy in Hamilton is open from 10 am to 2 pm on Sunday.

Doctors and Dentists Government Health Clinic ☎ *441/278–6460* .

Foreign Consulates American Consulate ✉ *Crown Hill, 16 Middle Rd., Devonshire* ☎ *441/295–1342* ⊕ *hamilton.usconsulate.gov.*

General Emergency Contacts Sea Rescue ☎ *441/297–1010* ⊕ *www.rccbermuda.bm.* **Police, fire, ambulance** ☎ *911.*

Hospitals and Clinics King Edward VII Memorial Hospital ✉ *7 Point Finger Rd.,*

outside Hamilton near the Botanical Gardens ☎ *441/236–2345.*

▌ HEALTH

The most common types of illnesses are caused by contaminated food and water. If you have problems, mild cases of traveler's diarrhea may respond to Imodium (known generically as loperamide) or Pepto-Bismol. Be sure to drink plenty of fluids; if you can't keep fluids down, seek medical help immediately.

Infectious diseases can be airborne or passed via mosquitoes and ticks and through direct or indirect physical contact with animals or people. Some, including Norwalk-like viruses that affect your digestive tract, can be passed along through contaminated food. Speak with your physician and/or check the CDC or World Health Organization Web sites for health alerts, particularly if you're pregnant, traveling with children, or have a chronic illness.

SPECIFIC ISSUES IN BERMUDA

Sunburn and sunstroke are legitimate concerns if you're traveling to Bermuda in summer. On hot, sunny days, wear a hat, a beach cover-up, and lots of sunblock. These are essential for a day on a boat or at the beach. Be sure to take the same kind of precautions on overcast summer days—some of the worst cases of sunburn happen on cloudy afternoons when sunblock seems unnecessary. Drink plenty of water and, above all, limit the amount of time you spend in the sun until you become acclimated.

The Portuguese man-of-war occasionally visits Bermuda's waters, so be alert when swimming, especially in summer or whenever the water is particularly warm. This creature is recognizable by a purple, balloonlike float sack of perhaps 8 inches in diameter, below which dangle 20- to 60-inch tentacles armed with powerful stinging cells. Contact with the stinging cells causes immediate and severe pain. Seek medical attention immediately: a serious sting can send a person into shock. In the meantime—or if getting to a doctor will take a while—treat the affected area liberally with vinegar. Ammonia is also an effective antidote to the sting. Although usually encountered in the water, Portuguese men-of-war may also wash up on shore. If you spot one on the sand, steer clear, as the sting is just as dangerous out of the water.

More recently, divers have encountered the highly poisonous lionfish, which is not a native of the waters. Swimmers will be extremely unlikely to come into contact with one, while divers should just exercise caution around the creatures, which are not aggressive unless provoked.

■ HOURS OF OPERATION

Most branches of the Bank of Bermuda are open weekdays from 9 to 4:30. All branches of HSBC Bermuda are open weekdays from 9 to 4. Bermuda Commercial Bank (⊠ 19 Par-La-Ville Rd., Hamilton) operates weekdays from 9 to 5. Capital G Bank (⊠ 25 Reid St., Hamilton) is open weekdays from 8:30 to 5 and Saturday from 8:30 to 4.

Many gas stations are open daily from 7 am to 9 pm, and a few stay open until midnight. The island's only 24-hour gas station is Esso City Auto Market in Hamilton, near the Bank of Butterfield, off Par-La-Ville Road.

Hours vary greatly, but museums are generally open Monday through Saturday from 9 or 9:30 to 4:30 or 5. Some close on Saturday. Check with individual museums for exact hours.

Pharmacies are open Monday through Saturday from 8 am to 6 or 8 pm, and sometimes Sunday from around 11 to 6 pm.

Most stores are open Monday through Saturday from around 9 until 5 or 6. Some Hamilton stores keep evening hours when cruise ships are in port. Dockyard shops are generally open Monday through

Saturday from 10 to 5, Sunday from 11 to 5. The Bermuda government recently made it legal for all stores to open on Sunday, although most shops have yet to take advantage of the change. Those that are open—mainly grocery stores and pharmacies—have abbreviated hours.

HOLIDAYS

On Sunday and national public holidays, all shops, businesses, and many restaurants in Bermuda close. Buses and ferries run on limited schedules. Most entertainment venues, sights, and sports outfitters remain open. When holidays fall on a Saturday, government and commercial offices close the following Monday, but restaurants and shops remain open.

Bermuda celebrates a two-day public holiday for Emancipation Day/Somers Day and Cup Match in late July or early August, when the whole island comes to a standstill for the annual cricket match between the East and West ends of Bermuda. National public holidays are New Year's Day, Good Friday, Bermuda Day (late May), National Heroes Day (mid-June), Labour Day (early September), Remembrance Day (early November), Christmas, and Boxing Day (December 26).

■ MAIL

Mail services in Bermuda can be erratic, so the following should be taken with a pinch of salt. However, generally allow seven to 10 days for mail from Bermuda to reach the United States, Canada, or the United Kingdom, and about two weeks to arrive in Australia or New Zealand.

Airmail postcards and letters for the first 10 grams to the United States and Canada cost 70¢. Postcards to the United Kingdom cost 80¢, letters 85¢ for the first 10 grams. Postcards to Australia and New Zealand cost 90¢, letters 95¢ for the first 10 grams.

If you want to receive mail but have no address in Bermuda, you can have mail sent care of General Delivery, General Post Office, Hamilton HM GD, Bermuda.

Main Branches International Data Express ☎ *441/297-7802.* **Parcel Post** ☎*441/297-7875.*

SHIPPING PACKAGES

Through Parcel Post at Bermuda's post office, you can send packages via either International Data Express (which takes three to five business days to the United States and Canada and three to seven days to the United Kingdom, Australia, and New Zealand) or Air Parcel Post (which takes seven to 10 business days to the United States, Canada, and the United Kingdom, or two weeks to Australia and New Zealand).

For the first 500 grams, International Data Express rates are $25 to the United States and Canada, $30 to the United Kingdom, and $38 to Australia or New Zealand. Air Parcel Post rates run $7.65 for the first 500 grams to the United States, $9.10 to Canada, $11.95 to the United Kingdom, and $14.95 to Australia or New Zealand.

Most of Bermuda's largest stores offer shipping of purchases. Some may ask you either to buy insurance or to sign a waiver absolving them of any responsibility for potential loss or damage.

Overnight courier service is available to or from the continental United States through several companies. Service between Bermuda and Canada takes one or two business days, depending on the part of Canada; between Bermuda and the United Kingdom, generally two business days; and between Bermuda and Australia or New Zealand, usually three.

In Bermuda, rates include pickup from anywhere on the island. Prices for a document up to the first pound range from $44 to $48 to the United States, from $44 to $48 to Canada, and from $45 to $60 to the United Kingdom, Australia, or New Zealand. For the fastest delivery, your pickup request must be made before about 4 pm. Note that pickups (and drop-off locations) are limited on Saturday, and

there's no service on Sunday. Packages sent to Bermuda may take a day longer than documents.

Express Services DHL Worldwide Express ☎ *441/294-4848.* **Federal Express** ☎ *441/295-3854.* **International Bonded Couriers (IBC)** ☎ *441/295-2467* ⊕ *www.ibc. bm.* **Mailboxes Unlimited Ltd.** ☎ *441/292-6563.* **Sprint International Express** ☎ *441/296-7866* ⊕ *www.sprint.bm.*

▌ MONEY

ITEM	AVERAGE COST
Cup of Coffee	$3
Glass of Wine	$11
Glass of Beer	$8
Sandwich	$10
One-Mile Taxi Ride in Capital City	$10
Museum Admission	Free-$20

The Bermudian dollar is on par with the U.S. dollar, and the two currencies are used interchangeably. (Other non-Bermudian currency must be converted.) You can use American money anywhere, but change is often given in Bermudian currency. Try to avoid accumulating large amounts of local money, which is difficult to exchange for U.S. dollars in Bermuda and expensive to exchange in the United States. ATMs are plentiful, as are the number of venues that will accept credit cards, even for small items.

Since Bermuda imports everything from cars to cardigans, prices are high. At an upscale restaurant, for example, you're bound to pay as much for a meal as you would in a top New York, London, or Paris restaurant: on average, $60 to $80 per person, $120 with drinks and wine. There are cheaper options, of course; the island is full of coffee shops, where you can eat hamburgers and french fries with locals for about $15. The same meal at a restaurant costs about $25.

Prices throughout this guide are given for adults. Substantially reduced fees are almost always available for children, students, and senior citizens.

ATMS AND BANKS

Your own bank will probably charge a fee for using ATMs abroad; the foreign bank you use may also charge a fee. Nevertheless, you'll usually get a better rate of exchange at an ATM than you will at a currency-exchange office or even when changing money in a bank. And extracting funds as you need them is a safer option than carrying around a large amount of cash.

■ TIP→ PIN numbers with more than four digits are not recognized at ATMs in many countries. If yours has five or more, remember to change it before you leave.

ATMs are found all over Bermuda, in shops, arcades, supermarkets, the airport, and two of the island's banks. Both HSBC Bermuda and the Bank of Butterfield are affiliated with the Cirrus and Plus networks. Note that both banks' ATMs only accept personal identification numbers (PIN) with four digits. Typical withdrawal amounts are multiples of 20 up to 100. Cash point robberies are a rarity in Bermuda, but if you're concerned, Reid Street and Front Street—which have the most banks—are Hamilton's busiest, and hence safest places to withdraw cash.

CREDIT CARDS

Throughout this guide, the following abbreviations are used: **AE**, American Express; **D**, Discover; **DC**, Diners Club; **MC**, MasterCard; and **V**, Visa.

It's a good idea to inform your credit-card company before you travel, especially if you're going abroad and don't travel internationally very often. Otherwise, the credit-card company might put a hold on your card owing to unusual activity—not a good thing halfway through your trip. Record all your credit-card numbers—as well as the phone numbers to call if your cards are lost or stolen—in a safe place, so you're prepared should something go wrong. Both MasterCard and Visa have general numbers you can call (collect if you're abroad) if your card is lost, but you're better off calling the number of your issuing bank, since MasterCard and Visa usually just transfer you to your bank; your bank's number is usually printed on your card.

If you plan to use your credit card for cash advances, you'll need to apply for a PIN at least two weeks before your trip. Although it's usually cheaper (and safer) to use a credit card abroad for large purchases (so you can cancel payments or be reimbursed if there's a problem), note that some credit-card companies *and* the banks that issue them add substantial percentages to all foreign transactions, whether they're in a foreign currency or not. Check on these fees before leaving home, so there won't be any surprises when you get the bill.

Dynamic currency conversion programs are becoming increasingly widespread. Merchants who participate in them are supposed to ask whether you want to be charged in dollars or the local currency, but they don't always do so. And even if they do offer you a choice, they may well avoid mentioning the additional surcharges. The good news is that you *do* have a choice. And if this practice really gets your goat, you can avoid it entirely thanks to American Express; with its cards, DCC simply isn't an option.

Most Bermudian shops and restaurants accept credit and debit cards. Some hotels insist on cash or traveler's checks, so check in advance whether your hotel takes credit cards. The most widely accepted cards are MasterCard, Visa, and American Express.

Reporting Lost Cards American Express ☎ *800/992–3404 in U.S., 336/393–1111 collect from abroad* ⊕ *www.americanexpress. com.* **Diners Club** ☎ *800/234–6377 in U.S., 303/799–1504 collect from abroad* ⊕ *www. dinersclub.com.* **Discover** ☎ *800/347–2683 in U.S., 801/902–3100 collect from abroad* ⊕ *www.discovercard.com.* **MasterCard**

☎ 800/622–7747 in U.S., 636/722–7111 collect from abroad ⊕ www.mastercard.com. **Visa** ☎ 800/847–2911 in U.S., 410/581–9994 collect from abroad ⊕ www.visa.com.

CURRENCY AND EXCHANGE

The local currency is the Bermudian dollar, which is on par with the American dollar. Both are accepted throughout the island. Bermudian dollar notes all feature the Queen's head and are smaller than their U.S. counterparts. It's worth being careful, as both the $10 and the $2 notes are similar in color (light blue) and could be easily mistaken for one another.

If you need to exchange Canadian dollars, British pounds, or other currencies, for the most favorable rates change money through banks. Although ATM transaction fees may be higher abroad than at home, ATM rates are excellent because they're based on wholesale rates offered only by major banks.

▌PACKING

As a rule of thumb, Bermudians dress more formally than most Americans. Leave your cutoffs, short shorts, and halter tops at home. In the evening, some of the more upscale restaurants and hotel dining rooms require men to wear a jacket and tie and women to dress comparably, so bring a few dressy outfits. However, increasingly venues are more accepting of the trend toward "smart-casual." In this case, women should be fine with slacks or a skirt and a dressy blouse or sweater. Bermudian men often wear Bermuda shorts (and proper kneesocks) with a jacket and tie for formal events and business meetings.

During the cooler months, bring lightweight woolens or cottons that you can wear in layers to accommodate vagaries of the weather. A lightweight jacket is always a good idea. Regardless of the season, pack a swimsuit, a beachwear cover-up, sunscreen, and sunglasses, as well as a raincoat (umbrellas are typically provided by hotels). Comfortable walking shoes

are a must. If you plan to play tennis, be aware that many courts require proper whites and that tennis balls in Bermuda are extremely expensive. Bring your own tennis balls if possible.

Bermuda-bound airlines commonly accept golf-club bags in lieu of a piece of luggage, but there are fairly stringent guidelines governing the maximum amount of equipment that can be transported without an excess baggage fee. The general rule of thumb is one covered bag containing a maximum of 14 clubs, 12 balls, and one pair of shoes.

▌PASSPORTS

U.S. citizens arriving by air and sea to Bermuda need a valid passport, though cruise-ship passengers on closed-loop cruises (those departing and arriving in the same U.S. port) need only have proof of citizenship and identity (a government-issued photo ID and a birth certificate with a raised seal). U.S. citizens do not need a visa to enter Bermuda for a period less than 90 days.

U.S. Passport Information U.S. Department of State ☎ 877/487–2778 ⊕ travel.state.gov/ passport.

▌SAFETY

Crime, especially against tourists, is extremely low in Bermuda. Purse snatching is the most common crime tourists should watch out for. While rare, more serious incidents do happen occasionally, so you should guard against being overly complacent. Don't leave unattended valuables on the beach while going for a swim. Exercise commonsense precautions with wallets, purses, cameras, and other valuables. If you're driving a moped, always travel with your purse or bag concealed inside the seat. Always lock your moped or pedal bike, and store valuables in your room or hotel safe. Although an ocean breeze through a screen door is wonderful, close and lock your hotel room's glass patio door while you're sleeping or out of your room. The "back-of-town" area, in particular Court Street, has a bad reputation historically, though the government has made a number of efforts to clean the area up. However, if you do want to go to a venue there it's worth taking a taxi, just to be on the safe side.

■ TIP➜ Distribute your cash, credit cards, IDs, and other valuables between a deep front pocket, an inside jacket or vest pocket, and a hidden money pouch. Don't reach for the money pouch once you're in public.

■ TAXES

Hotels add a 7.25% government tax to the bill, and most add a 10% service charge or a per-diem dollar equivalent in lieu of tips. Other extra charges sometimes include a 5% "energy surcharge" (at small guesthouses) and a 17% service charge (at most restaurants).

A $25 airport-departure tax and a $4.25 airport-security fee are built into the price of your ticket, as is a $4 passenger facility charge, whereas cruise lines collect $60 in advance for each passenger, again, normally included in the price of the ticket.

■ TIME

Bermuda is in the Atlantic time zone. Bermuda observes daylight saving time (from the second Sunday in March to the first Sunday in November), so it's always one hour ahead of U.S. eastern standard time. Thus, for instance, when it's 5 pm in Bermuda, it's 4 pm in New York, 3 pm in Chicago, and 1 pm in Los Angeles. London is four hours, and Sydney 14 hours, ahead of Bermuda.

■ TIPPING

Tipping in Bermuda is fairly similar to tipping in the United States. A service charge of 10% (or an equivalent per-diem amount), which covers everything from baggage handling to maid service, is added to your hotel bill, though people often still tip a few extra dollars. Most restaurants tack on a 17% service charge; if not, a 17% tip is customary (more for exceptional service).

TIPPING GUIDELINES FOR BERMUDA	
Bartender	$1 to $3 per round of drinks, depending on the number of drinks
Bellhop	$2 per bag, depending on the level of the hotel
Dive Instructor	5% to 10% of the total trip
Gas Station Attendants	$2
Grocery Baggers	$1 to $2 a bag
Hotel Maid	$10 at lower-end accommodations, $20 at higher-end accommodations
Porter at Airport	$1 per bag
Taxi Driver	15%, but round up the fare to the next dollar amount
Waiter	17%; nothing additional if a service charge is added to the bill

■ TOURS

SPECIAL INTEREST TOURS
GARDEN AND WILDLIFE TOURS
Free 75-minute guided tours of the Botanical Gardens depart from the visitor center Tuesday, Wednesday, and Friday at 10:30 am weather permitting.

In spring the Garden Club of Bermuda arranges tours ($30) to three homes and gardens each Wednesday afternoon from 1 to 4.

Byways Bermuda offers personalized off-the-beaten-path tours of Bermuda for $100 per person for a four-hour tour.

Contacts Botanical Gardens ☎ 441/236–5291. **Byways Bermuda** ☎ 441/535-9169 ⊕ www.bywaysbermuda.com. **Garden Club of Bermuda** ✎ gardenclubbermuda@northrock. bm ⊕ www.gardenclubbermuda.org.

HISTORICAL AND SOCIAL TOURS

The Bermuda Department of Tourism (BDT) publishes brochures with self-guided tours of Hamilton, St. George's, the West End, and the Railway Trail. Available free at all Visitor Information Centres and at hotels and guesthouses, the brochures also contain detailed directions for walkers and cyclists as well as historical notes and anecdotes. The BDT also coordinates walking tours of Hamilton, St. George's, Spittal Pond Nature Reserve, the Royal Naval Dockyard, and Somerset. The tours of Hamilton and St. George's, as well as most of the Royal Naval Dockyard tours, take in historic buildings, while the Spittal Pond and Somerset tours focus on the island's flora.

Tim Rogers Tours are run by a witty British transplant who has lived in Bermuda for more than a decade. Rogers leads exceptional walks (and seated talks) about various Bermuda topics that other historians or guides sticking to their textbooks may be hesitant to discuss. His humorous and conversational tours cover intriguing historical material on piracy, local ghosts and lore, and the island's more interesting geological and architectural features. A 90-minute walking tour costs $80 per couple and $10 extra for each additional person. Special group rates are also available.

The Walking Club of Bermuda is an exercise club that provides visitors with a social opportunity to meet Bermudians while seeing the island. Walks are of varied length, and refreshments included in the fee are served afterward. A $20 yearly membership fee is required for regulars, but donations are welcome from nonmembers at the beginning of the walk.

Segway Tours of Bermuda offers a historical tour of the Royal Naval Dockyard aboard a Segway—an electric two-wheel vehicle. The machines are the only vehicles that can tour the National Museum of Bermuda. Sites include the Clocktower Mall, Casemates Prison, the Victualling Yard, the Glassblowing and Rum Cake

Factory, and the Sail Loft. The 90-minute tour includes a brief orientation to the vehicle and costs $75. Tours depart daily at 10, 12, 2 and 4.

Contacts Bermuda Department of Tourism (*BDT*). ☎ 441/292–0023 ⊕ www.gotobermuda. com. **Segway Tours of Bermuda** ☎ 441/504–2581. **Tim Rogers Tours** ☎ 441/238–0344 ✉ trogers@northrock.bm. **The Walking Club of Bermuda** ☎ 441/236–6034, 441/737–0437 ⊕ www.walk.free.bm.

HORSE-DRAWN CARRIAGE TOURS

You can hire carriages on Front Street in Hamilton—a Bermuda tradition among the just-married. Rates for a one- or two-horse carriage for up to four passengers are $45 for 30 minutes. Each adult is charged an additional $5 per half hour when more than five people ride in one carriage.

TAXI AND MINIBUS TOURS

For an independent tour of Bermuda, a taxi is a good but more expensive alternative to a group tour. A blue flag on the hood of a cab indicates that the driver is a qualified tour guide. These cabs can be difficult to find, but most of their drivers are friendly and entertaining—they sometimes bend the truth for a good yarn—and well informed about the island and its history. Ask your hotel to arrange a tour with a knowledgeable driver.

Cabs seat four or six, and the legal rate for island tours (minimum three hours) is $40 per hour for one to four passengers and $55 per hour for five or six passengers. Two children under 12 equal an adult.

Taxi and Minibus Tour Operators Bee-Line Transport Ltd. ☎ 441/293–0303. **Bermuda Triangle Tours** ☎ 441/293–1334 ⊕ www. bermudatriangletours.bm. **Destination Bermuda Ltd.** ☎ 441/292–2325. **Island Taxi Services** ☎ 441/295–4141.

▍ VISITOR INFO

Have all your questions answered about what it's like to be a visitor to Bermuda by getting in touch with the island's

Department of Tourism. The Government-run department can offer help and advice on the best places to stay and visit. The Bermuda tourism Web site also offers lots of travel deals and has a calendar of events so you can plan your days and nights with the locals. If you are heading to St. George's in the East End, the St. George's Foundation can help you find your way around the Old Town.

Contact Bermuda Department of Tourism ☎ 441/292–0023 in Bermuda, 800/223–6106 in the U.S. ⊕ www.gotobermuda.com. **St. George's Foundation** ☎ 441/297–8043 ⊕ www.stgeorgesfoundation.org.

ONLINE TRAVEL TOOLS
One of the best Bermuda Web sites is Bermuda-online, which offers information on every aspect of life on the island, from history to transportation. The Department of Tourism's Web site is especially helpful during the initial stages of vacation planning. Bermuda.com has a great search engine and links to a number of Bermuda-related Web pages, plus listings. The Bermuda Hotel Association's Web site has a monthly events calendar and a search function to allow users to find events by date or type. To keep up with current affairs, the island has two newspapers; *The Royal Gazette* is a daily and the *Bermuda Sun* is twice-weekly. To find out about nightlife offerings, visit Nothing To Do In Bermuda, which will prove that there's lots to do in Bermuda, if you know where to look. And if you want to check out the types of people you will be partying with, take a look at the photos on the Black and Coke and Bermy Net Web sites.

All About Bermuda Bermuda Online (⊕ www.bermuda-online.org). **Bermuda Department of Tourism** (⊕ www.gotobermuda.com). **Bermuda.com** (⊕ www.bermuda.com). **Bermuda Hotel Association** (⊕ www.experience-bermuda.com). **The Royal Gazette** (⊕ www.royalgazette.com). **Bermuda Sun** (⊕ www.bermudasun.bm). **Nothing To Do In Bermuda** (⊕ www.nothingtodoinbermuda.

com). **Black and Coke** (⊕ blackandcoke.com). **Bermy Net** (⊕ www.bermynet.com).

INSPIRATION
Bermuda Moods is a compilation of Bermuda snapshots taken by professional and amateur photographers. As the title suggests, the pictures were chosen to reflect the various characteristics of the island. The book is a huge success locally.

Shakespeare, an Island and a Storm by David F. Raine mixes historical research with poetic storytelling to link the story of the *Sea Venture* and Shakespeare's *The Tempest,* which is believed to have been inspired by accounts of the storms that greeted the island's first settlers.

The Story of Bermuda and Her People by William Sears Zuill gives one of the best historical accounts of the island and its inhabitants, starting from the wreck of the *Sea Venture* in 1609 and ending in the modern era.

The Deep, starring Robert Shaw and Jacqueline Bisset, shows the island through Hollywood's eyes. Older locals remember the 1970s filming with pride. Rest assured, the shady international criminals in the film are purely part of Peter Benchley's imagination!

The documentary *Rare Bird* has enjoyed an exceptional response from both the Bermudian public and the international film scene after premiering at the Bermuda International Film Festival in 2007. The film follows the history of the cahow (Bermuda's national bird) and its present-day plight against extinction. It also explores the island's environmental and social issues, both past and present.

When Voices Rise tells the important but little-known story of how segregation was finally overcome in Bermuda in the late 1950s. The documentary has achieved widespread critical acclaim.

INDEX

PHOTO CREDITS

6 (left), Homer Martin/age fotostock, 6 (right), Howard Millard. 7, Rolf Richardson/age fotostock. 10, Homer Martin/age fotostock. 11 (left), Bermuda Department of Tourism. 11 (right), Ken Ross/viestiphoto.com. 12, Ken Ross/viestiphoto.com. 13, Bob Kriste/eStock Photo. 14. Bermuda Department of Tourism.15 (left), Bermuda Department of Tourism. 15 (right) Richard Cummins/viestiphoto.com. 16, Ken Ross/viestiphoto.com. 21, Joe Viesti/viestiphoto.com. 22, Bermuda Department of Tourism. 23 (left), Joe Viesti/viestiphoto.com. 23 (right), Bermuda Department of Tourism. 24, Bermuda Department of Tourism.

NOTES

NOTES

NOTES

NOTES

NOTES

NOTES

NOTES

NOTES